Honor Among Thieves

NEW TEXTS FROM ANCIENT CULTURES

Edited by

Traianos Gagos†
James G. Keenan, Loyola University of Chicago
Terry Wilfong, University of Michigan

Settling a Dispute: Toward a Legal Anthropology of Late Antique Egypt
by Traianos Gagos and Peter van Minnen

Women of Jeme: Lives in a Coptic Town in Late Antique Egypt
by T. G. Wilfong

Wine, Wealth, and the State in Late Antique Egypt: The House of Apion at Oxyrhynchus
by T. M. Hickey

New Literary Papyri from the Michigan Collection: Mythographic Lyric and a Catalogue of Poetic First Lines
by Cassandra Borges and C. Michael Sampson

Materia Magica: The Archaeology of Magic in Roman Egypt, Cyprus, and Spain
by Andrew T. Wilburn

Honor Among Thieves: Craftsmen, Merchants, and Associations in Roman and Late Roman Egypt
by Philip F. Venticinque

Honor Among Thieves

CRAFTSMEN, MERCHANTS, AND ASSOCIATIONS IN ROMAN AND LATE ROMAN EGYPT

Philip F. Venticinque

ANN ARBOR
UNIVERSITY OF MICHIGAN PRESS

Published in the United States of America by the
University of Michigan Press
Manufactured in the United States of America
♾ Printed on acid-free paper

2019 2018 2017 2016 4 3 2 1

A CIP catalog record for this book is available from the British Library.

Library of Congress Cataloging-in-Publication data has been applied for.

ISBN 978-0-472-13016-0 (hardcover : alk. paper)
ISBN 978-0-472-12243-1 (e-book)

For
Mom and Dad
and
Katie, Philip, and Madeleine

Preface

I had not planned to study craftsmen, merchants, or anything about the ancient economy. In fact, I distinctly remember trying to substitute as much Moses Finley as I could while going through my Greek history reading lists. Thankfully, or fatefully, Jonathan Hall knew better. Urging moderation and constraint, he told me to go read *The Ancient Economy* because the debate remained lively and there still was a story to tell. Later, when I was searching for a dissertation topic, David Martinez suggested that I take a look at the Michigan association texts (*P.Mich.* V 243–48) because "there might be something there." After reading those charters and lists, along with the important work of Onno van Nijf and Philip Harland, whose studies of groups in Asia Minor helped usher in what has become a vibrant period of scholarship on associations, I realized that Jonathan and David were right. There was a story to tell about the social and economic world of associations and individual craftsmen and merchants who had not figured in Finley's account, and Egypt's papyri read in conversation with the epigraphic, legal, and literary evidence could help illuminate their place in local communities and their approach to economic activities. This book is the product of my return to Finley, his critics, and his supporters, and a decade or so of trying to put the pieces together and tell the story from the perspective of the associations and their members as much as possible.

As I constantly remind my own students, research is not a solitary enterprise. Along the way from dissertation to book, I have incurred many debts and benefited from the collegiality and support of teachers, colleagues, and friends. David Martinez, Janet Johnson, Emanuel Mayer, and Cam Grey continued to offer assistance and guidance long after their duties as dissertation advisors had ended. David's and Jan's attention to what the documents could (and could not) reveal and their ever-present mindfulness of the realities of working with papyri have been formative and indispensable. Emanuel's and Cam's encouragement to think beyond Egypt and to keep my eye on larger social and economic questions that the papyri could help illuminate was equally crucial. I owe special thanks to Clifford Ando and James Keenan, who were all but members of my committee and have read more about craftsmen, merchants, and associations than they ever planned. That Cliff has a virtually unparalleled depth of knowledge about the Roman world may be common knowledge; he is also a strong advocate for his students. Not only did I benefit from all he knows and shares freely, but also from his support and interest in this project from its early stages. I first met Jim Keenan when he graciously accepted an invitation to speak at a conference I organized with Ari Bryen and Fanny Dolansky, focused on exploring life at the margins of the Roman Empire. Since then, I have learned a great deal about history, about how to be a historian, and a great many things besides from Jim, whom I am fortunate enough to count as a mentor and friend. Many others offered support and guidance to me first as a student and then as a young academic. Few could wish for better guides along academia's paths than Christopher Faraone, Jonathan Hall, Walter Kaegi, and Matthew Stolper. I also must thank Alain Bresson, Kent Rigsby, and Sofia Torallas-Tovar, who read and discussed portions of my work, and Terry Wilfong, who encouraged me to submit the manuscript for publication in the series he edits for the University of Michigan Press. I also owe a debt of thanks to Ellen Bauerle, the Classics editor at the press, and Marcia LaBrenz for their help during initial writing, revision, and production as well as Jill Butler Wilson, whose copy editing helped improve the manuscript.

I was lucky enough to work with and learn from a large group of critical thinkers and compassionate friends while at the University of Chicago. Ari Bryen, Vanessa Davies, Fanny Dolansky, Cameron Hawkins, John Hyland, Ray Kania, Paul Keen, John Paulas, Fran Spaltro, and Jennifer Westerfeld have each helped immensely over the years. Ari, Fanny, Paul, and Cam have been constant sounding boards about all manner of association-related (and nonassociation) matters; this book would not have been written without them. Ari, Paul, and Sofia also read the entire manuscript and improved it greatly, a debt I probably cannot repay.

Getting involved with the Copenhagen Associations Project provided me with another group of interlocutors, chief among them Vincent Gabrielsen,

Matt Gibbs, and Christian Thomsen, who have read, discussed, and shared comments on different aspects of my work. I must also thank John Gruber-Miller, my colleagues in the Department of Classical and Modern Languages, our student assistants Miranda Donnellan and Caitlin Conlon, and many other members of the Cornell College community. Without their help and support, this book, completed somewhere between Mount Vernon, Iowa, and Chicago, would not have been possible or finished.

Throughout my work on associations, I benefited from opportunities provided by foundations and fellowships to interact and work with students and scholars from across the humanities and social sciences. The seminars and workshops of the Martin Marty Center for the Advanced Study of Religion at the University of Chicago, my time as a Junior Fellow in Byzantine Studies at Dumbarton Oaks, and my participation in the Franke Institute workshops as a Mrs. Giles Whiting Dissertation Fellow all have left an indelible mark on the project. Generous fellowship awards from the Loeb Classical Library Foundation, the Center for Hellenic Studies, and the American Council of Learned Societies also supported a leave during the 2012–13 academic year during which the bulk of the manuscript was written. The manuscript that resulted draws from and expands upon work published in *Greek, Roman, and Byzantine Studies*, *The Center for Hellenic Studies Research Bulletin*, and volumes published under the auspices of the Copenhagen Associations Project.

Above all, I must thank my family, to whom this book is dedicated, for their love and support. To my parents, Philip and Janis Venticinque, who never wavered in their support and who were always at the ready to help in any number of ways throughout my life and made everything possible, I offer my sincere love and gratitude. Though my father did not live to see this book's completion, it is, in many ways, a tribute to him and what he taught me about work. To my wife, Katie, who lived with this project from start to finish, I offer all my thanks and love for her support, patience, and trust. My children, Philip and Madeleine, are too young to know that I do it all for them. I thank them for giving me a reason to put down my books and pick up theirs.

Contents

Introduction

At some point in the middle of the fourth century CE, a high-ranking imperial official with fiscal responsibility over Egypt, the *katholikos* (or perhaps a member of his staff), prepared a packing list in advance of a trip.[1] The list details the numerous luxury items he brought along, including fine linen tunics (some embroidered or decorated), towels, and cloaks that a person of means would have possessed. Besides the *katholikos* and his staff, a number of craftsmen, merchants, and the associations they formed to address economic, political, social, and legal concerns (referred to as *collegia*, *koina*, and *sunodoi* among other terms) had a hand in helping him dress for success on his trip. In this case, that would have included weavers and embroiderers who wove and decorated the tunics, dyers who colored the fabric decorations, and fullers who finished and later cleaned the items. The artisans, who produced the clothing primarily in their own workshops (or shops owned by or leased from others), also relied on any number of merchants to supply the linen, wool, dye, and other materials required to create finished garments. Linen and wool merchants would, in turn, have traded with owners of sheep as well as landowners (or tenants) who cultivated flax, the raw material from which tow workers spun linen and other items. Even the sacks that contained the items the *katholikos* brought with him would have been produced by specialized craftsmen. Still more people working with craftsmen and merchants would have provided and coordinated transport of raw materials and finished goods from workshops or fields to market spaces (by river and, over land, by donkey or camel) and would have managed payment of customs charges and taxes along the way.[2]

1. Venticinque 2016.
2. For craftsmen in Roman Egypt, see van Minnen 1987; E. Wipszycka 1965. For merchants, see Alston 1998; for transportation, Adams 2007.

In the process of producing the garments for the *katholikos*—or, for that matter, any item intended for either local consumption or a more distant market—craftsmen, merchants, and those involved in trade and production confronted economic, legal, social, and political challenges and faced risks and uncertainties in their personal and professional lives as they managed manufacture and sale of their goods in an economic environment in which the costs of doing business (transaction costs) were high.[3] The same can be said for carpenters, builders, and skilled craftsmen whose efforts were not confined to a single workshop and not sold or consumed like an article of clothing but whose services were contracted by individuals, groups, and local councils and officials to undertake new projects or repair existing structures. Everyone, whether a weaver, a merchant, or a builder, had to contend with asymmetric information not only about goods, prices, market conditions, and labor costs and its supply but also about colleagues, customers, agents, and even market and port officials collecting customs and taxes, whose actions, though ideally bound by precedent and law in the Roman world, could be unpredictable.

Once craftsmen and merchants overcame these difficulties, the marketplace posed its own challenges. Apuleius' description of his protagonist Lucius' bargain-hunting efforts to purchase dinner in Thessaly and his encounter with an old friend (and current market official) Pythias provides a humorous, often-quoted anecdote about buying and selling in the ancient world. After hearing about Lucius' encounter with a merchant and the price he paid for the fish he purchased for dinner, Pythias reacted with indignation.

> When he [Pythias] heard this, he grabbed my hand and led me straight back into the market square. "And from which of these men," he said, "did you buy this stuff?" I pointed to a little old man, who was sitting in the corner. Pythias, by the power vested in him as public works official, began right then to berate him harshly, shouting "So now, now your lot don't even spare our friends, or any strangers whatsoever, since you advertise your trashy little fishes at such a

3. For transaction costs, see R. H. Coase's classic 1937 study of firms (reprinted as Coase 1990: 33–55), where he explained transaction costs as "the cost of carrying out a transaction by means of an exchange on the open market" and "marketing costs." He later expanded his treatment, claiming that "in order to carry out a market transaction, it is necessary to discover who it is that one wishes to deal with, to inform people that one wishes to deal and on what terms, to conduct negotiations leading up to a bargain, to draw up the contract, to undertake the inspection needed to make sure that the terms of the contract are being observed, and so on" (Coase 1960 [= 1990: 114]). See also Frier and Kehoe 2007: 115–17.

> high price, and make the jewel of the region of Thessaly out to be some desert on a cliff, by the cost of its edibles? But you won't get away with it! I shall see to it that you learn right now how evildoers are to be treated when I'm in charge," and, emptying the basket out in the middle of the market, he ordered his officer to jump on top of the fish and to mash them all up with his feet. My Pythias was satisfied with this sternness of his character, and urged me to leave: "This great insult to the little old man," he said, "is good enough for me, Lucius." When this was over, I went on to the baths, confused and bewildered. My wise friend's clever plan had deprived me at once of both my money and my dinner, and after I had washed, I returned to my host Milo's and from there to bed.[4]

Though satirical, Apuleius' account of uncertainty in the marketplace points out some of the issues people faced doing business and securing goods and services in commercial spaces (be it a forum, agora, or *macellum*), periodic fairs, or workshops (*tabernae* or *ergasteria*) where production and sale of items took place.

Gaining information about prices, demand, and potential competitors at the marketplace and within the community and even about the legal constraints in a particular location was difficult, as suggested by a letter exchanged between associates in the second century CE concerning the state of affairs at Oxyrhynchus.

> Serapion to his dearest Potamon, greeting. Above all I think it is necessary to greet you through a letter. I urge you, dear, to write to me about the market near you. For the market in the Oxyrhynchos district is less favorable, since ordinances arrive every day. I greet all your family and your master Apollonios, the exceptional friend. Farewell.[5]

The problems that Serapion and his associates experienced, as well as those encountered by Lucius and Pythias, indicate the importance of market information and the deleterious impact of imperfect information for transactions and for developing a strategy to engage the ancient market. It would have been an experience approximating the conditions observed in a bazaar, famously described and analyzed by Clifford Geertz in his investigation of the Moroccan

---

4. Apuleius, *Metamorphoses* 1.24–25, trans. Lindsay.
5. *P.Oslo* II 49 (II CE), trans. Eitrem and Amundsen (adapted).

town of Sefrou. In such an economic environment, Geertz explained, information typically is "poor, scarce, maldistributed, inefficiently communicated, and intensely valued."[6] As George Akerlof made clear in his landmark study of asymmetrical information, the problem that Geertz highlighted is not limited to a bazaar, which certainly has its own rhythms and rules, but is a fundamental problem in any transaction.[7]

Beyond the professional challenges of the workshop or marketplace, personal financial crisis, sickness, injury, and other social and legal difficulties also complicated the efforts of craftsmen and merchants to provide for themselves and their households in order to live at or above subsistence level in a predominantly agrarian world, though one served by an important and not insignificant craft and merchant sector. Craftsmen and merchants needed to find ways to deal with economic and personal obstacles, navigate the Roman legal and political system, and defend their interests in the face of potential challenges from other artisans, traders, community members, and local and imperial officials. Relying on association membership and the benefits it provided was one method to overcome constraints on economic activity, including imperfect information and high transaction costs, and also to deal with a host of personal, legal, and social concerns no less vital to attaining economic success, because it allowed members to develop social capital with peers and the community. Described in various ways by economists, anthropologists, and sociologists, social capital has come to refer to trust, reputation, shared norms, and norm-supported social networks that facilitate access to scarce information about potential partners, customers, and goods, which gives individuals and groups "advantages in pursuing their ends," according to sociologist Ronald Burt.[8] Investment in social capital within the association network on the part of members enabled them to confront many risks, uncertainties, and challenges in their lives by providing both assurances that members would conduct themselves according to accepted norms and access to support in personal and professional contexts: loans, surety, and assistance with burial. Some Egyptian associations even appear to have collected market and price information, the type of information that Serapion had hoped to learn from Potamon through the letter quoted above.

How craftsmen and merchants accomplished their professional and per-

6. Geertz 1978: 29.
7. Akerloff 1970.
8. Burt 2005: 5. See also Coleman 1988; Putnam 2000: 19–22; Ogilvie 2011: 6–13.

sonal aims, relied on associations as part of a strategy to mitigate risk and uncertainty, and participated in the society and economy of their communities has generally not been the focus of economic studies of the ancient world. Instead, the story of the ancient economy has primarily been about the activities of elites like the *katholikos* who wore the expensive clothes, the estates they owned and managed, their investment in (and attitudes toward) agriculture, and their stated aversion to commercial activity. Craftsmen, merchants, and the way that the associations they formed operated have largely taken a backseat in analyses of an economy in which a majority of the population was engaged in or depended on agricultural production in some way and where an elite ideology that privileged agriculture as the only honorable pursuit structured economic relations, supposedly informed economic decisions, and impacted the overall performance of that economy.[9] Accordingly, economic activity at all levels of the social pyramid was motivated not by profit or economic advantages but by the acquisition and preservation of status and honor, characterized by J. E. Lendon as "a filter through which the whole world was viewed, a deep structure of the Graeco-Roman mind, perhaps the ruling metaphor of ancient society."[10] What determined elite behavior supposedly drove the actions of those farther down the social and economic scale who, it is assumed, desired to emulate their social and economic superiors. In the world created and perpetuated by such an ideology, economic, social, political, and legal power remained in the hands of the elite landowners on whom everyone else ultimately depended. Held in low regard by the elite authors whose texts have framed our understanding of the ancient economy, craftsmen and merchants have been relegated to a supporting role in the story, when they are mentioned at all.

As a result, throughout a good portion of the last century, associations have been thought not to be economic organizations at all, despite common ties of profession, and not to impact members' lives economically.[11] Scholars viewed associations primarily as social or religious groups that provided access to mutual support, proper burial, commiseration and sociability, and spaces where nonelite individuals could acquire and compete for the status and honor supposedly denied to them in ancient society. Believing that craftsmen and merchants occupied a less-than-advantageous position in the social and economic framework, at least in relation to elite landowners, scholars assumed that the

9. Finley 1999: 195.
10. Lendon 1997: 73.
11. For discussion of the previous scholarship, see Harland 2003: 68–72; Perry 2006; Liu 2009: 4–11.

associations formed by those people provided little besides compensation for exclusion from political society in their communities throughout the Greek and Roman world, and this remained the understanding for some time.[12]

By contrast, the following study of craftsmen, merchants, and associations in Egypt during essentially the first seven centuries CE seeks to insert these members of the nonelite into discussions of the society and economy of the ancient world and of the place associations occupied in that world, and it aims to do so not on the basis of elite texts and concepts alone but on their own terms. Accordingly, the analysis will concentrate on how craftsmen, merchants, and associations interacted with each other and with elite and nonelite constituencies; managed economic, political, social, and legal activities; represented their concerns to the authorities; and acquired and used social capital. Incorporating these aspects of a craftsman or merchant's life in the analysis is vital to further our understanding of how individual economic actors and the different pieces of the ancient economy worked together—sometimes in concert, sometimes in conflict—to manage and offset risks and uncertainties faced by everyone at all levels of the economic pyramid.

From its incorporation as a province in 30 BCE until the end of Roman rule in the seventh century, Egypt provides a plethora of evidence that documents the activities of associations and their members, preserved primarily in a large body of papyrological texts (and ostraca) written in Greek, Latin, Demotic, and Coptic but also, to a lesser degree, in inscriptions and archaeological material. Though papyri and ostraca are not without their difficulties when it comes to interpretation, the substantial body of documentary evidence from Egypt provides an opportunity to carry out a (more or less) bottom-up investigation of the ancient economy, using associations as a lens through which to examine the "small politics" of communities in more detail than in other regions or provinces.[13] The epigraphic material that Philip Harland and Onno van Nijf relied on in their excellent studies of associations in Roman Asia Minor or that provided the basis for Jinyu Liu's detailed study of a single professional association in the Roman west, the *centonarii*, mainly reveals the public face of these groups.[14] The papyrological documents—association charters, contracts, work orders,

12. Burford 1972; MacMullen 1974; 1992: 173; Hopkins 1983a: 211–17; Garnsey and Saller 1987: 156–57; Kloppenborg and Wilson 1996; Carroll 2006.
13. The phrase "small politics" is borrowed from Cam Grey, who used it in his study of peasants in the late Roman countryside; see Grey 2011: 1.
14. Van Nijf 1997; Harland 2003; Liu 2009. See also Arnaoutoglou 2011.

business receipts, accounts, petitions, tax documents, and private letters—provide the sort of information not usually revealed by monuments or recorded epigraphically. In this way, the papyri refine our understanding of association activities; the lives craftsmen, merchants, and members led; the decisions they made (economic or otherwise); and their interactions with and, to some extent, experience of the multiple layers of administration in the Roman world.

Although there have been detailed studies of association activities in recent years, there remains no extensive examination of associations in Egypt since San Nicolò's study of groups from the Ptolemaic and Roman periods (undertaken in 1913 and revised in 1972), which, like earlier foundational studies, focused on institutional, organizational, and legal questions.[15] The detailed evidence provided by late Roman Egypt has yet to be treated comprehensively; in fact, evidence of association activities typically has been omitted from discussions regarding the nature of associations, the organization of trade and production, the state's involvement in it, and their experience of and interaction with the apparatus of government during the late Roman period. Extending the analysis into the late Roman period and treating the period of Roman rule in Egypt as a whole (rather than breaking the period with Diocletian's reorganization of the Roman Empire, the rise of Christianity, or some other date) and examining the activities of associations, craftsmen, and merchants over the course of Roman rule allows for consideration of the ways that associations did or did not alter their activities, organization, and reliance on social capital in response to changes in the administrative and economic landscape of communities. Inclusion of material from the fourth century and beyond suggests parallels with the strategies that craftsmen, merchants, and associations adopted earlier to deal with problems that were common over the centuries.

Craftsmen, Merchants, and Associations in Egypt and the Ancient World

Evidence for craftsmen, merchants, associations, and their activities can be found documented on papyrus, carved in stone, detailed in legal codes and juristic commentaries, and discussed in literary sources throughout the ancient

15. San Nicolò 1972. See also Mommsen 1843; Foucart 1873; Waltzing 1895–1900; Poland 1909. More recently, see Arnaoutoglou 2005; Venticinque 2010, 2013; Gibbs 2011.

world from the Hellenistic into the late Roman period. The variety of associations attested is staggering. Some operated locally—like the *collegium* of ship caulkers (*stuppatores*) at Ostia,[16] the *sunodos* of weavers at Theadelphia,[17] the *sunedrion* of silversmiths at Ephesos,[18] and the *koinon* of spice merchants at Oxyrhynchus.[19] Others, such as nearly all those found in Ostia's square of corporations or those who maintained a presence on Delos and Rhodes, consisted of traders resident abroad, at least temporarily. People relied on these groups, like the *koina* of merchants from Berytus and Tyre on Delos and the networks to which they gave access, to accomplish their aims.[20]

Faced with such diversity, scholars have categorized groups based on a number of criteria. John Kloppenborg and Philip Harland have focused on the social composition of a group's membership and an association's social networks and rightly have concerned themselves less with outward appearances of a particular association's function.[21] Kloppenborg suggested three categories: associations organized around occupation and professional pursuits, shared cult or religious identity, and shared household or family connections.[22] Harland expanded the categories to five in his study of associations in Asia Minor: common household bonds or a household network, shared ethnic or geographic origins, neighborhood networks, occupation or profession, and what he calls "cult or temple connections."[23] Despite such analytically useful categories, it is difficult, in practice, not only to distinguish between a group's apparent function and purpose and its character as a religious or professional group, since such concerns could be and likely were fluid, but also to distinguish associations based on criteria derived from a membership profile. A neighborhood association could also be a professional association, given the tendency of craftsmen and merchants to concentrate in similar areas, and family and household bonds are not mutually exclusive in a religious group or an occupational one.

Even if typologies should not be the only key to interpreting association activities and the motivations of individual members, the proposed categories do roughly organize the associations encountered in Roman and late Roman

16. *CIL* XIV 4549.
17. *I.Fayum* II 122 (109 CE).
18. *I.Eph.* 2212 (41–54 CE or after).
19. *P.Oxy.* LIV 3731 (310–11 CE); for terminology, see Waltzing 1895–1900, vol. 4: 236–42.
20. *I.Délos* 1519–20 (153/2 BCE). For associations on Delos, see Rauh 1993; Trümper 2011. For Rhodes, see Gabrielsen 2001, 2007.
21. On typologies, see Harland 2003: 28–53.
22. Kloppenborg 1996: 23–26.
23. Harland 2003: 29.

Egypt. Broadly speaking, Egyptian associations belong to two categories: on the one hand are occupational or professional groups composed of craftsmen, merchants, and, in some cases, farmers and animal herders; on the other are cultic or religious groups. The two most common terms used in Egypt to refer to associations were *sunodos* and *koinon*, but many association members called their group a *thiasos* or a *plēthos* instead.[24] Some groups simply called themselves or were identified by others as "the carpenters" or "the dyers" of a particular location, such as the carpenters from Ptolemais or the weavers from Abydos.[25] Others made no geographical specification, as appears to have been the case with an association of specialty weavers in Alexandria, who identified themselves simply as the *tarsikarioi* when they honored an individual.[26] Tax registers and accounts indicate that such identification remained common during the late Roman period.[27]

Associations outside of Egypt identified themselves in a similar manner, including a group of dyers at Thyatira in Lydia who referred to themselves only as "the dyers" (*hoi bapheis*) in two honorary inscriptions.[28] Besides *sunodos* and *koinon*, the terms *sunergasia*, *homotechnon*, and *sustēma* also described associations in Asia Minor.[29] In Italy and the Roman west, groups were referred to as *collegia*.[30] The imperial edicts collected in the Theodosian Code and the writ ings of the jurists compiled in the Digest of Justinian used both *collegium* and *corpus* to refer to these organizations, regardless of location. Even within groups, terminology could be slippery. Members of the same association sometimes used multiple terms to identify themselves, such as the linen weavers of Saittai who described their group both as a *sunergasia* and as a *homotechnon*.[31]

Scholars themselves have discussed these organizations using many different terms. Some, such as A. H. M. Jones and Russell Meiggs, referred to them

---

24. For *thiasos*, see *I.Philae* II 157 (8 CE). For *plēthos*, see *I.Fayum* III 212 (3 CE); *I.Alex.Imp.* 97 (7 CE); *P.Mich.* V 244 (43 CE); *P.Oxy.* LXXVI 5097 (62 CE).
25. *IGR* I 1155 (45 CE); *I.Varsovie* 66 (257 CE).
26. *I.Alex.Imp.* 99 (III CE).
27. *P. Cairo Masp.* II 67147 (VI CE).
28. *CIG* 3496–97 (III CE).
29. For examples of associations referred to as a *sunergasia*, see *SEG* XXIX 1191 (183/4 CE), XXXI 1036 (202/3 CE); *TAM* V.1, 83 (205/6 CE, all linen workers in Saittai). For examples of associations referred to as a *homotechnon*, see *TAM* V.1, 82 (183/4 CE, linen workers in Saittai), 85 (145/6 CE, wool workers in Saittai), 86 (154/5 CE, dyers in Saittai); *SEG* XL 1045 (152/3 CE, dyers in Gordos). For *sustēma*, see *MAMA* III 770 (after III CE, linen merchants in Korykos).
30. Waltzing 1895–1900, vol. 4: 236.
31. For discussion, see van Nijf 1997: 10.

as "guilds."[32] Others have described them as "corporations," as "voluntary associations," or simply as "associations." In his study, van Nijf chose to label them "associations" but often used *collegium* as a blanket term; Harland opted to call them "associations" or "voluntary associations." In what follows, *association* is used as a general term to describe the different groups of individuals organized around common occupations or religious observances encountered in Egypt and elsewhere, whether labeled by *collegium*, *homotechnon*, *koinon*, *sunodos*, or any other term. Although each group faced unique challenges and enjoyed opportunities based on the particular time and place in which it was active, there was more that united a *homotechnon* of linen workers from Asia Minor and a *koinon* of linen workers from Oxyrhynchus than divided them.

The charters that associations devised to govern their operations reveal that groups met regularly, feasted together, marked major life events, celebrated religious rituals with colleagues, and relied on each other for financial assistance and support in their professional and personal lives. For many associations, financial assistance and mutual support extended to death and burial. Archaeological evidence from throughout the Hellenistic and Roman world—epitaphs, tombs, and burial monuments—indicates that membership held meaning and significance in life and death and that it was fairly common for a funeral to involve an association, in addition to or in place of a family.[33]

Associations routinely elected a presiding officer or cohort of officials for a period of time to administer association affairs and to interact with and represent the group's interests before local or Roman authorities. Those who served Egyptian associations in these capacities held various titles. Throughout the period under consideration here, one finds such an individual commonly styled as a *hēgoumenos*,[34] a *prostatēs*,[35] or, less often, an *epimelētēs*[36]; references to the *mēniarchēs*[37] (monthly president) and the *kephalaiōtēs*[38] become more

32. Jones 1964; Meiggs 1973.
33. On associations and funerals, see van Nijf 1997: 31–69; Harland 2003: 84–86; Venticinque (forthcoming).
34. *P.Ryl.* II 94 (14–37 CE), line 1 = *Sel.Pap.* II 255; *P.Mich.* II 121r (42 CE), col. IV, line 6; II 123r (45–49 CE), col. XIV, line 16; II 124r (46–49 CE), col. II, line 19; V 246 (mid-I CE), line 1; V 247 (early I CE), line 1.
35. See, for example, *I.Alex.Imp.* 96 = *AGRW* 279 (30 BCE–14 CE), lines 1–3; *I.Fayum* III 212 (3 CE), line 7; *I.Alex.Imp.* 93 (14/15 CE, line 1); *P.Mich.* V 243 (14–37 CE), line 3; *P.Oxy.* LXXVI 5097 (62 CE), line 6.
36. *P.Mich.* V 244 (43 CE), line 4; 245 (47 CE), line 5.
37. *P.Oxy.* I 84 = *Sel.Pap* II 374 (316 CE), line 6; *P.Leid.Inst.* 62 (late IV CE), line 3. Some associations, such as the tow or flax merchants, had multiple monthly presidents: see *P.Oxy.* XLV 3261 (324 CE), line 4; LIV 3753 (319 CE), lines 8–11; *P.Harr.* II 216 (343 CE), lines 6–10.
38. *PSI* XII 1265 (426 CE, an association of goldsmiths in Oxyrhynchus); *P.Cair.Masp.* III 67283 (before

common beginning in the fourth century CE. Sixth-century associations of fullers and iron workers referred to their officer as the *epistatēs*, although this term appears to have been less common.[39] Some groups, like the weavers in the Fayum village Theadelphia, had a board of elders called the *presbuteroi*.[40] In addition to an association's presiding officer, a treasurer or, more often, a scribe (*grammateus*) assisted in running organizations.[41]

Access to the perquisites of membership came at a price; associations required members to pay monthly dues and sometimes fees upon admission. Part of the price entailed nonfinancial obligations: more specifically, associations expected members to abide by a set of rules and regulations (outlined in their charter) that specified ethical and behavioral norms. For instance, members agreed to conduct themselves in a specific manner at banquets and meetings, pledged not to slander or prosecute colleagues, and promised not to withhold aid when another member found himself in financial or legal difficulties. Failure to follow the regulations was supposed to result in a fine. Associations did not employ only negative reinforcement; the ways in which they honored those members who played by the rules and acted admirably on the group's behalf included erecting portrait statues, awarding extra portions at banquets, and reciting honorary decrees at their events.[42]

Associations were not a Roman innovation imposed from above to help better manage the province and coordinate the productive efforts of the population; groups had a particularly long history in Egypt. The same can be said of associations in Asia Minor and the Greek east under Roman rule, as van Nijf pointed out in opposition to earlier, yet persistent, claims.[43] Although the number of associations in Egypt (and evidence of their activities) does appear to have increased during the Roman period, collegial organizations existed well before the annexation of the province in 30 BCE. A Demotic financial account produced by a group of Theban mortuary priests and dating to the sixth century BCE provides the earliest evidence for organizations of this sort.[44] A variety of Greek and Demotic texts (association charters, membership lists, ac-

547 CE, associations of cloak weavers, ship builders, wine merchants, fullers, bronzesmiths, and carpenters in Aphrodito).

39. *SPP* VIII 850, 852 (both VI CE).
40. *I.Fayum* II 122 (109 CE).
41. *P.Ryl.* II 94 (14–37 CE), line 3 = *Sel.Pap.* II 255.
42. *SB* V 8267 = *I.Prose* 49 (5 BC); *I.Fayum* III 212 (3 CE); *I.Alex.Imp.* 91 (3/4 CE), 99 (III CE).
43. Van Nijf 1997: 8.
44. De Cenival 1986; for the Theban mortuary priests, see de Cenival 1972: 103–7.

counts, receipts, dedications, and honorary inscriptions) attest to the activities of associations over the course of many centuries and throughout the Ptolemaic period.[45] Prior to the Roman period, groups typically identified themselves with a particular deity or temple, such as the association of crocodile mummy bearers affiliated with the temple of Sobek in Tebtunis.[46] Groups like the crocodile mummy bearers appear to have been priests and personnel attached to temples. Some associations, however, did identify themselves with a particular trade during the Ptolemaic period. The groups of funerary workers (*nekrotaphoi*) and mortuary priests (*choachytai*) that existed during the Ptolemaic period likely constituted professional associations.[47]

Associations continued to affiliate themselves with temples in the Roman period, even with the perceived increase of professional groups identified with a trade. An account detailing the expenditures for feasts and other costs of a *sunodos* of *pastophori* perhaps affiliated with the god Thonis, in whose temple the group held their meetings, indicates that the association participated in social and convivial activities similar to those of any other association. Payments listed in the account, including those made to other associations, emphasize the fact that groups did not operate in a vacuum, even those groups presumably with ties to a temple.[48] Other groups dedicated to or affiliated with a deity also existed in villages during the Roman period.[49] A connection between the association of Harpocrates in first-century Tebtunis and a specific temple is not necessarily apparent. But based on an account recording banquet expenses—which includes designation of members as officers—this group of sixteen individuals structured its activities similarly to other craft, merchant, or religious groups and probably also provided familiar social, religious, political, and economic benefits to their membership.[50]

The relationship between an association's religious, social, political, and economic undertakings, often regarded as distinct spheres of activity, has

45. For Greek evidence of Ptolemaic associations, see Boak 1937; Nock, Roberts, and Skeat 1936. For Demotic charters of priestly associations, see de Cenival 1972; see also Muszynski 1977.

46. For the crocodile mummy bearers, see de Cenival 1972: 45–51 (=*P. Cairo dem.* II 30606), 59–61 (= *P. Hamburg dem.* 1), 63–68 (= *P. Cairo dem.* II 31179), 73–78 (= *P. Cairo dem.* II 30605), 93–97 (= *P. Cairo dem.* II 30619); see also Muhs 2001.

47. *OGIS* II 729 (221–205 BCE). See also Derda 1991; Pestman 1993.

48. *P.Oslo* III 143 (I CE); on Thonis see Frankfurter 1998 : 161.

49. See *P.Mich.* II 124r, col. II, line 24, which mentions a payment made for writing or copying a charter for the *sunodos* of the god recorded in the Tebtunis *grapheion* register. See also *I.Philae* II 139 (13 BCE); *IGR* I 1084 (25 CE), 1106 (30 BCE–14 CE); *I.Portes* 111 (160 CE), 83 (209/10 CE).

50. *P.Mich.* V 246 (mid-I CE).

proved problematic in the past, although recent analyses have increasingly argued otherwise.[51] Drawing lines between religious, social, political, or economic activities carried out under an association's auspices is no less difficult than distinguishing between religious, professional, neighborhood, or family associations. Many associations centered on a common occupation had an overtly religious character and celebrated banquets and made dedications in honor of a particular deity. One of the more telling examples from Egypt involves an association of ironsmiths based at Hermonthis in the Theban area during the early fourth century CE.[52] The ironsmiths probably gathered together regularly in their own community, feasted together, and carried out standard association activities. The group is known to us, however, from a collection of six texts spanning half a century and inscribed on the walls of a room within the temple of Hatshepsut at Deir el-Bahari, where the group met to conduct religious rites and feast together. Each year, the group traveled some twenty kilometers from Hermonthis to hold a banquet and carry out a donkey sacrifice. The mix of common craft, pilgrimage, and shared religious ritual indicates overlap between craft production, trade, and religious ceremonies. Both occupational and religious associations also provided support to their members for funerals and marked celebrations of births, marriage, and occasions in their members' private lives.[53] Members of religious groups and members of occupational associations would have enjoyed similar benefits from association membership, in terms of access to credit, loans, reduced transaction costs, and mitigation of risk and uncertainty in personal and professional life. Consideration of outwardly religious groups thus complements and helps us better understand the approaches to and activities of craftsmen and merchants as well.

Regardless of location and exact nomenclature, associations from the Roman period under discussion here worked within similar institutional frameworks provided not only by charters but by factors that helped shape their responses to challenges and the economic environment in which they lived and worked. Those factors included the predominance of agriculture, imperfect information, high transaction costs, social norms, and Roman law and administration. Associations and their members were also united by a common experience of living and working in communities under Roman rule, which, in this

51. Van Nijf 1997; Hawkins 2006; Venticinque 2010; Gibbs 2011; Verboven 2011.
52. Łajtar 1991. See also Bagnall 2004; Łajtar 2006: 242–64.
53. *P.Mich.* V 243 (14–37 CE); for the commemorative activities of *collegia* in Italy, see Waltzing 1895–1900, vol. 4: 505–22; see also van Nijf 1997: 31–69.

context, largely meant relying on the social and financial capital of a particular community's leading members for local administration and tax collection.

Association Membership

Ancient authors and Roman jurists often made a link between association membership and financial hardship, specifically among those at the lower levels of society, the *homines tenuiores*.[54] During Pliny's term as governor in Bithynia, a group of people in Amisus sought to form an association and petitioned him concerning their request.[55] The response Pliny reports he received from Trajan granting permission suggested that the association and the monthly fees collected were aimed at compensating for the social and economic deficiencies experienced in the lives of the poor (*ad sustinendam tenuiorum inopiam utuntur*), at least from an elite perspective.[56]

The response Pliny reported also speaks to the status distinctions and social structures so often invoked to explain the ancient economy in general and the economic activities and goals of individual actors, particularly those operating outside the world of the wealthy elite. The way in which Pliny approached the question of associations and association membership may not necessarily have mapped onto the reality on the ground or matched up with how members thought about belonging to a group or about their own economic capacities. The financial obligations of membership indicate that belonging to an association was actually an expensive privilege not open to or affordable by everyone, certainly not to the truly poor. The total annual contribution for members outlined in the charter of an association in Tebtunis supposedly composed of sheep and cattle herders (*probataktēnotrophoi*), for instance, amounted to 144 drachmas.[57] Another association in Tebtunis active at roughly the same time, a group of tenants who held leases on imperial estate land (including at least one person identified also as a carpenter), expected the same level of payment: twelve drachmas a month.[58] An annual payment of 144 drachmas was a significant amount of money that equaled or approached the estimated expenditures

54. *Dig.* 47.22.1, 47.22.3.2.
55. Pliny, *Ep.* 10.92.
56. Pliny, *Ep.* 10.93.
57. *P.Mich.* V 243 (14–37 CE).
58. *P.Mich.* V 244 (43 CE).

required to support a hypothetical family of four during a single year, a sum that ranged between 140 and 320 drachmas on grain, depending on regional and seasonal variation.[59] Certain members were expected to contribute more, based on their position in the group. Such was the case with the *presbuteroi* of the weavers in Theadelphia in the early second century CE. They provided the money to outfit the space that their group used for meetings and feasts, according to the inscription commemorating the dedication of the room.[60] The head of an association of weavers active during the middle of the first century CE in the Fayum village of Kerkesoucha Orous contributed ninety-two drachmas for the group's banquet, a sum that is 66 percent of the minimum costs enumerated above.[61] The economic profile of members was not uniform, but in the most basic sense, association membership was costly, since all members contributed large sums.[62] That it was so expensive suggests that members had attained and were able to maintain an elevated economic status relative to the very poor of a given community's population. This aligns with the economic reality of association membership in Ptolemaic Egypt and throughout the Roman world, as van Nijf has asserted.[63]

Based on membership lists, dedicatory and honorific inscriptions, and other documents from Roman and late Roman Egypt, those who belonged to associations were predominately male and freeborn. There are some indications, however, that women belonged to groups or participated in association activities. A petition from two members of a woman's immediate family complaining that the members of a women's association failed to pay a burial benefit makes clear that women's groups existed during the Ptolemaic period.[64] A statue base with a dedication made by two women reveals the involvement of women in associations during the Roman period.[65] The group that benefited

59. Duncan-Jones 1990: 144–45. Duncan-Jones estimated that the cost of wheat in the first century averaged 3.5 drachmas per artaba (a measurement for dry goods equal roughly to 30 kg) for upper Egypt and 8 drachmas per artaba for lower Egypt. Estimates suggest that, on average, a person consumed ten artabae of wheat per year, worth thirty-five to eighty drachmas. A hypothetical family of four would require resources amounting to 140 to 320 drachmas based on expenditures for grain alone. Duncan-Jones also pointed out that the records of the *grapheion* in Tebtunis (*P.Mich.* II 127 [45/6 CE]), indicate that the price of grain varied between 4.4 and 8 drachmas per artaba during September and October. Based on these figures, association members in Tebtunis would have required expenses similar to the average range, if not slightly higher on the low end.

60. *I.Fayum* II 122 (109 CE).

61. *P.Mich.* II 121r (42 CE), col. IV, line 6.

62. See chapter 1, n. 54.

63. Monson 2006: 228; van Nijf 1997.

64. *P.Enteuxis* 21 (218 BCE).

65. *I.Alex.Imp.* 70 (early I CE) = *SB* III 6211 = *AGRW* 282.

from their donation might have been composed exclusively of women, based on its name (*Apolloniakē gunaikea sunodos*).[66] Evidence for participation of women in craft and merchant associations is sparse, but women, along with children and other household members, contributed to production and would have been involved in association affairs on some level.[67] The association of linen weavers in Oxyrhynchus in the late third century CE, for instance, referred to the participation of wives and children in the production of items that had been contracted by the local council.[68] Yet it is important to note that gender norms and expectations constrained the participation of women in trades and occupations in antiquity.[69] Although greater numbers of women may have participated in linen weaving and other production (often of luxury goods like jewelry and perfumes) that could be located within a domestic context or in retail, this might not be necessarily true for the whole of the craft and merchant sector.

The presence of slaves or freedmen in Egyptian associations is not well documented. There are no examples from the Ptolemaic period and only a few references to freedmen in later texts. A freedman named Narkissos belonged to the *sunodos* of Harpocrates in Tebtunis and contributed twenty-one drachmas for one of the group's banquets, somewhat more than the average contribution of just under seventeen drachmas for this particular celebration.[70] Two of the three weavers who represented a weavers' association in Philadelphia and to whom a local official made payment for clothing that the Roman prefect ordered were freedmen.[71] The lack of involvement of slaves and freedmen in Egyptian associations corresponds to what we know about slavery in Egypt. Compared to the rest of the ancient world, the slave population in Egypt was low. Bagnall and Frier estimated that 13.4 percent of the population in the *metropoleis* and an even smaller 8.5 percent of the population in villages were slaves.[72]

The picture is quite different in the Roman west. A more significant number of freedmen belonged to associations in Ostia, to offer just one example,

66. The group may have had a counterpart Apollonian association that was comprised of male members; see *I.Alex.Imp.* 65 (I CE).
67. Treggiari 1979; Saller 2003: 193–97; Clarysse and Thompson 2004: 201–3.
68. *P.Oxy.* XII 1414 (271-72 CE).
69. Saller 2007: 101–7.
70. *P.Mich.* V 246 (mid-I CE), line 15.
71. *BGU* VII 1564 = *Sel.Pap.* II 395 (138 CE).
72. Bagnall and Frier 1994: 70–71.

both as regular members and as group officials.[73] Social composition may have differed according to geographic location and the peculiarities of a specific population group. Wealthy freedmen who belonged to associations in the west operated under different social and economic constraints than their largely freeborn counterparts in Egypt.[74] Nevertheless, membership remained a significant investment and required a good deal of expendable income, which marked members out as more than poor and downtrodden craftsmen, merchants, and farmers.

Egyptian associations averaged ten to twenty-five members, but there would have been some variation.[75] Larger associations may have existed, but little, if any, Egyptian evidence indicates that groups grew as large as the *collegium* of builders (*fabri tignarii*) in Ostia, whose membership numbered over three hundred, or the *collegium* of builders in Rome, whose membership Royden suggested may have approached thirteen hundred.[76] As a major center of trade, however, the membership numbers for Ostian associations or those from Rome may not provide the best comparanda for what is found throughout Egypt, where smaller groups were the norm.

Arriving at an exact number of associations active in Egypt (or anywhere else) is, in many ways, just as difficult. Inscriptions, papyri, archaeological evidence, and Roman legal sources suggest that associations were ubiquitous. Associations were common in large cities and centers of trade for obvious reasons, but groups also were active in smaller communities. Tebtunis, a village of several thousand inhabitants located in the Fayum, was home to many associations during the first century CE: wool merchants, linen weavers, goldsmiths, dyers, fullers, salt merchants, oil makers, herders/owners of sheep and cattle, farmers, tenants on imperial estates, shepherds, fishermen, and builders, in addition to the *sunodos* of the great god and the association of Harpocrates. Fourth-century price declarations submitted by the associations of Oxyrhynchus indicate at least thirty-three groups active in what was a well-populated capital city (metropolis) of its administrative district (nome).[77] The actual number of associations may have been much higher, given Fikhman's estimate that

73. Meiggs 1973: 311–36; Royden 1988: 25–62.
74. Joshel 1992: 32–33; see also Mouritsen 2011.
75. Wipszycka (1965) suggested ten as an average; Poland (1909: 287) suggested twenty-five to thirty as the average, based on evidence not limited to Egypt or to craft and merchant associations.
76. *CIL* XIV 4569 (198 CE); Royden 1988: 127.
77. For the associations mentioned, see *P.Oxy.* LIV, appendix II.

documents mention more than 190 different trades and occupations.[78] Associations continued to play a vital and influential role in local communities well into the late Roman period. Sixth-century Aphrodito, a rather large village of perhaps seven thousand people, appears to have supported many associations: fullers, shipbuilders, cobblers, masons, smiths (including bronzesmiths), tailors, weavers, cloak makers, carpenters, bakers, barbers, wine merchants, shepherds, and oil workers. The presence of so many groups in places like Tebtunis, Aphrodito, and Oxyrhynchus also indicates that associations were not exclusively an urban phenomenon. The Egyptian documents even detail apparent links between association activities in villages and cities. Charters from first-century Tebtunis, for instance, stipulate that meetings of the associations of sheep and cattle herders and salt merchants would be held in the village and the nome's metropolis, Arsinoe.[79]

It has been estimated, based on census registers, that between one-third and one-half of the population of a metropolis like Oxyrhynchus during the third or fourth century CE consisted of individuals engaged in some sort of craft or merchant activity and not only involved in agricultural pursuits.[80] The small size of the sample provided by registers like *P.Oxy.* XLIV 3300 and *P.Oslo* III 111 and inconsistencies present in individual entries—in how scribes chose to record information such as profession (or how that information was provided to them)—still make it difficult to draw firm conclusions. Peter van Minnen estimates that even during the late Roman period in Oxyrhynchus, when overall population levels declined somewhat, six to nine thousand individuals may have worked in a "productive craft." Agricultural activities predominate in smaller communities, but Michael Sharp has pointed out, based on the trades described in documents, that "something of a service and commercial sector" seems to have existed in Theadelphia, a village in the Fayum.[81] The variety of associations in Tebtunis appears to indicate the existence of a similar sector there. Though none of these estimates mention association membership specifically, they suggest that a significant portion of the population may have been either a member of an association or employed by one.

78. Fikhman 1969: 151; Zimmerman (2002) suggests the possibility of close to three hundred different associations, based on references to occupations in documentary texts.
79. *P.Mich.* V 243 (14–37 CE), line 4; 245 (47 CE), lines 36–37.
80. Van Minnen 1987: 45; van Minnen concludes that 25 to 30 percent of the house-owning population of fourth-century Panopolis was engaged in some sort of productive craft, based on *P.Oxy.* XLVI 3300. See Alston 1998: 183–84; 2002: 274–75; Bagnall and Frier 1994: 72–74.
81. Sharp 1999: 164–65; Hobson 1985, 1986. For Karanis, see Alston 1997: 170.

Associations, the Ancient Economy, and Elite Ideology

Keith Hopkins famously characterized the ancient economy debate as an academic battleground over three decades ago.[82] Perhaps this characterization remains true today, although participants less frequently adopt either a strict "primitivist" or "modernist" approach, most clearly identified with the work of Moses Finley and Michael Rostovtzeff respectively. In fact, it has become common to castigate as overly reductionist both extreme positions adopted in the debate between the primitivist model, which sees the ancient economy as predominately agrarian, underdeveloped, vastly different from our own, and constrained by ideology and status concerns, and the modernist model, which emphasizes quantitative, rather than qualitative, differences. Critics of the ideologically determined models articulated by Finley, whose book *The Ancient Economy*, first published in 1973, has come to stand as the definitive statement of the primitivist position, often refer to the engagement of members of the elite in trade and commercial activity.[83] Others, such as Joseph Manning and Ian Morris, have pointed out Finley's exclusion of the Near East from his models and have made a persuasive case for expanding the data set brought to bear on issues regarding structure and performance that have been raised by Finley and by historians of the ancient economy applying both primitivist and modernist approaches.[84]

Regardless of one's location on the spectrum between the primitivist and modernist positions, Finley's work still defines the debate, determines research agendas, and influences approaches to a variety of economic topics beyond agriculture, including craft production, trade, and market activity, something Manning and Morris emphasize.[85] The place of trade and nonagricultural production in primitivist models (or the lack thereof) has prompted continued efforts by those working within both primitivist and modernist frameworks to measure the scale of production and the quantity of goods traded, in an attempt to refine their models.[86] The focus, however, has not necessarily extended to the artisans and merchants who contributed to the production and trade mea-

82. Hopkins 1983b: ix.
83. See, for example, D'Arms 1981; Pleket 1983; Wallace-Hadrill 1991; Patterson 1998; Andreau 1999, Rosenstein 2008; Craver 2010. On the extent of elite participation, see Garnsey and Saller 1987: 47–48.
84. Manning and Morris 2005.
85. Manning and Morris 2005: 12–15; on Finley's impact, see Andreau 2002.
86. See, for example, Bowman and Wilson 2009b.

sured. The social and economic decisions made by craftsmen and merchants (and others traditionally labeled nonelite), the frameworks in which they operated, their approach to economic activity on their own terms, and the impact these factors had on their economic decisions have essentially been overlooked or have seemed to matter less. Instead, the elite approach and explanation of economic activity has remained largely the only approach and explanation.

It is no surprise, then, to find that Finley's work has influenced our understanding of associations. As the following passage shows, Finley was among those who believed that associations existed primarily to fulfill social and convivial functions and that they bore no resemblance to any sort of economic organization.[87]

> Not only were there no guildhalls in antiquity, there were no guilds, no matter how often the Roman *collegia* and their differently named Greek and Hellenistic counterparts are thus mistranslated. The *collegia* played an important part in the social and religious life of the lower classes, both free and slave; they sometimes performed benevolent functions, as in financing burials; they never became regulatory agencies in their respective trades, and that, of course, was the *raison d'être* of the genuine guilds, medieval and modern.[88]

Ramsey MacMullen echoed this sentiment and claimed that *collegia* were "more interested in the pursuit of honor than economic advantage."[89] As Finley himself maintained, neither he nor Max Weber, whose work had a strong influence on him, had overlooked the numerous craftsmen who inhabited the cities and manufactured the goods used by urban populations. However, according to Finley, the overall impact of these manufacturers on an economy dominated by local agricultural production and income derived from land owned by elites was not significant.[90] In analyses of the economy and society of the ancient world, the emphasis on agriculture and the importance of rural production for ancient economic models from Weber to Finley, coupled with the antipathy expressed by members of the elite toward labor, has led to further marginalization of individual craftsmen, merchants, and the groups they formed.

87. Finley 1999: 137–38.
88. Finley 1999: 138.
89. MacMullen 1974: 76. For similar views, see Garnsey and Saller 1987: 156–57; Hopkins 1983: 211–17.
90. Finley 1999: 139.

This marginalization is based on the important place that status occupies in Finley's model of the ancient economy. The discussions of social status and the ancient economy have remained intertwined since Weber first took up the topic of the ancient economy and society, but Finley's approach has set the parameters of the debate for decades. Finley strove for a holistic model of the Greco-Roman economy and society and sought to incorporate dominant cultural values—including the low regard in which elites held craftsmen and merchants—in his economic and political models.[91] He viewed these cultural values as powerful determining factors in the economic decisions and behavior of individual actors at all levels of society. Finley asserted that an individual's social status and economic activities were inextricably linked. Therefore, he insisted that all economic endeavors were embedded in a larger web of social relationships that were determined and, in a sense, structured by an elite ideology that privileged agricultural economic activity as a source of prestige and honor, over commercial activities.[92] For Finley, an understanding of the economy and society of the ancient world could only be based on an examination of social status and the ways in which status hierarchies were formed, functioned, and perpetuated. Perhaps nothing illustrates this more than Finley's own choice to begin his analysis in *The Ancient Economy* with a discussion of status and attitudes regarding wealth and its proper acquisition.[93]

Finley (and others) found no shortage of spokespersons for these elite attitudes toward craft and merchant activities. A lack of trust for merchants and commercial activity pervades Greek and Latin literature. Herodotus, for instance, used the trope against Greek and non-Greek alike. According to Herodotus, when the Persian Cyrus was preparing to do battle against the Greeks, he expressed confidence because he "never yet feared men who set apart a place in the middle of their city where they perjure themselves and deceive each other."[94] Herodotus also counted as an initial volley in the conflict between Greece and the Near East the abduction of Io and other women from Argos by Phoenician merchants while they haggled over the merchandise that had been laid out on the beach.[95] Finley, though, based much of his analysis of

91. Finley 1983: 27.
92. Finley 1999: 49–52. On the role social status plays in Finley's analysis, see Andreau 2002: 43–49. For discussion of "embedded" social relationships in society and the economy, see Granovetter 1985; Granovetter and Swerdberg 2001; Swerdberg 2003: 33–37.
93. Finley 1999: 35–61.
94. Herodotus 1.153, trans. Waterfield (1998).
95. Herodotus 1.1.2–4.

the relationship between status and economic activities on an often-cited passage of Cicero's *De officiis* that outlined honorable and dishonorable economic pursuits.

> Now in regard to trades and employments, which are to be considered liberal and which mean, this is the more or less accepted view. First, those employments are condemned which incur ill-will, as those of collectors of harbour taxes and money lenders. Illiberal, too, and mean are the employments of all who work for wages, whom we pay for their labor and not for their art; for in their case their very wages are the warrant of their slavery. We must consider mean those who buy from merchants in order to re-sell immediately, for they would make no profit without much outright lying. . . . And all craftsmen are engaged in mean trades, for no workshop can have any quality appropriate to a free man. Least worthy of all are those trades which cater to the sensual pleasures: 'fishmongers, butchers, cooks, poulterers and fishermen' as Terence says; to whom you may add if you please, perfumers, dancers, and all performers in low grade music halls. But the occupations in which either a higher degree of intelligence is required or from which society derives no small benefit—such as medicine or architecture or teaching—they are respectable for those whose status they befit. Commerce, if it is on a small scale, is to be considered mean; but if it is large scale and extensive, importing much from all over and distributing to many without misrepresentation, is not to be greatly censured. Indeed, it even seems to deserve the highest respect if those who are engaged in it, satiated, or rather, I should say, content with their profits, make their way from the harbor to a landed estate, as they have often made it from the sea to a harbour. But of all things from which one may acquire, none is better than agriculture, none more fruitful, none sweeter, none more fitting for a free man.[96]

Investment in land and the adoption of an elite lifestyle was preferred not only in an economic sense but also in social and political terms, by elite Roman patricians who filled the senatorial and equestrian ranks. Commerce on a grand scale—such as, perhaps, that undertaken by the associations of *navicularii*, shipping magnates of sorts who were involved in trade across the Mediterranean—was approved or at least, according to Cicero, "not to be

96. Cicero, *De officiis* 1.150–51, trans. Finley (1999: 41–42). For the role of agriculture in an "underdeveloped economy," see Garnsey and Saller 1987: 43–46; on this passage in general, see Dyck 1996: 333–38.

greatly censured." But it was better to convert commercial profits into an investment in agriculture. Those who engaged in the work of the "mean trades" would have found themselves excluded from elite circles and political power, and members of the landholding elite would not have engaged in any dishonorable activities, themselves constrained no less by this elite ideology.

Cicero's statement finds ready parallels in the writings of Cato, Varro, and Columella. Striking a similar chord are Lucian's preference for literary endeavors rather than toil in his uncle's workshop, as he related in his *Somnium*,[97] and the following remarks, from Plutarch's *Life of Pericles*, about craftsmen who can be admired but never emulated.

> In other things there does not immediately follow upon the admiration and liking of the thing done any strong desire of doing the like. Many times, on the very contrary, while taking delight in the work, we slight the craftsman, as in the case of perfumes and purple dyes; we are pleased with these things themselves, but we consider dyers and perfumers to be of low status and vulgar people.[98]

Similar attitudes persisted into late antiquity. Two centuries after Plutarch and Lucian, Libanius invoked standards of honor in orations bemoaning the plight of councilors and the newfound wealth and, apparently, respect of merchants.

> I am no councilor: I have immunity because of my concern with rhetoric, but I can still be upset at the poverty of the councilors and the wealth amassed by the lackeys of the governors. Some of these, only recently hawkers of meat, bread or vegetables, have grown great on the property of the councilors and enjoy just as much respect as they, so great is the wealth they possess.[99]

By using stock tropes to abuse his political opponents, Libanius used models, set down in his own rhetorical handbooks, that extolled the innate and superior virtues of agriculture as an economic pursuit and way of life.[100] It is also clear that in his orations and rhetorical manuals, Libanius was following a long tradition of

97. Lucian, *Somnium* 1.8.
98. Plutarch, *Life of Pericles* 1.4, trans. Dryden (adapted).
99. Libanius, *Oration* II.54, trans. Norman (Loeb).
100. Libanius, *Progymnasmata*, comparisons 4 ("On Seafaring and Farming"), 5 ("On the Country and the City").

invective that likened opponents to craftsmen and merchants or denigrated them as the progeny of such individuals. None other than Cicero himself was besmirched by opponents because his father supposedly owned fulleries.[101] The reality of elite participation in the economy beyond agriculture suggests that even for members of the elite, however, the ideology espoused in texts like Cicero's *De officiis* was not an absolute constraint on their economic activities or behavior.

Finley employed Cicero's social analysis and the sentiments expressed by authors like Plutarch and Lucian as evidence for what he described as the "rigidly restricted" life of craftsmen and merchants, who "could think of leisure and independence only as Utopian."[102] Of course, such a negative assessment leaves little room for craftsmen and merchants or the associations they formed. A need to compensate for a lack of status has been seen as the driving force behind the organization, proliferation, and operation of associations. By considering them to be more or less entirely dependent on the main actors on the ancient economic stage, as reacting and never acting, it has been easy to view associations as social and religious organizations that focused on recouping this sense of status loss, or on a perceived status anxiety first and foremost, and not on economic matters. It has been assumed, then, that acquisition of status and honor thus remained the central preoccupation within these groups, left to play the role of a shadow society operating in parallel to but separated from the elite society in their communities.

A number of scholars have recently and rightly challenged this position as a suitable framework for approaching not only craftsmen and merchants but also associations.[103] In particular, in their studies of associations in Roman Asia Minor, Onno van Nijf and Philip Harland questioned the marginality of craft and merchant groups. In the process, they helped, to a great extent, to inaugurate a new wave of studies focused on the associative phenomenon. It is difficult to overlook the large number of public monuments and dedications to association benefactors that are set up along thoroughfares, near or within temple precincts, and in prominent civic spaces, as well as the monuments erected in cemeteries commemorating deceased association members, which attest to the social and political connections of many associations. Based on detailed analysis of the epigraphic and archaeological evidence that documents activities

101. Plutarch, *Life of Cicero* 1.1.
102. Finley 1999: 4.
103. See, for example, Joshel 1992; van Nijf 1997; Harland 2003; Hawkins 2006; Liu 2009; Holleran 2012; Mayer 2012; Flohr 2013.

such as commemoration and honorific exchange, van Nijf and Harland concluded that associations participated actively in local civic life. As a way of elucidating this participation, van Nijf examined the ways people chose to identify themselves, with which groups they sought to align, and how this translated into an important means of fashioning an identity for themselves and their groups, claiming,

> The epigraphy of private associations is an important constituent of the wider epigraphic representation of the *plebs media* in the first centuries of our era, and it opens a door for us upon the concerns and aspirations of craftsmen and traders in the post-classical polis. The fact that an increasing number of individuals chose in varying ways to commemorate their membership of collegia shows that this type of sociability was becoming an important element of popular self-identification. Relationships with the world at large (the post-classical polis) were increasingly defined through the mediating factor of membership of an association centered on occupational activities.[104]

The links that these monuments show with patrons and a wealthy segment of society and the connections that the craftsmen and merchants sought to commemorate are of particular importance. The reciprocal exchange of honors, goods, and benefits played a large role in van Nijf's investigation of the complexities of life within associations and within the society of the Roman world.[105] For Harland, associations provided an important way to integrate these different groups within local society. Like van Nijf before him, Harland stressed what he has viewed as the positive interaction between associations and society in general.[106]

Attention must now turn toward examining in a more detailed fashion how social, political, religious, and economic activities operated together as part of a system that guided action on the part of associations and their individual members. Analysis of documents from Egypt reveals that any single association activity—a funeral, a banquet, honoring a member or local official, collecting taxes, coordinating interactions with the authorities—was not simply a social, legal, political, or economic endeavor but all of the above. Nor were the very structures adopted to govern association actions, as laid out in their charters, intended to

104. Van Nijf 1997: 28.
105. Van Nijf 1997: 73.
106. Harland 2003: 87.

impact only one aspect of life. A more systematic approach to associations and the evidence that makes their actions clear will help hone our understanding of the relation between economic, social, religious, and political aims and experiences on both nonelite and elite levels in communities in the Roman Empire.

Beyond Elite Ideology: Honor among Thieves

It goes without saying that the ancient world and its economy were quite different from our own. Any number of demographic, social, legal, and political factors impacted that economy's scale and performance, even taking into consideration more generous estimates of the volume of trade and production.[107] The market economy that Peter Temin argued existed in the Roman world still would have operated under a number of constraints.[108] Be that as it may, some tools and concepts developed by economists, sociologists, and anthropologists and increasingly used to explain social and economic activity in medieval and modern contexts can also be applied to antiquity in order to analyze and better understand the actions of individuals and groups like associations. Social capital—however defined—and the access to it that associations provided and sought to maintain through shared norms and reciprocity within a multistranded network was of critical importance. In addition, trust, reputation, and esteem, which Geoffrey Brennan and Philip Petit have referred to as the "intangible hand" in economic activities, were no less vital to combat high transaction costs and to navigate what Peter Bang described as the "rough trading world" of antiquity.[109] This is perhaps not surprising, since, as Robert Putnam extolled in *Bowling Alone* (his classic discussion of social capital in modern American communities), "trustworthiness lubricates social life."[110]

Economic historians have suggested that reliance on social capital and the access to trust networks provided by medieval guilds and trade organizations were important factors in successful long-distance trade in the medieval world. Avner Greif has argued that medieval trade guilds relied on reputation-based mechanisms to deal with moral-hazard problems endemic to principal-agent relations, asymmetric information, and high transaction costs, among other

107. Chapters 2–6 of the *Cambridge History of the Greco-Roman Economy* are concerned with a description and analysis of different constraints on economic activity: ecology, demography, gender, law, economic institutions, and technology; see Scheidel, Morris, and Saller 2007:15–171.

108. Temin 2012.

109. Brennan and Pettit 2004: 245–88; Bang 2008: 131–32.

110. Putnam 2000: 19.

concerns.[111] Greif sums up the potential benefits of a trust-based and reputation-based strategy as follows: "When effective, this intertransactional linkage enables an individual to credibly commit himself ex ante not to behave opportunistically ex post. In the case of agency relationships, the agent can commit to honesty and hence be trusted."[112] In turn, Greif maintains that guilds had a salutary impact on the economy as a whole. Sheilagh Ogilvie has challenged this claim, highlighting the exclusionary character of guilds and the rent-seeking behavior that guilds engaged in while pursuing monopolies and their own advantages.[113] Putnam also pointed out that social capital primarily serves and benefits those within a particular network and does not always have a positive impact in all senses; what is good for an association is not necessarily good for others, in an unqualified sense.[114]

Nevertheless, the discussion about how craftsmen, merchants, and guilds attempted to harness social capital for their own benefit invites a similar investigation of ancient associations and their reliance on trust, reputation, esteem, and social capital in their public and private endeavors. The importance of trust and reputation was not only understood by craftsmen, merchants, and association members, whose group charters reveal that they understood it quite well. Even Cicero acknowledged it, as detailed in another passage (less often cited) from the *De officiis*.

> So also to buyers and sellers, to employers and employed, and to those who are engaged in commercial dealings generally, justice is indispensable for the conduct of business. Its importance is so great, that not even those who live by wickedness and crime can get on without some small element of justice. For if a robber takes anything by force or by fraud from another member of the gang, he loses his standing even in a band of robbers; and if the one called the "Pirate Captain" should not divide the plunder impartially, he would be either deserted or murdered by his comrades. Why, they say that robbers even have a code of laws to observe and obey.[115]

To say that there was nothing free about a workshop, to characterize craftsmen and merchants as incapable of honesty, and to exclude them from the world of

111. Greif 1989, 1993, 2006.
112. Greif 2006: 58.
113. Ogilvie 2011: 2–4, 315–43; see also Ogilvie 2007.
114. Putnam 2000: 21–22.
115. Cicero, *De officiis* 2.40, trans. Miller (Loeb).

honor in which members of the elite operated ideally, as Cicero did earlier in the *De officiis*, does not preclude the existence of a sense of honor among thieves, so to speak.[116] If not honor, Cicero would at least grant that buyers, sellers, and employers understood or should have understood the importance of justice, which he considers necessary not only for transactions, as stated above, but also for establishing trust (*fides*).[117]

Analyses of associations and individual craftsmen and merchants by Sandra Joshel, van Nijf, and Harland, carried out on the basis of Latin and Greek epigraphy and focused on group or individual identity and the ways in which associations allowed members of the nonelite to claim a place in society, have helped realign our understanding of these groups and their members. Such an approach can be refined further by considering the importance of social capital and trust, reputation, and esteem in the public sphere within communities. How associations and their members managed collective or individual reputations can be part of economic, social, and political strategies aimed at more than acquiring status or honor that had been denied to them. The honorific activities groups carried out—honoring patrons and colleagues, erecting statues in public, maintaining individual or common graves used by the group and its membership—point not to a focus on honor at the expense of profit, in keeping with an ancient elite ideology, but to an interest in profit and advancement through developing and perpetuating a trustworthy reputation and exploiting social norms and the rhetoric of honor in the process. Considering these concepts can push beyond the primitivist and modernist debate and, at the same time, shed new light on and open up new avenues of interpretation for the actions of craftsmen, merchants, and associations. Studying groups on their own terms, to the extent possible, facilitates a move away from status as an ideologically constructed absolute. Status should instead be conceived as something that is continually negotiated and used in a number of contexts and impacted by economic, social, legal, and political concerns.

Outline of This Book

This book analyzes the activities of craftsmen, merchants, and associations essentially from the bottom up, a privileged perspective on social and economic

116. Cicero, *De officiis* 1.150.
117. Cicero, *De officiis* 2.34.

life that the papyri afford. The first two chapters focus on association organization and collaboration, the economic aspects of membership and association activities, and how members conceived of and approached economic actions. Chapter 1, which argues that associations were economic organizations that aimed at enhancing the success of individual and collective actions, contends, on the basis of group charters and other texts documenting association activities, that establishing a trustworthy reputation was construed as a vital strategy for managing risk and uncertainty by association members themselves. As foundational documents that described how groups hoped to interact with colleagues and the community, outlined group activities, and detailed the financial and behavioral obligations incumbent upon members, charters provide an entry point not only to investigate the economic nature of associations but also to understand how their members approached decisions. More important, these texts allow us to examine the actions and decisions of association members largely in their own words.

Chapter 2 examines collaboration between association members and explores how trust, reputation, and working within an association framework mattered in the lives of members beyond meetings, celebrations, or funerals. Although the papyri provide significant detail, the evidence does not necessarily allow for easy answers. Archives and dossiers from the first-century Fayum, fourth-century Oxyrhynchus, and sixth-century Aphrodito, paired with documents from throughout the Roman world, indicate that members did attempt to adopt the business practices outlined in charters. Tracing the connections and business partnerships within and between associations, families, and individuals in contracts, leases, receipts, and related documents throughout the Roman and late Roman periods reveals that association members tended to pool resources and collaborate with each other.

Chapters 3 and 4 move beyond the immediate circle of an organization and explore important questions of self-presentation and the participation of associations in the community. These chapters examine the expression and perception of the identity and reputation that craftsmen, merchants, and their associations crafted for themselves, on the basis of texts they created and those prepared for official use. Chapter 3 extends the analysis of individual and group identity further than the funerary and commemorative context and focuses on what sociologist Erving Goffman termed the "presentation of the self in everyday life." More specifically, the analysis in that chapter concentrates on the ways in which individuals and groups communicated information about themselves, their behavior (economic or otherwise), and their social capital, as part of a strategy that had an economic and social impact beyond identity formation.

The perspective that Egyptian papyri provide on the participation of associations and their membership in their communities complements and refines our understanding of associations and craftsmen and merchants in Asia Minor, Italy, and the Roman west, which have been the subject of recent analyses based primarily on inscriptions and public monuments. Chapter 4 concentrates on their involvement in local public life, by analyzing interactions between local officials and elites and craftsmen, merchants, and association members, made clear by documents produced in the course of administering communities under Roman rule. Contractual relationships between associations and local officials demonstrate that these individuals and their groups were important and influential constituencies. Nominations to and appeals for relief from official posts and obligations indicate that being a craftsman, merchant, or association member did not preclude participation in Egyptian communities; evidence of office holding by craftsmen and merchants suggests that elite ideology regarding their unsuitability and untrustworthy nature may have been less of a determinant of political and economic decisions. Not only do contested nominations point to the expectation of participation by wealthy craftsmen and merchants, but the legal drama that followed invites analysis of larger questions: how such individuals and, presumably, the associations to which they may have belonged negotiated and defended their place in society and managed interactions with local elites. The language used in petitions and in the legal proceedings forces us to examine the reality and the rhetoric of how elites and nonelites alike viewed and interpreted this participation.

The final chapters of this book examine the impact of law on associations. The examples of two often-discussed public disturbances in Ephesos—the protest of a group of silversmiths reported in the Acts of the Apostles and the marketplace disruption instigated by the city's bakers during the second century—prompt questions about what craftsmen and merchants could expect from the imperial authorities. These episodes and their ultimate resolutions also invite consideration of how associations and their members understood policies and responded to legal regulations and of the extent to which imperial authorities and Roman law facilitated or constrained craft, merchant, and association activities. The actions of the silversmiths and bakers in Ephesos provide a starting point for a more detailed analysis of the impact of law on associations, craftsmen, and merchants; their conflicts with those in power; and how associations managed these relationships. As such, chapter 5 examines discrete incidents of conflict between associations and the authorities within Egypt and beyond, as well as the legal framework in which these disputes played out.

Chapter 6 evaluates associations, craftsmen, and merchants in the late Roman world. The consensus has been that life lived outside of elite circles was bleak. The rules of the game did not seem to favor those farther down the economic scale, compared to the power wielded by the Roman aristocracy and wealthy landowners or to the growing influence of Christian ecclesiastical establishments during this period, following the third-century economic crisis. As part of a systematic response to economic and social upheaval, it has been assumed, based on a selective reading of the Theodosian Code's restrictions and orders to "drag back" association members to cities, that the authorities and members of the local elite sought to limit the mobility of craftsmen (socially and geographically) and did so to preserve sufficient numbers who could provide necessary services and to increase the efficiency of tax collection.[118]

Texts from Egypt, particularly tax registers and account books, again offer another perspective, however, and suggest that associations did not suffer disproportionately under the weight of imperial legislation. Instead, associations and their members continued to be engaged in and were thought to be integral to the process of administering late Roman communities. Chapter 6 examines the relations between associations and the local and imperial authorities from the fourth century onward, by investigating the extent to which the authorities intervened in association activities and the lives of individual craftsmen and merchants. The evidence examined—primarily inscriptions, the legislation of the Theodosian Code, and papyri—suggests that associations continued to be active in their communities, remained influential constituencies, acquired privileges, and participated in the process of government on a local level.

History in Fragments: A Note on Papyrological Sources

Although the abundance of papyri (including ostraca) provides an unparalleled opportunity to examine life in the ancient world at both elite and nonelite levels, papyri are not without difficulties and quirks that complicate their interpretation. The papyrological documents do offer perspectives on social and eco-

118. *C.Th.* 10.20.6, 14.7.1.

nomic activity besides those of the Roman literary and political elite. Yet the bottom-up accounts that the papyri would seem to afford do not always begin at the rock bottom, as Roger Bagnall and Todd Hickey have reminded us.[119] The papyri offer something other than the points of view of Cicero or philosophical discussions of proper social and economic behavior, but they do not fill the gap in our understanding of the economy with the thoughts and ideas of the truly poor. The poorest peasants, craftsmen, and day laborers remain essentially absent from the documentation. Associations, however, were populated by relatively well-off members of the nonelite, whose lives are illuminated by papyri in ways not recovered so easily or in quite the same way through other evidence.

The textual evidence that Egypt provides is also fragmentary in a number of senses beyond the actual torn pieces of papryus on which the documents, receipts, leases, accounts, association charters, and tax registers are preserved. Certain areas of Egypt are better documented, which impacts our overall picture of the society and economy of Roman and late Roman Egypt. The largest number of texts that have been excavated, edited, and published come primarily from the Fayum region and Oxyrhynchus, and thousands of texts from Oxyrhynchus and its surrounding area await study and publication. The study that follows necessarily draws heavily on evidence from these two regions, along with papyri from Aphrodito, a village particularly rich in papyri from the late Roman period. Fewer documents have survived from areas where the water level has impacted the preservation of the otherwise durable papyri, such as Alexandria and the Nile delta. Our understanding of places like Alexandria, at least from a papyrological perspective, thus depends greatly on texts that were written or copied there and later brought elsewhere. The chronological spread of the papyri, though extensive, also contributes to the fragmentary nature of the picture that the texts provide. The published documents are concentrated in certain time periods, making some centuries better documented than others. The first several centuries of Roman rule in Egypt are documented best, while significantly fewer texts are available from, for instance, the fifth century.[120]

Even the most complete texts are fragmentary in another sense: documents essentially represent one moment in time in the lives of the parties involved, sometimes the only moment visible in the record. Details of a single receipt or

---

119. Bagnall 1993: 5; Hickey 2008: 120–24. See also Hickey 2009.
120. See Hickey 2008: 120–23 on chronology and geographical distribution in the late Roman period.

lease, including whether the terms actually were met, often remain obscure. In other instances, such as legal suits and petitions, only one side of an argument survives. Personal letters preserve wishes of health or condolence exchanged by friends and family, inquiries about business matters, and other details of daily life; however, for most of these letters, no reply exists. Dossiers and archives alleviate some of this fragmentation, but even a dossier or archive, which can consist of as few as two documents, is, in some sense, less than complete. The reality of working with papyrological documents, no matter how rich, ultimately reveals how much information has been lost, elided, or simply not recorded by the parties involved or the scribes who prepared the texts.

Yet, in some ways, papyri are no more fragmentary than other sources. Inscriptions that record and monumentalize official decrees, decisions, and political careers provide information that also complements the literary record and has proven invaluable for documenting the public life of associations. Nevertheless, honorific inscriptions can and do omit details pertaining to the relationship between those mentioned. Epitaphs saluting a member of an association or documenting someone's inclusion or affiliation with a group leaves the reader to assume a great deal about that person's relationship with the professional or religious group mentioned. Papyri can fill this gap. While a papyrus document often was composed by a scribe, inscriptions, too, would have been mediated by scribes and stonecutters.

The special place of Egypt or the purported uniqueness of papyri, once commonly invoked to exclude their consideration, should not hinder the reliance on papyri to write a history of associations under Roman rule.[121] It is true that Egypt can be said to differ from other provinces in certain political, social, and environmental aspects: with the exception of those in four privileged "Greek cities," there were no councils (*boulai*) familiar from other parts of the eastern empire until the time of Severus; slavery existed there on a smaller scale; and life on the Nile presented its own environmental benefits and constraints—to name only a few considerations. But each Roman province would have been peculiar in many ways, and each would have had its own local traditions, history, and social and economic hierarchies, as well as its own environmental and geographical constraints.

Upon closer examination, many factors make Egypt seem more or less simi-

121. For discussions of and the need to move beyond Egypt's "special place," see, among others, Bagnall 2005a; Keenan 2009.

lar to other parts of the Roman Empire and the ancient Mediterranean, as a growing body of research has attempted to show. From an economic perspective, agriculture remained the dominant pursuit even with an active craft and merchant economy. The administrative and political structure of individual communities was similar to what was in place in other provinces.[122] If there were no *boulai* in name, local bodies that acted like councils did exist at least from the advent of Roman rule, and communities continued to rely on local elites to fulfill administrative duties. Although the epigraphic and archaeological evidence has not survived in the same quantity or detail for Egypt as for other areas, the existing evidence does not seem to differ drastically in character, although there certainly are some regional differences. All of this suggests that seeking to better understand Egypt, its communities, its various associations and professional groups, and Roman interactions with its elite and nonelite populations as evidenced through the papyri will help us better understand other provinces in comparison and the functioning of the empire as a whole.

122. Bagnall 2005a: 198; Bowman and Rathbone 1992.

CHAPTER 1

Charters, Transaction Costs, and Trust

Ancient craft and merchant associations have been called many things, but the designation economic organization rarely makes the list. Instead, they have been characterized as religious groups, burial societies, and social clubs. Their goals, we have been told, remained predominantly social and religious: to offer a setting for commiseration; to compensate for political impotence with their own offices, titles, and passing honorary decrees; and to commemorate departed members with a funeral and burial celebrated and paid for by the group. Faced with pervasive deficiency in all aspects of life, living on the social and political margins of their communities, and unable to rely on family and friends, craftsmen and merchants, it has been asserted, resorted to mutual aid societies like associations to make their nonelite existences manageable.[1]

This is certainly how some members of the Roman elite understood these groups and their function.[2] Jurists assumed that associations existed primarily to offer support to *homines tenuiores*, echoing the language and sentiment that Pliny employed to describe these groups in his letters.[3] Given the primacy of agriculture and its place as the dominant and most ethically proper source of wealth and power in antiquity, combined with a negative appraisal of commercial activity, elite attitudes toward these groups and their purposes is not surprising. Such ideas have shaped our models not only of the ancient economy but also of the place associations, craftsmen, and merchants occupied in society and how they operated in that economy. Since associations were not deemed

1. For discussion, see introduction, n. 12.
2. Pliny, *Ep.* 10.32, 33. On attitudes toward work, see D'Arms 1981: 20–47; Joshel 1992: 63–91.
3. *Dig.* 3.4, 47.22; Pliny *Ep.* 10.92, 93.

active players in local, provincial, or imperial society, scholars have supposed that association membership, association activities, and operating within the organizational framework described by charters mattered little to the ancient economy. Any potential economic impact that membership had on individuals who belonged to associations has been considered less important and secondary to the groups' social goals.

In his magisterial survey of social relations in the Roman world, Ramsey MacMullen echoed much of this sentiment and maintained that association activities were not economic but, instead, social in nature.[4] He expressed surprise that given what seemed to be shared economic interests among association members, the texts he examined contained little specifically pertaining to economic concerns, and there was little evidence of actions taken on the part of these groups to further or defend economic interests. Surveying the evidence with an eye to elite ideology and ancient ideas about work and labor, MacMullen saw only the constant struggle for status—perhaps at the expense of economic activity—and a lack of sophistication in ancient economic practice.

More recently, although accepting the existence of some group economic activities, Sandra Walker-Ramisch, following MacMullen, cautioned us not to be misled by the "economic focus of guild records," and placed the emphasis on the social and convivial elements of association membership.

> As Ramsey MacMullen warns, one should not to be misled by the economic focus of the records; *collegia* were not constituted for economic purposes. Although there could be an economic advantage to the incorporation of herders or weavers or longshoremen, even the professional guilds assembled for social purposes. It was primarily the experience of conviviality and *communio* provided by *collegia* which drew people together, and this is reflected in the names they gave to their societies—"Mates and Marble Workers," "Brother Builders," "the Comrade Smiths," "The Late Drinkers."[5]

Although Walker-Ramisch emphasized the brotherhood of the builders and the camaraderie of the smiths, she discounted both the central aspect that their trade may have played in adopting a particular organization and any economic impact membership might have had.

4. MacMullen 1974: 78.
5. Walker-Ramisch 1996: 133.

Yet charters and other documents make it clear that economic concerns—including prices, taxes, and credit relationships—were no less a focus of association activities. The rules and regulations that groups adopted in their charters also reveal that their regard for the economic matters that membership helped individuals manage was intertwined with, not separate from, what is often considered the social and religious aspects of membership. It is thus important to remember that the "mates and marble workers" whom Walker-Ramisch discussed were not either mates or marble workers, nor were they primarily mates, as she suggested. They were both.

Since charters outline group activities and obligations, these documents provide an ideal entry point not only to investigate the economic nature of associations but also to understand how members approached decisions and to explore the relationship between economic concerns and financial matters, on the one hand, and celebrating feasts and funerals, on the other. In addition to the financial expectations of members and internal organization, charters also define accepted social and economic norms. The framework that charters created and that members relied on thus linked individuals through various relationships (economic, social, and legal), shared celebrations, participation in rituals, and reciprocal obligations.

Ideally, by acting in accordance with the rules laid out in the charters, associations fostered the creation of what Charles Tilly has called trust networks. Tilly described a trust network as a group of closely connected individuals who "carry on major long-term enterprises such as procreation, long-distance trade, workers' mutual aid or practice of an underground religion" and who work in concert to offset risks, economic or otherwise, and the potential for failure in their enterprise.[6] Operating within an association's institutional framework—indicated by charters and other documents related to group activities—enabled members to amass social capital by establishing interpersonal trust and developing a trustworthy reputation through repeated interaction, whether via feasts, funerals, meetings, loans, or other transactions. Abiding by norms spelled out in charters also likely helped members secure credit and financial assistance and acquire and disseminate information about goods, services, prices, and potential partners. Ultimately, relying on trust, reputation, and social capital allowed members to further individual and group goals; to manage

6. Tilly 2005: 4. For ancient associations as trust networks, see Hawkins 2006: 101; Monson 2006; Venticinque 2010, 2013.

risk and uncertainty in economic, political, social, and legal contexts; and, in short, to reduce transaction costs.[7]

Egypt has preserved some of the most detailed examples of group charters (*nomoi*), as well as documents related to association activities beyond honorific inscriptions and epitaphs, including receipts, accounts, leases, letters, contracts, petitions, and official declarations.[8] Charters have survived from the Ptolemaic, Roman, and late Roman periods.[9] Although groups operated within different economic and political systems during these time frames, the charters that associations crafted and the activities in which these groups engaged compare well with other association charters and evidence of their activities drawn from communities throughout the Greco-Roman world. This is perhaps not surprising. Regardless of economic and political constraints, trust, reputation, esteem, and access to market information and to information about those with whom people maintained economic, social, and legal relationships remained vital and would have been sought after, if possible, in any context.

This does not lessen the economic nature of funerals and the rituals leading up to or following a burial, of regular celebrations or feasts, or of the rules devised to govern these activities; rather, the reliance on social capital would seem to raise the economic stakes of participation for all involved. Charters and other documents that show how associations structured their affairs offer an opportunity to investigate the relationship between economic, social, and religious activities and the impact that the social and religious rituals had on economic activity and behavior. Far from only involving participants in social or religious events, celebrating banquets, honoring people (members, patrons, and local officials), and attending funerals were part of how groups operated and how individual craftsmen and merchants plied their trades. Taking into account the embedded nature of the economy—something even Finley main-

7. For transaction costs, see introduction, n. 3. Risk and uncertainty have been defined in numerous ways. Frank H. Knight, one of earliest to discuss the distinction between the two, defined "risk" as random outcomes with known factors and probabilities and defined "uncertainty" as random outcomes with unknown factors and probabilities, basic definitions that remain useful for conceptualizing risk and uncertainty in antiquity; see Knight (1921) 2006. The discussion of risk and uncertainty, however, has progressed a great deal since Knight. On risk in general, see Lupton 1999; on risk in late Roman communities, Grey 2011.

8. In general, see Boak 1937; de Cenival 1972; Muszynski 1977; San Nicolò (1913) 1972; Muhs 2001; Arnaoutoglou 2005; Monson 2006, 2007a, 2007b; Gibbs 2008; Venticinque 2009.

9. For Greek evidence from the Ptolemaic period, see Nock, Roberts, and Skeat 1936; for Demotic *nomoi,* de Cenival 1972. For Roman and late Roman examples, see *P.Mich.* V 243 (14–37 CE), 244 (43 CE), 245 (47 CE); *PSI* XII 1265 (426 CE); *SB* III 6704 (538 CE).

tained—it is important not to view these activities otherwise.[10] As a result, associations must be considered not only religious groups or social groups or burial societies or economic organizations; they were, in fact, all of these things.

Charters, Membership Obligations, and Financial Support

The charters that have survived, inscribed on stone or written on papyrus in Greek, Latin, or Demotic, offer a different perspective on association activities than public honorific inscriptions, epitaphs, and legal discussions.[11] Charters describe the organization of associations, define members' financial obligations and behavioral expectations, and detail group celebrations, meetings, and involvement in funerals. By specifying privileges and obligations of membership, charters indicate how associations and their members intended to interact, as well as the concerns that occupied their minds in the marketplace, the meeting hall, and the workshop and at home.

Some charters were erected in the houses that groups possessed or in spaces they used for meetings (referred to as *scholae* or *oikoi*).[12] Association officials kept copies of charters written on papyrus, and other copies might have been filed in public archives, as seems to have been the case for the charters from first-century Tebtunis. Membership lists were sometimes inscribed along with charters and displayed in houses and were expanded or emended as needed.[13] An association of weavers from Coptos, for instance, inscribed the names of their officials and members on the stele that displayed their charter in the temple of Geb.[14] Egyptian charters written on papyrus also included membership rolls and individual signatures, which turned charters into contracts.

Three first-century charters belonging to groups active in Tebtunis provide a representative sample of how associations structured their activities and accomplished their aims. The charter of an unidentified group believed to have been an association of sheep and cattle herders (based on language in the text

10. Granovetter 1985; Granovetter and Swerdberg 2001.
11. See, for example, *IG* II² 1369 (II CE, Attica); *SEG* XXXI 122 (ca. 121/2 CE, Attica); *IG* II² 1368 (164/5 CE, Attica), IX/1² 670 (early II CE, Locris); *CIL* XIV 2112 (136 CE, Lanuvium) = *ILS* 7212 = *FIRA* III 35; *ILS* 7213 (153 CE); *P.Mich.* V 243–45 (I CE, Tebtunis). On evidence for charters and on references to charters in other documents, see Kloppenborg and Ascough 2011: 4.
12. For example, *CIL* XIV 2112 (136 CE, Lanuvium); *IG* II2 1368 (164/5 CE, Attica). On *scholae*, see Bollmann 1998; Hermansen 1982: 61-87.
13. See *CIL* XIV 4569 (198 CE), a membership list found in the *schola* of the builders in Ostia.
14. *Stud.Demotica* V 158 (30 BCE).

pertaining to the acquisition of livestock) was signed by seventeen men (*P.Mich.* V 243 [14–37 CE]).[15] Another charter belonged to a group of twenty-four men who leased land from an imperial estate and were referred to as the *apolusimoi*, assumed to be a reference to their freedom from certain taxes and duties (*P.Mich.* V 244 [43 CE]). That one of the *apolusimoi* was identified as a carpenter invites speculation that others among them may have also been tradesmen. The third charter belonged to a group of salt merchants who had at least five members and maybe more; damage to the portion of the document containing their signatures makes certainty on total membership impossible (*P.Mich.* V 245 [47 CE]). These charters, all written in Greek, along with membership lists of three other associations (*P.Mich.* V 246–48), were part of an archive of 192 texts that spanned seventy-six years (20 BCE–56 CE). The archive belonged to the village scribe Kronion, who had taken over the scribal position (and the archive) from his father. All but forty-three of the texts have been published.

Tebtunis was one of many villages in the Fayum (a region southwest of the Delta, linked to the Nile by the Bahr Yusef) and belonged administratively to the Arsinoite nome.[16] Despite the agricultural focus of the economy of Tebtunis, this village of several thousand people also supported a lively craft and merchant economy, evidenced by the variety of associations mentioned in the texts of Kronion's archive.[17] Other documents relating to Tebtunis and the Fayum (one of the best-documented regions in Egypt) confirm the image provided by the archive's texts. In addition to the salt merchants, the *apolusimoi*, and the sheep and cattle herders, associations of dyers, fullers, wool merchants, weavers, builders, oil makers, and goldsmiths operated in Tebtunis, and a similar variety of associations can be found in other communities.[18]

Any extant charter was probably one of several copies. The charter of the sheep and cattle herders stated that the group returned the document into the possession of their president after its ratification.[19] Other groups may have done likewise. The texts give the impression that associations composed the

15. In addition, the accounts of the *grapheion* in Tebtunis also contain references to associations of sheep and/or cattle herders (*probatoktēnotrophoi*): see *P.Mich.* II 123r (45–46 CE), col. iii, line 40; col. viii, line 26.
16. On the Fayum, see Bagnall and Rathbone 2004: 127–54. See also Capasso and Davoli 2007; Lippert and Schentuleit 2008.
17. For population estimates, see Rathbone 1990.
18. *P.Mich.* II 123r (45–47 CE), col. VI, line 16; *P.Mich.* II 123r (45–47 CE), col. VI, line 17; *P.Mich.* II 123r (45–47 CE), col. VI, line 18; *P.Mich.* II 123r (45--47 CE), col. IX, line 35; *P.Mich.* II 123r (45–47 CE), col. XVII, line 38; *P.Mich.* II 124r (46–49 CE), col. II, line 15; *P.Mich.* II 124r, col. II, line 19,
19. *P.Mich.* V 243 (14–37 CE).

regulations in communal fashion, and approval by a vote seems to have been a common final step. Nevertheless, scribes like Kronion may have helped prepare the documents.[20] The copy of the charter of the sheep and cattle herders might even have been a draft by Kronion himself; it appears to have been a copy kept on file at the *grapheion*. Another of Kronion's accounts indicates that charters belonging to associations of shepherds (*poimenes*), oil workers (*elaiourgoi*), wool merchants (*eriopōloi*), and builders (*oikodomoi*) were also prepared at the *grapheion*, for fees ranging from several obols to eight drachmas.[21] However charters were composed and ultimately disseminated to the group and displayed, they functioned as contracts that bound members to each other and reminded them of their obligations and responsibilities to abide by and to enforce the provisions among themselves.

The organizational framework and the mutual obligations agreed on by the cattle herders contain elements that were common among associations in the ancient world. The sheep and cattle herders planned to meet regularly, pledged mutual support, offered financial assistance for funerals, and reserved the right to punish members who violated the rules, missed meetings, or misbehaved. The sheep and cattle herders also elected a colleague—Heron, son of Orseus—to serve as the presiding officer for the year, to whom responsibility fell to organize meetings and enforce the charter's rules.

> [. . .] have chosen as president for the *x* year of Tiberius Caesar Augustus Heron, son of Orseus, in whose company they shall hold a banquet each month on the twelfth, each one contributing for his monthly dues the twelve silver drachmas assigned equally to each. If anyone fails to meet his obligations in these or the other matters, the president has the right to exact pledges. If anyone misconducts himself, let him be fined whatever the society may decide. If anyone receives notice of a meeting and does not attend, let him be fined one drachma in the village, but in the city four drachmas.[22]

The *apolusimoi* and the salt merchants also met monthly and designated elected officers to oversee their activities and enforce their rules according to their charters.[23] Other groups in Tebtunis (and elsewhere) for whom no charter has

20. For the *grapheion*, see Husselman 1970.
21. *P.Mich.* II 123 (45–49 CE).
22. *P.Mich.* V 243 (14–37 CE), lines 1–4, trans. Boak.
23. *P.Mich.* V 244 (43 CE), lines 14–16; 245 (47 CE), lines 34–35.

survived, including the builders, oil workers, and wool merchants mentioned in Kronion's accounts, may have adopted similar structures. References in Kronion's accounts to individuals identified as a *grammateus* or *hēgoumenos* of associations of weavers, cloth beaters, and fishermen suggest as much.[24]

Regular attendance (and proper decorum) at meetings and celebrations was expected, as evidenced by fines, but associations also assumed that members would interact with colleagues in a certain way beyond banquets and offer assistance when needed. The sheep and cattle herders, for instance, required members to provide aid and financial support to their colleagues spelled out in their charter.

> If anyone neglects another in trouble and does not give aid to release him from his trouble, let him pay eight drachmas. And each one who in taking seats at the banquets shoves in front of another shall pay an extra three obols for his own place. If anyone prosecutes another or defames him, let him be fined eight drachmas. If anyone intrigues against another or corrupts his home, let him be fined sixty drachmas. If anyone is given into custody for a private debt, let them go to bail for him up to one hundred silver drachmas for thirty days, within which he will release the men.[25]

The *apolusimoi* outdid the cattle herders' promise to help with private debts up to one hundred drachmas during a span of thirty days, by extending support for debts up to sixty days.[26] The charters of associations active during the Ptolemaic period emphasized similar obligations to assist colleagues, and the associations fined those who neglected to do so, as did groups in Greece.[27] These provisions most likely applied to loans and debts among group members, as well as to obligations outside the association. Loans may not have been readily available to cover regular dues payments, however, since associations reserved the right to punish delinquency.[28]

Given the financial profile of members, helping someone in need, extend-

24. *P.Mich.* II 121r (42 CE), col. IV, line 6; 123r (45–47 CE), col. XIV, lines 16, 37; 124r (46–49 CE), col. II, line 19; 127, line 20; *PSI* VIII 901 (46 CE). For other examples in the Arsinoite nome, see *P.Fouad* 18–19 (53 CE).
25. *P.Mich.* V 243 (14–37 CE), lines 6–8, trans. Boak.
26. *P.Mich.* V 244 (43 CE), lines 9–11.
27. For Egyptian comparisons, see, for example, *P.Lille.Dem.* 29 (223 BCE), lines 15–17 = de Cenival 1972: 3–38; *P.Prague* (137 BCE), lines 25–26 = de Cenival 1972: 83–91. See also *IG* II2 1275 (325–275 BCE), lines 7–10.
28. *P.Mich.* V 243 (14–37 CE), lines 2–3; 244 (43 CE), lines 18–20; *SEG* XXXI 122 (II CE), lines 43–45; *IG* II² 1368 (164/5 CE), lines 67–72.

ing credit, and making loans probably were not always a last resort for colleagues in dire straits. Loans provided by the group itself appear to have been one way associations used their common fund, which offered a source of ready capital.[29] Alleviating financial hardship and low economic status might not have been the chief attraction leading people to join or form an association. The provisions in charters more likely indicate that members decided to pool resources and depend on each other to manage economic concerns, including money shortages and burial expenses, as part of a larger strategy to offset risk and uncertainty, not out of need, but because they could.

That does not mean that a personal or financial disaster was not sometimes the impetus for using association funds. Five weavers from Euhemeria, another village in the Fayum, apparently were in legal or financial distress when the president and secretary of their association provided surety on their behalf to the local magistrate presiding over their dispute with a wool worker.[30] No matter the circumstances, association membership provided an additional avenue to confront economic setbacks and helped members maintain a position of strength relative to the rest of the community. Although mutual aid and support was a concern, all association members had an interest in and benefited economically from preserving a colleague's credit. The fact that groups tried to protect a colleague's credit through loans and surety, even in the short term, suggests that members of associations understood this fact.

Financial Management

Group charters also reveal that associations possessed and managed a common fund into which members contributed their various payments, whether for dues or fines. Associations may have used these funds for a number of purposes, but several honorific inscriptions indicate that groups may have done more than just safeguard the money contributed. A number of groups in Hellenistic and Roman Greece routinely honored the efforts of their officials for prudent management of their resources and for increasing the treasury.[31] Man-

29. See *P.Ryl.* IV 586 (99 BCE); *BGU* IV 1137 (6 BCE) = *W.Chr.* 112; *P.Stras.* IV 287 (VI CE). See also *SEG* XXXI 122 (II CE), lines 42–43. On loans, see Martinez and Williams 1997; Martinez 1997; Gabrielsen 2005. On common funds, see Liu 2008.

30. *P.Ryl.* II 94 (14–37 CE) = *Sel.Pap.* II 255.

31. *IG* II^2 1271 (299/8 BCE), 1298 (248/7 BCE), 1292 (215/4 BCE), 1323 (194/3 BCE), 1343 (37/6 or 36/5 BCE).

aging the common fund with an eye to preserving and, perhaps, adding value helped associations defray expenses as a group and provide a larger resource pool for unexpected needs, whether providing aid to a member or covering an unanticipated tax increase.

In addition, charters detail other economic activities that associations coordinated, beyond what might appear to be mutual aid or dues payments. The *apolusimoi*, for instance, expected their officer to manage tax payments and group expenses.

> The third year of Tiberius Claudius Caesar Augustus Germanicus Imperator, on the third supplementary day of the month Kaisareios, at Tebtunis in the division of Polemon of the Arsinoite nome. Having met together, the undersigned men of Tebtunis, *apolusimoi* of an estate of Tiberius Claudius Caesar Augustus Germanicus Imperator, voted unanimously to elect one of their number, an excellent man, Kronion, son of Herodes, to be superintendent for one year from the month Sebastos of the coming fourth year of Tiberius Claudius Caesar Augustus Germanicus Imperator, the same Kronion to collect the public revenues of the poll-tax of the same *apolusimoi* and all the expenses of the said association.[32]

The salt merchants made a similar provision for trade taxes.[33] Additional texts suggest that group payment was common and that the sums levied could be quite large: documents in Kronion's *grapheion* archive indicate that the salt merchants, as a group, made payments of 576 and 208 drachmas.[34] By the late Roman period, if not sooner, associations managed tax collection as a group, in coordination with local and imperial officials.[35] This was the case with the *chrysargyron*, a trade tax collected every five years from the reign of Constantine into the reign of Anastasius (491–518 CE), as well as other taxes.[36] An association of goldsmiths in fifth-century Oxyrhynchus, for example, designated their officer (*kephalaiōtēs*) to collect and pay the trade tax according to regulations they adopted.[37] Demotic

32. *P.Mich.* V 244 (43 CE), lines 1–7, trans. Boak.
33. *P.Mich.* V 245 (47 CE), lines 5–9.
34. *P.Mich.* II 123r, col. xxii, line 27; col. vii, line 27; *P.Grenf.* II 43 (92 CE); *P.Tebt.* II 287 (161–69 CE) = *W.Chr.* 251. On trade taxes, see Gibbs 2011: 298–99.
35. *P.Leid.Inst.* 62 (370, 385, or 399 CE); *SB* XVIII 13916 (386 CE), XVI 12260 (421 CE); *P.Rain.Cent.* 122 = *SB* XVIII 13883 (429 CE); *SPP* VIII 850, 852 (both VI CE); *P.Rain.Cent.* 138 (VI CE). See also Bagnall and Worp 1985.
36. For the *chrysargyron*, see Johnson and West 1949: 318–20; see also Wallace 1938: 214–19.
37. *PSI* XII 1265 (426 CE)

receipts dating to the reigns of Augustus and Tiberius from the Theban area, however, indicate that some trade taxes were paid by individual weavers, sellers of hay, and builders.[38] Greek texts from Oxyrhynchus and the Fayum similarly attest to individual payments.[39] Individual tax payments by craftsmen and merchants suggest that not all groups may have chosen to pay as collectives or were able to do so or that each craftsman did not necessarily belong to an association. This fact might, in turn, reveal some strategy behind decisions by association members to pool resources for tax assessments.

Associations also managed the fees and taxes for market access, as detailed in a second-century register from Oxyrhynchus that was prepared for official use. According to the register, seventeen different types of craftsmen and merchants paid for stalls at the Serapeum market, including several explicitly identified as associations (*koina* of vegetable sellers, butchers, and, possibly, shoe makers) and many others for which associations are known.[40] Although extant charters do not include such a provision, it seems to complement association efforts to manage other imposts. Inscriptions from Asia Minor that designate the market stalls that associations occupied and were granted by officials point toward a role that associations played in securing space to sell goods and organize other economic aspects of their trade.[41] When disputes regarding financial burdens like tax assessment arose, associations coordinated interactions with the authorities as well. Believing that they had been assessed unfairly, for instance, a group of dyers and fullers from the Fayum submitted a petition about their payments, which prompted a review of records by the authorities.[42] The actions of the dyers and fullers make it clear that their responsibilities, at least to the group, continued beyond collection of taxes and fees.

Market Activities and Information

Charters reveal that beyond the management of tax assessments and the coordination of payments on behalf of the group, members used associations to organize trade, collect price and market information, and, presumably, dissem-

38. *O.Medin.HabuDem.* 54–58 (I CE).
39. *P.Oxy.* II 288 (25 CE); *P.Fay.* 58 (155–56 CE), 59 (178 CE).
40. *SB* XVI 12695 (143 CE), lines 13, 15, 19; on the text, see Rea 1982. See also *P.Köln.* IV 195 (II/III CE), V 228 (176 CE).
41. See, for example, *I.Eph.* 2076–82 (200–210 CE).
42. *P.Tebt.* II 287 = *W.Chr.* 251 (161–69 CE).

inate this information within the group. The charter of the salt merchants indicates how associations sought to manage these processes.

> The seventh year of Tiberius Claudius Caesar Augustus Germanicus Imperator, the 25th of the month Kaisareios. The undersigned men, salt merchants of Tebtunis, meeting together have decided by common consent to elect one of their number, a good man, Apynchis, son of Orseus, both supervisor and collector of the public taxes for the coming eighth year of Tiberius Claudius Caesar Augustus Germanicus Imperator, the said Apynchis to pay in all the public taxes for the same trade for the same coming year, and (they have decided) that all alike shall sell salt in the aforesaid village of Tebtunis, and that Orseus alone has obtained by lot the sole right to sell gypsum in the aforesaid village of Tebtunis and in the adjacent villages, for which he shall pay, apart from the share of the public taxes which falls to him, an additional sixty-six drachmas in silver; and that the said Orseus has likewise obtained by lot Kerkesis, alone to sell salt therein, for which he shall likewise pay an additional eight drachmas in silver. And that Harmiusis also called Belles, son of Harmiusis, has obtained by lot the sole right to sell salt and gypsum in the village of Tristomos also called Boukolos, for which he shall contribute, apart from the share of the public taxes which falls to him, five additional drachmas in silver; upon condition that they shall sell the good salt at the rate of two and one-half obols, the light salt at two obols, and the lighter salt at one and one-half obol, by our measure or that of the warehouse. And if anyone shall sell at a lower price than these, let him be fined eight drachmas in silver for the common fund and the same for the public treasury; and if any of them shall be found to have sold more than a stater's worth of salt to a merchant, let him be fined eight drachmas in silver for the common fund and the same for the public treasury; but if the merchant shall intend to buy more than four drachmas worth, all must sell to him jointly. And if anyone shall bring in gypsum and shall intend to sell it outside, it must be left on the premises of Orseus, son of Harmiusis, until he takes it outside and sells it. It is a condition that they shall drink regularly on the 25th of each month each one a chous of beer . . . in the village one drachma, outside four drachmas, and in the metropolis eight drachmas. But if anyone is in default and fails to satisfy any of the public obligations, or any of the claims that shall be made against him, it shall be permissible for the same Apynchis to arrest him in the main street or in his house or in the field, and to hand him over as aforesaid.[43]

43. *P.Mich.* V 245, lines 1–42, trans. Boak.

The salt merchants apparently thought of themselves as more than a group that looked after tax payments and provided mutual aid to members. They attempted to monitor the particulars of the trade in salt and gypsum (a construction material) in Tebtunis and its surrounding area.[44] Each member did have the right to sell salt in Tebtunis, but as the charter stipulates, the merchants divided up other areas and made specific arrangements regarding the sale of gypsum. The right to trade in other locations was decided by lot. But this may not be as egalitarian as it appears; for this access, the group assessed additional fees, quite significant in some cases: one Orseus mentioned in the charter paid sixty-six drachmas for the privilege of selling gypsum in Tebtunis—the equivalent of dues paid by the sheep and cattle herders or the *apolusimoi* over five and a half months. The same Orseus also obtained the right to sell salt in the neighboring village of Kerkesis. The charter mentions two men named Orseus, one of whom was the father of the current association president. It is unclear which Orseus held these concessions. The list of signatures at the bottom of the text might have given more information, but it is torn. If the Orseus who was the father of Apynchis held the costly concession for selling gypsum in Tebtunis, this arrangement may suggest something more than chance and, instead, allude to an internal hierarchy. Despite association claims of equality among members, differentiation within their ranks was common. The opinions of some members, if not the actual votes, may have carried more weight.

According to the charter of the salt merchants, prices were also a concern. The merchants set prices for the salt varieties they sold. Good salt traded at 2.5 obols, but light salt and lighter salt were priced at 2 obols and 1.5 obols respectively. This may look like an attempt to limit members' profits, but these were only minimum prices. The group placed no upper ceiling on prices (or profits), and individuals were apparently free to sell above minimum levels.

Several considerations may have influenced the salt merchants' concern for prices. Maintaining a base price to avoid undercutting other merchants in the group and damaging profits for all was probably a factor. Setting prices also indicates that the association hoped to play a role in gathering and exchanging information pertaining to the salt trade. To set and manage prices, the merchants had to collect information from each other about the demand for salt and gypsum and, presumably, about other variables related to their trade, including potential buyers and sellers. Attempts to set a baseline for prices sug-

44. For other examples of organizing trade activities, see *P.Fay.* 93 (161 CE), an agreement for a share in the trade of spices and perfumes; *P.Grenf.* II 68 (247 CE), an agreement for a share in an association of funerary workers (*nekrotaphoi*).

gest that the salt merchants might have succeeded in managing this information within their network and intended to use it to support their individual and collective efforts.

The salt merchants were not the only group to collect, monitor, and manage information related to their trade. A transcript of the proceedings of the council of Oxyrhynchus concerning petitions submitted by the linen weavers and the linen merchants may indicate that associations gathered and used information regarding prices for labor and materials in contract negotiations.[45] In this instance, both the weavers' and the merchants' associations requested additional money from the council to cover increased costs that rendered an initial allocation insufficient. The council ultimately awarded the weavers the full amount requested, and the merchants received only a partial increase; nevertheless, the involvement of the associations in gathering information seems clear.

A series of price declarations from Oxyrhynchus submitted to local authorities during the fourth century CE by thirty-three craft and merchant associations, detailing the costs of their goods and raw materials, paints a similar picture.[46] If associations like those of the glass workers, spice merchants, and wool merchants, to name a few, were collecting this information and sharing it with local officials to be kept on file, it is conceivable that the associations were exchanging and using the information among themselves as well.[47] Such efforts would have increased access to information and thereby lessened the transaction costs, risks, and uncertainties presented to craftsmen or merchants with respect to the market for and manufacture of their goods.

Concerns beyond setting prices and controlling distribution also drove the salt merchants. A need for information guided their activities—information about demand, about goods, and about those with whom individual members of their association transacted business. Obtaining this information is challenging and expensive in any environment and was even more so in the ancient world, where the economic reality that confronted craftsmen, merchants, and associations approximated Geertz's bazaar economy.[48] As Geertz maintained, information was "poor, scarce, maldistributed, inefficiently communicated,

45. *P.Oxy.* XII 1414 (271-72 CE).
46. For a list of price declarations, see *P.Oxy.* LIV, appendix II, 230–32.
47. *P.Oxy.* LIV 3742 (317 CE), 3731 (310–11 CE), 3733 (312 CE), 3751 (319 CE).
48. Bang has suggested Geertz's bazaar economy as an interpretive approach for the Roman economy; see Bang 2006, 2007, 2008.

and intensely valued"; it was also imperfect.[49] Business letters indicate some of the difficulty involved in dealing with prices, demand, and access to credit.[50] Trade manuals like the *Periplus Maris Erythraei* preserve attempts to compile information about trade routes and specific cities and ports.[51] Gaining access to information about demand, costs, and reliable sellers and buyers would have given associations and their members an advantage and would have helped them to protect their own interests.

That the merchants penalized failure to share information with the association about large orders (defined as any amount worth more than four drachmas) indicates that the group focused on sharing market information in addition to sharing the wealth. The group expected members to exchange information collected while trading in Tebtunis, Tristomou, and Kerkesis and in Arsinoe, the nome capital and probably the "city" to which the charter referred. Withholding information hindered efforts to manage prices and could have resulted in penalties for offending members up to sixteen drachmas, a sum that was 25 percent above the monthly dues of other associations in Tebtunis. For the sake of comparison, the sheep and cattle herders of *P.Mich.* V 243 assessed a fine of eight drachmas for slandering another or neglecting someone in need (two-thirds of the monthly dues).[52] Failing to share information or selling below agreed-on prices was a significant breach of decorum and accepted economic norms within the association of salt merchants, on par with slander and making false complaints against another member. Beyond violating norms, such actions amounted to a breach of trust.

Feasting and Commiseration

Charters also attest to the important place that commiseration and commemoration occupied in association life in Egypt and elsewhere. It would be wrong to disregard social and religious elements of association activities and to isolate them from the economy or our understanding of ancient approaches to economic activities. Charters not only describe regular feasting and socializing (sometimes in honor of a patron, a divinity, or the emperor's birthday, such as

49. Geertz 1978: 29. See also Geertz 1963; Akerloff 1970; McMillan 2002: 41–52.
50. For instance, see *P.Oxy.Hels.* 48 (II/III CE).
51. Casson 1989.
52. *P.Mich.* V 243 (14–37 CE), lines 6–9.

the celebrations held by the *apolusumoi* on the "day of the god Augustus"); they also establish the rules of decorum for such occasions.[53] Lists of contributions and receipts detail the substantial resources individuals devoted to these occasions.[54] Contributions to groups also marked significant moments in members' personal and financial lives; the sheep and cattle herders, for instance, were supposed to make contributions to the common fund to celebrate births, marriages, and purchases of property or livestock.[55]

> If anyone marries, let him pay two drachmas, for the birth of a male child two drachmas, for a female child one drachma, for the purchase of property four drachmas, for a flock of sheep four drachmas, for cattle one drachma.[56]

In this way, the gains of one member turned into gains for the group. But more than additional revenue, these moments may have given the group another opportunity to meet, celebrate together, solidify their network, and build social capital.

Social and religious activities and the rules governing these and all aspects of association life were intimately related to the way groups approached economic activity. Religious and social elements of membership provided the social glue, in a sense, and helped further create an environment that nurtured trust in a positive way.[57] Religious, social, and economic aspects of association rules, rituals, and activities were thus connected to building trust networks and developing, marking out, and perpetuating a trustworthy reputation within the group. Participation in rituals and regular celebrations (whether on the occasion of a marriage, the birth of a child, acquisition of property, or a funeral) fostered the creation and maintenance of the trust networks on which associations relied. Repeated interactions and celebrations with colleagues renewed these bonds.

Hierarchies, too, were definitely at play within groups, as evidenced by honorific decrees, inscriptions, and other papyri that attest to the importance of at-

53. For celebrations of the emperor's birthday, see *P.Mich.* V 244, lines 14–16; for celebrations on behalf of gods and Ptolemaic rulers, see *P.Lond.* VII 2193 (69–58 BCE); compare with *CIL* XIV 2112 = *ILS* 7212 (136 CE), lines 43–45.
54. *P.Mich.* V 246 (mid-I CE), *P.Mich.* II 121r, col. IV, 6 (42 CE); see also *P.Oslo* III 143 (I CE), *P. Lund.* IV 11 (169/70 CE).
55. The Iobacchoi in Athens made contributions for acquiring a legacy or other honor listed in the charter; see *IG* II^2 1368 (164/5 CE), lines 125–35.
56. *P.Mich.* V 243 (14–37 CE), lines 5–6, trans. Boak.
57. Sennett 2012: 86–93; see also Bang 2008: 255–57.

taining rank and status distinctions within a group. Membership lists and charters not only from the Greek east under Roman rule but also from the western half of the empire reinforce these ideas.[58] A group from Tebtunis associated with the god Harpocrates organized themselves in a rank-based manner for their banquets, as the list of contributions for one such event makes clear.[59] The list recorded each member's contributions in money, food, and drink and placed them at a particular position around one of three dining tables. That there was some order besides giving pride of place at the first table to the association's presiding officer (*hēgoumenos*)—Pasipsemis, son of Orseus—is revealed by the numerals placed next to each members' name, ranked one (alpha) through five (epsilon). The seating arrangement did not neatly correspond to the amount contributed either: the second position at the first table belonged to Orseus the son of Herakles, who contributed ten drachmas; the third position went to an older man named Eutychos the son of Soterichos, who contributed twenty-two drachmas; and Pasipsemis, the *hēgoumenos,* provided two types of spices, vegetables, and other items but no financial resources.[60] The leading position at the third table went to a man described as the "master of the banquet" (*kleisiarchēs*).

> Master of the banquet,twenty silver drachmas;
> 2nd. Narkissos, freedman of the sons of Maron also known as Marous, son of Herakles, about 36 years old, with a mole on his nose on the right side, twenty-one silver drachmas;
> 3rd. Herodes, son of Eutychos, about 46 years old, with a scar on his nose below the eyebrows, seventeen drachmas;
> 4th. Serapas, son of Ptolemaios, about 36 years old, with a scar on the left side of his neck, fourteen drachmas 3 obols;
> 5th. Last (at the table of the) master of the banquet, Pastoous, son of Pastoous, about 38 years old, with a scar on his left shin, twelve silver drachmas.[61]

As was the case with the provision of aid, honors and ranks should be placed in context. Honors, including designated seats at a banquet, were intended to represent the end result of successful interactions with colleagues and a trustwor-

58. *CIL* XIV 2112 (136 CE); *IG* II² 1368 (164/5 CE). See also Royden 1988.
59. *P.Mich.* V 246 (mid-I CE); *BL* VIII 213; XII 120.
60. *P.Mich.* V 246, lines 1–4.
61. *P.Mich.* V 246, lines 14–19, trans. Boak.

thy reputation earned over time. Therefore, statues, decrees, and honors should be seen as part of a larger system by which associations disseminated information about members and perhaps tried to influence (and sometimes control) behavior. More than a struggle for status (as MacMullen maintained), that system speaks to a struggle for establishing trust.

Funerals and Commemoration

Association participation in funerary rituals and subsequent commemoration appears to have been a fairly standard practice in the Greco-Roman world. Verboven deemed commemoration one of the "three pillars" of association life, along with conviviality and cult.[62] Association members typically contributed to a common fund to offset some funeral expenses, and many groups paid for and maintained the funerary monuments of deceased members and the land on which those monuments were built.[63] Egyptian charters also make clear that members considered funerals and commemoration an important part of their structure and organization, even if epitaphs contain fewer references to trades or membership than are found elsewhere. Associations from the Ptolemaic and Roman periods outlined expectations that members would mourn not only the deaths of colleagues but also deaths in members' families. A group of priests active in Tebtunis during the mid-second century BCE, for instance, stipulated that they would drink with the father, father-in-law, and son of a deceased member and offer a benefit payment to help offset funeral costs.[64] In addition to attending funerals, the *apolusimoi* planned to host a feast for members in mourning and fined those who absented themselves.[65] Among the sheep and cattle herders, funerals and mourning called for contributions and memorial feasts. Like other groups, the herders also assigned fines for not participating.

> May health prevail! If one of the members dies, let all be shaved and let them hold a feast for one day, each bringing at once one drachma and two loaves, and in the case of other bereavements, let them hold a feast for one day. Let him who

62. Verboven 2011: 342. On association participation in funerals, see van Nijf 1997: 31–69; Venticinque, forthcoming. See also Waltzing 1895–1900, vol. 4: 505–22.
63. The examples are numerous: for Asia Minor, see, for example, *I.Eph.* 2212 (silversmiths), 2402 (potters), 2446 (weavers), 211 (dyers); for Italy, *CIL* XIV 2112 (136 CE).
64. *P.Prague* (137 BCE), lines 24–25; on this group, see Monson 2007b: 772.
65. *P.Mich.* V 244 (43 CE), lines 16–19.

> is not shaven in case of a death be fined four drachmas. Whoever has taken no part in the funeral and has not placed a wreath on the tomb shall be fined four drachmas. And let the other matters be as the society may decide. Let the law be valid when subscribed by the majority. When validated let it be returned to the president.[66]

The burials that associations provided were sought-after privileges and were defended, sometimes with legal action.[67] Some associations promised even more than what Egyptian charters outlined: the association of Diana and Antinous based in Lanuvium (located about twenty kilometers south of Rome) pledged to hire mourners with part of the three hundred sesterces that the group planned to provide as a benefit payment (referred to as a *funeraticum* or *taphikon*). The same association also promised to make arrangements to transport the body of the deceased back home if necessary.[68] Such arrangements signaled the desire for a lasting relationship among the group, the families, and the individuals who chose to be buried in this manner.

Group participation in a colleague's burial has often been viewed as necessary in order to meet individual needs, funerary or otherwise, that could not be met due to the financial constraints experienced by nonelite craftsmen, merchants, and association members and a perceived lack of assistance from family. Peter Garnsey and Richard Saller listed a lack of familial support, the absence of available financial resources, and a desire for a decent burial as factors motivating a decision to join the various *collegia* found throughout Italy and the Roman west.[69] In her study of funerary practices and epitaphs, Maureen Carroll maintained that anxieties over memory and commemoration were intertwined with burial habits, customs, and identity formation and remained a concern at all levels of society.[70] With regard to associations, Carroll specifically emphasized the "comfort" that members would have felt in knowing that appropriate commemoration awaited them thanks to membership in an association, despite their "humble means" and potentially absent or nonexistent family members.[71]

---

66. *P.Mich.* V 243, lines 9–12, trans. Boak.
67. *P.Enteux.* 20 (221 BCE), 21 (218 BCE).
68. *CIL* XIV 2112 = *ILS* 7212 (136 CE), lines 22–27.
69. Garnsey and Saller 1987: 156–57. See also Toynbee 1971: 54–56; Hopkins 1983: 211–17; Kloppenborg 1996; Seland 1996.
70. Carroll 2006: 18–20.
71. Carroll 2006: 45.

Members of associations might not have been immune to the concerns Carroll describes. Financial hardship should not be entirely dismissed. Burials could, after all, be quite expensive. Based on the reported costs in Italy and North Africa compiled by Duncan-Jones, costs averaged around one thousand sesterces in North Africa and two thousand sesterces in Italy, although there is a wide range of expenses reflecting a variety of burials and commemorative practices.[72] A smaller sample of burial costs reported in Egyptian papyri places the average around two hundred drachmas, itself not an insignificant sum.[73] The burial costs reported for Egypt approach the amount Scheidel suggested as the average wages an unskilled worker could earn annually (250–88 drachmas) and over half of the amount that he estimated would be required to support a hypothetical household of four members at "bare bones subsistence" during the period from 50 to 150 CE (roughly 350 drachmas).[74]

However, given the upfront costs for entry and dues that members assumed simply to belong to these organizations, which approached the wage and expenditure estimates Scheidel calculated, economic constraint might not have provided the primary impetus to seek membership or celebrate funerals in this way. The presence of relatives within groups, inferred from the evidence membership lists provide, would also seem to mitigate concerns commonly expressed over deficiencies within a support network, although traders operating abroad might have profited from the burial assistance (and other benefits) that an association could provide, as Carroll has suggested. Be that as it may, it is unlikely that any association membership was of uniformly "humble status." Compared to the Roman elite, association members could not be seen otherwise; but given the economic profile of association members, they might not have been destined for anonymous burials in the first place. Available funds to maintain membership in an association would have marked them out within their own circles and communities while they were alive and after death.

Beyond fears for proper burial, other concerns may have factored not only into how associations participated in funerals and all their public activities but also into an individual's decision to be commemorated in this manner and to participate in this kind of commemoration of others. Participation in association funerals allowed members to evaluate the reputation of their colleagues based on adherence to agreed-on standards of behavior, at a time when the

72. Duncan-Jones 1982: 79–80, 127–31.
73. Montserrat 1997.
74. Scheidel 2010: 434.

group or an individual member experienced loss. Associations' decisions to treat death, funerals, and commemoration as described by their charters relate to larger strategies that members adopted to establish or perpetuate trust, esteem, and a specific reputation and to communicate this information about themselves (or their group as a whole) to others within their network and to the community at large.

Regulations, Reputation, and Accounting for Trust

The rules devised by groups to organize and regulate members' behavior at feasts and funerals and to structure their interactions have not always been seen in economic terms, at least not in the same way as rules specifically dealing with prices. Prevailing opinion has considered association regulations to be primarily rules for socializing, perhaps relegated to the realm of Emily Post's etiquette manual, George Washington's *Rules of Civility*, or the written (and unwritten) rules for tenure-track professors.[75] But there is an economic import to these, too. Like people on the road to tenure, association members were encouraged and expected to attend meetings, invite colleagues to weddings, say yes when asked to do things by the group's leader, and be careful not to take anyone's seat at a meeting. Within an association setting, these rules had a larger significance and addressed the reality of working over time with colleagues in different economic, social, political, legal, and religious contexts, in which loans, various forms of assistance (with contracts, trade, and production), and mutual aid were part of a strategy for success within the group and beyond. Charters thus defined the parameters for establishing a trustworthy reputation that was continually tested, measured, and evaluated not only at meetings, banquets, and funerals but also in private interactions and in public.

The confluence of economic, social, religious, and legal factors in typical association activities makes notions of reputation and trust particularly important for understanding the economic strategies that members employed to structure individual and group activities. Prior to becoming the symbol of profit and capitalism guided by self-interest, Adam Smith discussed factors relating to reputation and esteem in his *Theory of Moral Sentiments*, published

75. Post's book (originally published in 1922) is now in its eighteenth edition (2011). Washington was not the author of the precepts in his book but a compiler building on previous editions and publications; see Brookhiser 1997.

over a decade and a half before his more famous *An Inquiry into the Nature and Causes of the Wealth of Nations*. In *Theory of Moral Sentiments*, Smith championed the idea that it was in an individual's self-interest to pay heed to reputation and to attune one's actions to expected norms, since people undertake transactions in a social and economic context, not in a vacuum. Smith emphasized that nature had provided individuals "with an original desire to please, and an original aversion to offend his brethren. She taught him to feel pleasure in their favorable, and pain in their unfavourable regard."[76] Prudence was central to Smith's social and economic thought and for what he deemed successful and profitable outcomes. For members of associations, abiding by the written and unwritten rules within the group and acting in accordance with the demands of a situation would have been prudent.[77]

Economists, sociologists, and philosophers have returned to Smith and have incorporated reputation and esteem into their analysis in order to investigate the impact that both have on economic decisions.[78] For Brennan and Pettit, esteem provides an "intangible hand" in transactions, alongside the invisible hand of the market and the iron hand of the state.[79] Society and its rules and norms, in addition to the regulations spelled out in an association charter, inform estimations of someone's reputation and trustworthiness. Association regulations therefore provided members with a blueprint for acting in a trustworthy fashion as defined in economic and social terms.

If this is the case, violations of the rules and the penalties that groups imposed are just as illuminating for describing economic strategies. Associations commonly employed a sliding scale for violations. This feature of association charters allows us to uncover, perhaps, which aspects of the rules most significantly impacted members' economic decisions and their interactions with others, not only within the group, but also in all of their economic and social relationships. Neglecting to offer support, slandering another, failing to attend meetings and funerals, or selling below agreed-on prices (as the salt merchants penalized) incurred monetary fines, but violations probably impacted a member's standing within the group proportionally, too.

76. Smith 2009 [1759]: 140; on Smith, see Solomon 2008.

77. On prudence, economic change, and ethical approaches to economic activities, see McCloskey 2006, 2010.

78. The bibliography on these points has become increasingly large. On esteem, see Brennan and Pettit 2004; on trust, Tilly 2005; on reputation, Klein 1997. Avner Greif has emphasized reputation in his analysis of medieval trade associations; see, for example, Greif 1989, 1993, and 2006.

79. Brennan and Pettit 2004: 245–88.

Attendance at meetings and funerals was crucial for how groups operated, but infractions in this area did not necessarily receive the stiffest penalties. The sheep and cattle herders assigned a fine of eight drachmas for failure to provide surety or help colleagues in need, two-thirds of the cost of dues members paid each month; they leveled smaller fines for violating rules of decorum at or missing meetings (four drachmas if the meeting was in the city, one if it was in the village – presumably Tebtunis).[80] The *apolusimoi* employed a sliding scale for absences, depending on whether the meetings were held in Tebtunis (two drachmas), in another village (four drachmas), or in the metropolis (eight drachmas).[81] The associations may have derived some additional benefit from a public display of strength when holding meetings away from Tebtunis, which therefore called for higher fines to encourage attendance.

Absence from and misbehaving at meetings, then, impacted one's social capital within the group and certainly marked someone out as less than reliable. It is no surprise, however, that groups reserved the highest penalties for infractions that most significantly damaged interpersonal trust: intrigue, plots against colleagues, and corruption of another member's household. The cattle herders, for instance, assigned a penalty of sixty drachmas for these violations, equal to the cost of membership fees for five months.[82] They were not alone. Groups in Ptolemaic Egypt, Hellenistic and Roman Greece, and Italy also assigned the highest penalties to this behavior.[83]

Many associations tried to limit abuse at meetings and banquets beyond basic rules of etiquette, too. The association devoted to Zeus Hypsistos, active in the Fayum during the final years of Ptolemaic rule, prohibited arguments about lineages and using other abusive language.

> It is not permissible for anyone to cause a disturbance, or to establish divisions within the group or to depart from the group of the leader to join another, or for one to argue about another's lineage at the banquet or to abuse another verbally at the banquet, or to chatter or to indict or to accuse another.[84]

80. *P.Mich.* V 243 (14–37 CE), line 4.
81. *P.Mich.* V 244, lines 7–9.
82. *P.Mich.* V 243, line 8.
83. See, for example, *P.Cair.Dem.* 30606 (158/7 BCE); *P.Lond.* VII 2193 (69–58 BCE), line 17; *IG* II^2 1275 (325–275 BCE, Piraeus), lines 14–15; IX,1^2 670 (150 BCE, Lokris); II^2 1368 (164/5 CE, Athens), lines 73–83; *CIL* XIV 2112 = *ILS* 7212 (136 CE, Lanuvium), lines 60–61.
84. *P.Lond.* VII 2193 (69–58 BCE), lines 13–17 = *AGRW* 295, trans. Kloppenborg (adapted).

The Iobacchoi in Athens declared that no one was allowed to make a speech without permission of the officers, perhaps for similar reasons.[85] Such regulations suggest a feeling among association members that competition within an association network was waged properly in the display of ethical behavior toward colleagues and the group, not by boasting about one's family background. Perhaps this expectation about conduct was even intended as a distinct departure from elite behavior and indicates something other than an attempt to mirror elite virtues.

Considerations beyond assuring pleasant and enjoyable banquets impacted how groups fashioned these rules. Slander and plots against colleagues damaged the business endeavors and personal standing of other members and were to be avoided for good reason. Impugning another exposed the perpetrator's reputation to attack, too, which had social, legal, and economic repercussions across the entire association network. Slander (*diabolē* in Greek papyri, *iniuria* in Latin legal discussions) was also actionable at law.[86] Such behavior was a potential source for lawsuits that strained the relatively compact networks of associations in Egypt, networks that also probably shared overlapping familial bonds.[87] Therefore, groups sought to discourage behavior that damaged trust across a network.

Slander, intrigue, and plots threatened the group in other ways. Whether someone made formal complaints of abuse or merely spread gossip, charges of this sort could have damaged the reputation of individual members within the group and, presumably, the community at large.[88] The association as a whole suffered as a result. Since associations punished those that made public charges against colleagues, members may have assumed that allegations also damaged the reputation of the complainant. Associations accordingly sought to limit prosecution of members that would make this information public.

Handling complaints and accusations in this way may also have been a strategic attempt to keep the authorities out of association business.[89] But this presupposes an antagonistic relationship between associations and society. Adopting such a stance also presumes that associations could not defend their own interests. Evidence suggests that this was not the case; groups repeatedly tried

85. *IG* II^2 1368 (164/5 CE, Athens), lines 107–8.
86. Bryen 2008.
87. On family connections, see Venticinque 2010: 277–79.
88. For discussions of ancient evidence, see Hunter 1990; Grey 2011: 84–90. Parallels from the medieval and early modern period suggest the complicated implications of slander and gossip for social and economic activities: see Wickham 1998; Farr 1988: 163–64.
89. Monson 2006: 236.

to defend their own interests and those of their members before local and imperial authorities (sometimes successfully).[90]

Attempts to mediate disputes internally might have aimed at limiting legal actions that cost time and capital (personal and financial) and avoiding the potential problems involved in legal action.[91] The decisions of a Roman official, though supposedly bound by precedent, could be capricious and unpredictable. The reason to keep disputes internal might not have been linked only to a desire for expediency. Associations hoped to limit negative economic impact among all members of the group (not just those involved in the dispute), so as to ensure continued cooperation within the group as a whole.

Managing discord in this manner reflects concerted efforts to protect the esteem and reputation of members, regardless of an accusation's validity. Nevertheless, other motivations remain possible. To protect the reputation of members in general, particularly in the face of specious claims, associations had an incentive to make sure that members who violated the rules would not go unpunished. Given the potential unpredictability of a legal action's outcome, groups may have sought more control over the situation; some might have even imposed additional sanctions on offending members.

Trust and a reputation for following accepted norms clearly mattered within association circles. It should not be surprising, then, that business letters between associates were quick to point out that proper observances had been carried out, even at a distance, in the event of a death in the family or extended network.[92] Charters also make clear that reputation mattered beyond the association's immediate network. Penalties that the salt merchants devised for violations turned concerns for reputation against offenders. Selling goods below agreed-on prices resulted in a fine of eight drachmas paid to the common fund. Undercutting the price also called for payment of an additional eight drachmas to the town's treasury.[93] The same penalty applied to selling quantities of salt worth more than a stater, presumably without sharing the information with the rest of the group.[94] At sixteen drachmas, these fines totaled more than a month's worth of membership dues for groups in Tebtunis and were larger than the fines the salt merchants assigned for missing meetings.

90. See, for example, *P.Phil.* 1 (103–24 CE); *P.Tebt.* II 287 = *W.Chr.* 251 (161–69 CE); *P.Oxy.* XII 1414 (271–72 CE).
91. For private arbitration in Egypt, see Gagos and van Minnen 1994.
92. *P.Oxy.* I 115, 116, 187 (all I CE).
93. *P.Mich.* V 245 (47 CE), lines 24–26.
94. *P.Mich.* V 245, lines 26–28.

Of consequence here is not so much the amount of the fine as the fact that part of the penalty included payment to the public treasury. Devising such a punishment reveals the group's intention to impose a penalty that inflicted damage to a member's reputation in a public way and exposed an individual offender as a rule breaker to those outside the group. Since many provisions adopted by associations express a desire to limit making internal disputes public, this arrangement seems all the more interesting. The salt merchants adopted additional regulations that would have resulted in damage to a member's reputation. Penalties included the threat of violence, beatings, and accosting members who had failed to follow through on their obligations to the group in public. Officials like Apynchis possessed the authority to confront delinquent members in the *plateia*, at home, or in the fields.[95] The same penalty also covered failure to fulfill public obligations, which could refer to public contracts or arrangements made with nonmembers.

Other groups resorted to violence, too, and sometimes even expulsion. The charter of the *apolusimoi* allowed the president to seize those who had failed to meet public obligations.[96] A fragmentary charter of an association from Attica in the second century CE imposed expulsion, fines, and potential beatings as penalties for members who fought or caused a disturbance.[97] Kloppenborg and Ascough have asserted that the threat of beatings alludes to the presence in the group of free members, who paid fines, and slave members, who received physical punishments.[98] Membership composition in groups did vary, but it is difficult to determine in many cases. This clause might simply refer to the penalty's severity: rule breakers will receive servile treatment and the diminution of reputation that such a penalty carried with it.

Whether enforcing beatings and public abuse damaged the reputation of the group or just that of the offending member can be debated. Punishing delinquent members may have helped maintain the positive reputation of a group in the eyes of the community. Competing interests might have made it difficult to balance these concerns. Nevertheless, the mere threat of physical coercion elucidates the meaning that association members attached to violence, as well as the way in which violence was perceived by other community members.[99]

95. *P.Mich.* V 245, lines 37–42.

96. *P.Mich.* V 244 (43 CE), lines 18–20.

97. *IG* II^2 1369 (II CE), lines 40–44; for translation and discussion, see Kloppenborg and Ascough 2011: 229–34.

98. Kloppenborg and Ascough 2011: 233.

99. Ari Bryen's work is instructive on these points; see Bryen 2008, 2013.

Although not all missteps resulted in physical punishment or public exposure of a bad reputation, every infraction mattered. Even smaller mistakes with less substantial fines, like taking someone's seat at a banquet, could and probably did add up over time. For those sponsoring celebrations, usually the group's officers, the arrangements were costly in terms of time, money, and effort. Causing a disturbance did more than ruin a celebration; it risked offending influential members of the association. In the process, it exposed someone as a less-than-reliable member of the group.

Disturbing or missing meetings had other consequences. While some groups made efforts not to discuss business during a banquet, conversations probably turned toward such concerns.[100] But meetings need not devolve into conspiracy or foment rebellion. Meetings were where groups decided on honors for their own members and those that acted for the good of the group.[101] Banquets and meetings also provided the setting at which members enjoyed honors doled out by the group. Common privileges included the right to wear crowns or distinctive dress, receiving extra portions of food and drink, portrait statues, and honorific decrees, often recorded on stelai. Some associations even mandated that honorary decrees and accounts of an individual's good deeds be recited during celebrations.[102]

Meetings and celebrations may have provided conviviality and contained a religious element. However, debating whom to honor and in what manner and celebrating individuals who had cemented a trustworthy reputation were still decisions of a political and economic nature. More important, meetings and the decisions made there were part of the association's process of disseminating information about members, benefactors, and other individuals. Therefore, more than mimicking elite values, honors and the decrees that members exchanged among themselves reflected an aspect of the way associations chose to operate. Given the regional scope of groups like the salt merchants and other associations based in Tebtunis, regular meetings also provided opportunities to gather and share information about their economic activities, with the goal of improving members' collective and individual efforts. The relatively large fine of eight drachmas that the salt merchants as-

100. *IG* II² 1368 (164/5 CE, Attica).
101. *TAM* V.2 972 (50 CE, Thyatira), 989 (120–30 CE, Thyatira); 966 (II/III CE, Thyatira), 933 (undated, Thyatira); *MAMA* VI 164 (98–117 CE, Akmoneia); *I.Hierap.J.* 40–41 (III CE, Hierapolis).
102. For example, for Egypt, see *OGIS* 50 (269–246 BCE, Ptolemais Hermou); *I.Delta* I 446 (65/4 BCE, Psenamosis); *SB* XXII 15460 (5 BCE, Alexandria). For Greece, see *SEG* XLII 716 (90/89 BCE, Macedonia); *I.Beroia* 22 (7 BCE, Macedonia).

signed for missing meetings in the metropolis suggests that they interpreted missing these sessions as a serious infraction.

In his treatment of association regulations in Ptolemaic Egypt, Andrew Monson suggested that ethical rules allowed groups to deal with free-rider problems, among other issues.[103] Monetary penalties thus encouraged compliance. Some fines were indeed steep and equaled or surpassed the monthly dues that members paid into the common fund. But there is no way of knowing whether a fine equal to the dues for a month would have been large enough to prevent breaking the rules or checking opportunistic actions when a substantial gain could be had that justified moral hazard in someone's mind. Since this was a segment of the population that was relatively secure, monetary fines might not have been the prime motivating factor for promoting compliance. Association members were driven by more than immediate damage to their finances at any one time. A desire to maintain their reputation as members in good standing, to preserve network ties, and to keep multiple avenues open to manage the risks they faced in their lives may have provided stronger motivation.

Conclusions

Groups like the salt merchants could never have been entirely sure that their colleagues would respect specified trading zones, sell at agreed-on prices, or even make good on their promises to contribute for monthly meetings. Similar concerns would have presented themselves to members of any group who trusted that their colleagues would not make false accusations, slander each other, or damage a colleague's reputation in public, as the *apolusimoi* and the sheep and cattle herders stipulated in their charters. Imperfect information hampered the activities of associations and their members, and the risk of a member breaking the rules in exchange for an immediate short-term gain remained ever present.

Charters and other evidence of association activities indicate that groups tried to dispel as much uncertainty as possible inside and outside the meeting hall. Information on prices like that gathered by the salt merchants or the associations in Oxyrhynchus helped individual members manage aspects of their financial and market activities. The behavioral regulations that groups devised, including promises of mutual aid and attendance at funerals, helped reduce risk

103. Monson 2006: 232.

and uncertainty in transactions with colleagues, by creating an environment of enhanced trust between members. Even with specific regulations and penalties for failure to follow through on loans, make tax payments, provide surety, fulfill obligations, and honor contracts, uncertainty remained in day-to-day transactions. Association regulations, however, aimed at creating a setting that would lessen the blow of these contingencies by allowing individuals to collect and share information about the social and economic activities and habits of colleagues. Evaluating the actions of colleagues according to expectations and obligations outlined in association charters enabled group members to measure an individual's reputation, esteem, and relative trustworthiness. Knowledge about a member's social capital was gained over repeated interactions and participation in meetings, celebrations, funerals, and other group activities and allowed association members to manage imperfect information, at least partly. Ideally, through participation in an association's activities, a member came to understand who was more likely to abide by the rules in order to obtain larger gains and long-term financial benefits, rather than to break a deal for a short-term gain.

Reliance on trust and reputation helps bring the rules for behavior at banquets, funerals, and social events into finer focus. On the surface, what seems to have been a confusing web of personal obligations to the group and its membership in terms of money, time, effort, etiquette, and attendance at gatherings reveals the role that trust and information about reputations played in individual members' efforts to manage economic concerns. The regulations associations crafted, the honors they voted for group benefactors, and the crowns and extra portions they granted to members who had shown devotion to the group were not inconsequential mimes of elite activity that only helped individuals claim a symbolic place in society or make up for deficiencies in their lives.[104] Charters reveal that a sense of honor, defined in terms of esteem and a trustworthy reputation, was important among craftsmen, merchants, and those living and working outside the realm of the Roman elite.

Association charters assumed that members engaged actively in the pursuit of this type of honor, and the organizations to which they belonged sought to cultivate and reward such behavior. Statues and portrait busts of esteemed members, honorific decrees, and extra portions at banquets were tangible signs of trust and of a good reputation earned. Erecting monuments in spaces used

104. See, for example, *SB* V 8267 = *I.Prose* 49 (5 BC).

by the group or in public can be seen, then, as a normal way of disseminating reputation-based information to members and the public at large—whether a group of bakers erected a statue and portrait of their president or a group associated with Isis thanked an individual for his efforts to reestablish the association.[105] Groups outside of Egypt operated in similar fashion. For instance, an Athenian association honored the man they credited with founding their group in the late first century BCE with a decree in their sacred enclosure.[106] In this respect, the rules described in charters and the decisions made by associations to honor benefactors and members who acted in accordance with those regulations were, in fact, quite consequential. Charters should thus be seen as complex documents embedded within and responding to concerns in a larger economic, social, political, and ethical world. Charters and the regulations contained therein did more than create and reinforce social hierarchies or reflect promises to behave according to accepted norms practiced by elites.[107] Economic concerns impacted by ethical, social, and religious factors and obligations lie behind these regulations.

In many ways, MacMullen, Walker-Ramisch, and others were not entirely mistaken when discussing the importance that associations placed on social and religious activities. Not only were commemoration, commiseration, and the dispensing of honors to members and patrons important actions in and of themselves, but these activities were also vital components of the economic strategies that associations adopted and expounded on in their charters. Funerals, banquets, and the rules, regulations, and ethical and behavioral norms described in their charters should therefore be conceived of as part of an association's overall approach to economic, political, and social activity. Charters further reveal that this approach was simultaneously focused inward on the association and directed outward toward their communities. Charters structured relationships between members, who relied on associations to do a number of things beyond funerals. Associations provided surety, legal assistance, access to credit, representation before the authorities, and, in some cases, management of trade and market information. Emerging through the activities outlined and the provisions contained in their charters, particularly the fines and penalties for noncompliance, is the structure of a system devised

105. For the bakers, see *I.Fayum* III 212 (3 CE); for the association related to Isis, *I.Fayum* II 121= *SB* I 5793 (93 CE).
106. *IG* II^2 1343 (37/6 or 36/5 BCE); see now Kloppenborg and Ascough 2011: 224–29.
107. For discussion, see Arnaoutoglou 2002: 29.

to encourage and facilitate cooperation between members under the watchful eyes of their colleagues.

This last point is perhaps the most important. From the moment members affixed their signatures on the charter and it was inscribed on stone and displayed for all to see, associations set up mechanisms in which members acquired, assessed, and used information about the reputation not only of members but also of family and friends connected to the group through wider social networks. Such an approach that used knowledge about reputation lowered transaction costs and offered association members a means to manage the uncertainties and risks they confronted in their lives, including problems with contracts, legal disputes, temporary lack of funds, injury, illness, imperfect information, and numerous other concerns related to deriving a profit and continuing to live at or above the subsistence level.

Crafted as multifaceted documents that organized association activities across many spheres, charters illustrate the relationship between different modes of interaction often thought of as separate. Social, religious, economic, and political elements were all part of the strategies employed by members not only to manage risk and uncertainty but to plot out the ways in which they, as a group, interacted with the community around them. Associations and their members did not see these as separate categories. The rituals, banquets, and ethical regulations were no less important to the successful operation of a particular group and its membership than other features. Beyond simple fines and fees for behavioral violations at banquets and meetings or mandated contributions for celebrations of important moments in a member's life, continued participation in these activities helped solidify links between members and marked individuals out as trustworthy to their colleagues.

Sustaining membership in an association and perpetuating the trust networks that it helped support would have provided an incentive for individuals not to violate group charters. Likewise, working within the network and abiding by group expectations would aid in the management of their collective economic resources and balance out the risks involved in trade with each other and with other individuals and groups. Reliance on bonds between association members helped lower transaction costs and increased the security of individual economic endeavors by enhancing the effectiveness of their contracts. Far from being distinct aspects of association life, the knowledge and experience gained from the interplay of the social and religious aspects of association life and from observing how members behaved helped inform economic decisions.

Conscious that their actions were being evaluated by the group, members were expected to moderate their behavior and planned their actions accordingly.

In theory, associations and the charters they adopted also offered a means of mediating conflict when it occurred. Considering that members would have to interact with individuals repeatedly over time, the same regulations and rituals that promoted trust may have also offered a way to reestablish it. Provided someone was not summarily expelled from the association, granting loans, regular attendance at meetings, participation in the funeral of a colleague, offering support to a member in need, or just paying the mandated fine could have helped rehabilitate a tarnished image. In this sense, the charters gave members an additional guide whether they aimed to establish trust or to renew it after transgressions.

Either way, the importance of performing rituals and abiding by the rules is related to the value that individual craftsmen, merchants, and association members placed on trust and reputation. Although subsistence, access to reliable business partners, supply of labor, and credit were probably concerns for everyone, those who belonged to associations were likely better equipped to handle the precarious nature of life in comparison to other members of the nonelite. Motivation to join an association need not stem from the disintegration of the family or a lack of financial resources, as has often been supposed. Instead, associations provided an additional source of social and economic strength not afforded to those who staffed workshops or stomped in vats of fuller's earth in Ostia, Pompeii, North Africa, Asia Minor, or Egypt.

Previous studies have seen associations primarily as a means to compensate for weakness in communities and for deficiencies in individual support networks. These approaches do not answer key questions about dynamics within the group and between an association and the other members of its community or about the underlying significance of honorific decrees for their colleagues or members of the community. Association activities have been seen as a game for honor, cut off from the surrounding community, without any anchor to a real social, economic, or political lived experience. Based on an examination of group charters, that is not what associations intended. Ultimately, the charters indicate that there was a sense of honor among thieves—or, in this case, craftsmen, merchants, and those that belonged to associations. This particular type of honor, however, had more to do with ideas of trust and a reputation for following through on agreements and obligations, concepts around which charters were organized.

CHAPTER 2

The Business of Trust

Around the same time that the associations in Tebtunis were crafting rules to govern their activities, limit harmful business practices, and assure access to support, groups were testing their trust networks elsewhere in the Fayum. For instance, five members of the weavers' association in the village of Euhemeria fell afoul of a wool-worker named Paninoutis. Paninoutis had submitted a petition alleging misconduct by these weavers. The petition has not survived, but the agreement that the president and secretary of the weavers' association submitted to local officials pledging surety on their behalf has. According to the text written by Aphrodisius, the association's secretary (the president apparently could not write), these two men promised an agent of the presiding local magistrate (*exēgētēs*) that they would make sure the weavers answered claims against them.

> Heracles son of Petesouchos, head of the weavers of Euhemeria, and Aphrodisius son of Asclepiades, secretary of the same weavers, to Heron agent of Sotas, exegetes, greeting. We acknowledge that we are sureties to you for Apheus son of Apheus, Harpagathes son of Orsenouphis, Heras son of Orsenouphis, Melas son of Hergeus, and Heracles son of Apollonius, all five weavers of the said village of Euhemeria, and that it is incumbent on us to produce them for you whenever you choose, to answer the claims stated in the petition of Paninoutis son of Aphrodisius, wool-worker. I the aforesaid Aphrodisius have written for Heracles because he is illiterate.[1]

1. *P.Ryl.* II 94 (14–37 CE) = *Sel.Pap.* II 255, trans. Hunt and Edgar.

With no specific details given in the surety agreement, it is unclear what caused the dispute. The weavers may have encroached on or damaged Paninoutis' property or business interests. Perhaps they failed to supply Paninoutis with material he had purchased and violated an agreement. Whatever the conflict, the five weavers had been collaborating and had somehow irked Paninoutis; now they found themselves in legal and financial trouble.

As a group, the five weavers also belonged to a larger network that they could expect to benefit from in the form of credit, loans, and support, if necessary. The conflict with Paninoutis would have been an applicable situation. Although providing surety may have been expected, it also exposed men like Herakles and Aphrodisius to risks of their own. As a result, all seven weavers were taking economic, social, and legal risks that opened them up to reprisals not only from Paninoutis and the wool workers but also from each other and the authorities, should any one of the weavers fail to honor the agreements they had made.

Membership in an association helped lessen the risks surrounding a surety agreement like this one. The five weavers counted on their colleagues for assistance, but the two officers also entered into the agreement with certain expectations: they trusted that these five men would honor their pledge to appear and sort out whatever mess they had created. Despite expectations that they would do so, the decision to enter into this agreement was presumably made easier for Herakles and Aphrodisius because they could rely on shared bonds of trust cultivated through repeated celebrations, transactions, and collaborations with their colleagues. Herakles and Aphrodisius also knew the weavers' reputations and whether they had proved themselves trustworthy in the past. Ideally, the officers assumed that the five weavers, who operated within the same institutional framework of obligations and expectations, would comply and not damage their standing within the group by violating the agreement.

As far as these weavers in Euhemeria were concerned, trust and reputation mattered a great deal. Other individuals in a similar situation might not have had the same luxury of depending on association membership to secure surety. Although reliance on previous interactions within an association context never eliminated the possibility of opportunistic behavior by a fellow member, it provided an enhanced safety net for people like Herakles and Aphrodisius. What separated the officials of the weavers' association from others called on to provide surety was the trust fostered between colleagues and the information that association membership gave them about their associates.

In order to understand how association membership impacted the activities of individual members and fostered cooperation between members and others within their colleagues' networks, this chapter will examine collaborations of all sorts between colleagues, not just surety provided in times of financial need. It also explores how trust, reputation, and operating within an association framework mattered in the lives of members beyond the confines of meetings, celebrations, and funerals, as described in charters . The documentary evidence, detailed though it may be, does not always allow for easy answers. Yet archives and dossiers from the Fayum, Oxyrhynchus, and Aphrodito, along with documents from throughout the ancient world, reveal the cooperative strategies that association members adopted to support collaborations within their own networks.

Assessing Ancient Collaboration: Production, Construction, and Trade in Cities and Villages

The extent to which members of ancient associations relied on trust and reputation, acted on the rules and regulations outlined in charters, collaborated with one another, and forged meaningful ties outside of a formal setting is difficult to measure, whether looking at inscriptions or papyri. Charters suggest that associations sought trustworthy individuals with good reputations as members and officers. Members of an Athenian association (*sunodos*) in the second century CE who described themselves as *eranistai* (another common term for groups) stated that prospective members had to establish a reputation as "pure [*hagnos*] and pious [*eusebēs*] and good [*agathos*]."[2] The rules of the association of Iobacchoi in Athens asserted that no one could gain entry unless he was "worthy" (*axios*) and "suitable" (*epitēdeios*).[3] Egyptian groups also identified these qualities in their leaders, in whom significant trust would be placed. The members of the association of Zeus Hypsistos, active during the mid-first century BCE, selected a man named Petesouchos as their president and touted that he was "worthy [*axios*] of the place and of the company of men."[4] The salt mer-

---

2. *IG* II^2 1369 (II CE), lines 31–34; for discussion and translation, see Kloppenborg and Ascough 2011: 229–34.
3. *IG* II^2 1368 (164/5 CE), line 36; for discussion and translation, see Kloppenborg and Ascough 2011: 235–57.
4. *P.Lond.* V 2193 (69–58 BCE), lines 6–7.

chants from Tebtunis described their elected official as a "good man" (*anēr agathos*) who would benefit both the association and its members.[5] Honorary monuments and the accompanying inscriptions erected by Egyptian groups also commend members for excellence (*aretē*), generosity (*philotimia*), and goodwill (*eunoia*) toward a group and suggest attempts to identify and reward behavior alluded to in charters.[6]

Such monuments, so common among associations throughout the ancient world, may not necessarily point to actual collaboration with or reliance on the group, individual members, or their networks in social, legal, or economic contexts. Yet several Athenian inscriptions do salute and document collaboration in a sense. One association in Hellenistic Athens saluted their secretary for speaking on behalf of the association and on behalf of individual members, which would seem to indicate support or assistance that the secretary offered members.[7] An association of *Dionysiastai* from the Piraeus, composed of Athenian citizens, commemorated the life of their founder, Dionysus, not only by highlighting his donations to the group and the offices he held but also by touting his character and his efforts to help other members.[8] Concerning Dionysus' assistance of others, the group claimed that "when he was asked he was always the cause of some good thing, both for individuals and for the common good being a benefactor at all times."[9] The praise of his assistance suggests that Dionysus provided the sort of support that associations came to expect from members, but what it might actually refer to is unclear.

Turning to the documentary record, one finds that the peculiar methods of record keeping and individual address used in public and private contexts compound the usual problems experienced when dealing with the fragmentary nature of ancient evidence. Identification of association membership in formal contracts or agreements that included the authorities in some way, such as the surety agreement with which the discussion in this chapter began, would have been expected and appears to have been fairly standard. But association members did not regularly identify themselves as such in private contracts, leases, accounts, and receipts, even in interactions with a colleague, though there are exceptions.[10]

5. *P.Mich.* V 245 (47 CE), line 4.
6. *I.Alex.Imp.* 94 (I CE), 97 (7 CE); *I.Portes* 83 (209/10 CE), 111 (160 CE); *IGR* I 1314 = *SB* I 1013 (I CE).
7. *IG* II² 1263 (300/299 BCE), lines 13–16.
8. *IG* II² 1326 (176/5 BCE).
9. *IG* II² 1326, lines 7–9; for text and translation, see Kloppenborg and Ascough 2011: 179–84; for similar honors, see also *IG* II² 1327 (178/7 BCE), lines 5–6.
10. *P.Mich.* IX 575 (184 CE); *P.Oxy.* XLV 3262 (328 CE).

Despite these obstacles, evidence suggests that members relied on colleagues and benefited from access to association networks in their individual economic, social, legal, and political undertakings. The occasional letter between people who identify themselves as members and allude to involvement in a joint venture may indicate collaboration and reliance on association ties that reduced transaction costs, though it is difficult to know all the details of what Sarapion and his associates were up to in the example provided by *SB* XIV 11898 (II CE). In that case, how the matter concerned those referred to as belonging to an association in the letter and why it was left to Sarapion to handle the situation are far from clear.[11] Another example, a first-century letter exchanged between an estate owner and his manager, reveals that the men shared more than an employer-employee relationship: it would seem that Chairemon, the owner (and a gymnasiarch), and Apollonius, his estate manager, belonged to the same association.[12]

A good deal of the evidence for collaboration and reliance on association ties has to do with construction and public contracts. While craftsmen and merchants operated their own workshops and managed their own trading activities (as even the charter of the salt merchants implied), individual craftsmen and merchants also worked together and relied on associations to help manage larger contracts. Collaborating with colleagues and coordinating across workshops on public contracts and construction projects was common in Egypt into the sixth century CE, as illustrated by contracts with specific associations and receipts addressed to officials.[13]

This seems to have been the case with groups of weavers in villages across the Fayum. Individual weavers collaborated with each other on large orders contracted by local and imperial officials. For instance, three weavers working in Philadelphia, a village in the northwest Fayum, received payment from local officials through a banker, for clothing the prefect ordered in the second century.[14] That the group received (partial) payment in advance and presumably managed its disbursement to individual weavers for their costs incurred in crafting the garments reveals reliance on their association. Additional documents show that a weavers' association in Philadelphia was called on by the authorities and that

11. On this text, see Parassoglou 1973; Tsantsanoglou 1975.
12. *BGU* I 248 (75–85 CE).
13. *P.Stras.* VII 678 (568/9 CE); see also *SB* XX 14985 (VI CE), line 1.
14. *Sel.Pap.* II 395 (138 CE) = *BGU* VII 1564.

members worked together at other times to complete orders.[15] A second-century order for clothing needed by the military in Judea is addressed to the weavers of Soknopaiou Nesos, another Fayum village, and makes clear that this association coordinated production efforts between individual workshops to complete an order for nineteen tunics and five white cloaks.[16]

The copy of council proceedings held at Oxyrhynchus late in the third century indicates that associations of weavers and linen merchants in cities also relied on their colleagues to fulfill contracts.[17] Among nominations to new posts and other matters discussed at this meeting, the council considered requests from these two groups to modify their agreements, based on difficulties encountered in completing contracts. The linen weavers and linen merchants had claimed that increased costs of materials and labor made them unable to fulfill the orders for which the council had already paid them. Each group requested additional funds from the council to cover the difference in the initial allocation. The discussion recorded in the proceedings suggests that the weavers (*linuphoi*) at least coordinated work across their network to realize the demands of their contract.

> A petition of the city linen-weavers [*linuphoi*] having been read, to the effect that, besides the . . . drachmae paid to them in the last year (for each . . .) . . . more drachmae should be given them on account of the rise in the value of the materials and in the wages of their workmen. After reading the prytanis said, "Let . . . drachmae be given to the cloth-weavers, making 200 drachmae in all, on account of the rise in value of materials.[18]

The linen merchants (*linemporoi*) who had been contracted to supply linen to the local temples, presumably for the priests to make vestments or other garments, also seem to be coordinating their efforts to procure the necessary raw materials.[19] At the very least, the council seems to be dealing with the linen merchants and their funding request as a collaborative venture coordinated by the group. Additionally, it would seem that the associations of both the linen weavers and the linen merchants played a role in gathering or sharing across

15. *BGU* VII 1572 (139 CE).
16. *P.Ryl.* II 189 (128 CE); see also *BGU* VII 1615 (84 CE).
17. *P.Oxy.* XII 1414 (271–72 CE).
18. *P.Oxy.* XII 1414, lines 12–14, trans. Grenfell and Hunt.
19. *P.Oxy.* XII 1414, lines 3–11.

their networks information that individual merchants and weavers had acquired about the costs of labor and goods and the availability of raw materials. The associations, then, used this information to make their cases to the council, though with different results: the merchants did not receive their entire request, but the weavers did.

Several documents prepared for official use show that associations apparently helped craftsmen coordinate work on creative projects commissioned by the authorities (and likely by others too). For instance, the council of Oxyrhynchus contracted the goldsmiths' association to fashion a crown intended to be presented to Licinius.[20] An account that details payments to a painter for creating an imperial portrait also lists payments to three officials of the goldsmiths' association for gold, although the reason for the expenditure or their involvement is not specified.[21] Earlier in the third century, the council of Oxyrhynchus also appears to have paid a group of artisans (described only as the *techneitai*) for a crown made on the occasion of Aurelian's ascension.[22] No association is mentioned explicitly in that case, but given that the circumstances would have been similar to work performed or coordinated by an association, the involvement of one is entirely possible.

More evidence documents collaboration on various construction projects—much of it from Oxyrhynchus. For instance, iron workers coordinated repairs of the baths in Oxyrhynchus, as a fourth-century receipt addressed to the *koinon* makes clear; a text from the third century makes no specific reference to an association, but a text addressed to two individuals "and the lead workers with them" may suggest an association.[23] In another third-century text, an association of bronzesmiths from Oxyrhynchus requests payment for repairs undertaken at the baths.[24] Five ironsmiths, who may have been acting on behalf of their association in Oxyrhynchus, received payment for work done on the public baths in the mid-fifth century.[25] Glass workers were also involved in bath upkeep at Oxyrhynchus. When asked by the *logistēs* for an account of work that their association was carrying out on the baths and the gymnasium, a represen-

20. *P.Oxy.* XLIII 3121 (316–18 CE).
21. *P.Oxy.* LV 3791 (318 CE), lines 4–8.
22. *P.Oxy.* XII 1413 (272 CE), lines 25–27.
23. *P.Oxy.* I 84 (316 CE), XLIV 3185 (III CE). See also *P.Oxy.* XLIV 3173 (222 CE), XLIV 3176 (222–34 CE); these two texts deal with the same craftsmen working on the baths but make no explicit mention of an association.
24. *P.Laur.* IV 155 (283–92 CE).
25. *P.Oxy.* XXXIV 2718 (458 CE).

tative named Aurelius Zoilus filed a report detailing total raw materials needed and costs: six thousand pounds at 1,320 talents.[26] The report, intended to detail "everything pertaining to our trade" for the work, probably included labor costs as well. Documents like the report from the glass workers reveal that associations not only may have played a role in coordinating work but continued, into the fourth century, to provide their members with a mechanism to gather price and market information. This was presumably the case in other civic centers, such as Panopolis, although a detailed payment request submitted there by three men identified only as glass workers (*uelourgoi*) does not specifically mention an association.[27]

These texts represent discrete points in a process that involved craftsmen and merchants in a string of transactions for which documentation is scarce. It is important to remember that the framework provided by associations operated in the background. Trust factored into their endeavors in many ways, including the trust that merchants and craftsmen had that their colleagues would share information and manpower (either their own or that of those working for them). Members also trusted their officers and each other not to violate agreements or hamper efforts to realize a contract. They trusted that their colleagues would not act in an opportunistic manner to obtain short-term gains (if there were any to be had) and would not endanger ongoing business relationships with each other or with the authorities.

Assessing Ancient Collaboration: Associations and Estates

It is hard to assess a formal relationship between associations of craftsmen and merchants, on the one hand, and large landowners and their estates, on the other, during the Roman and late Roman periods. Evidence for the operations of the Appianus estate's holdings in the Fayum, contained in the Heroninus archive, suggests that some of those who worked for the estate had organized themselves as collectives. Entries in the mid-third-century accounts mention groups identified as *sunodoi*, one of the terms frequently used to denote associations. In his authoritative study of the Heroninus documents, Dominic Rathbone argued that these *sunodoi* were groups of cattle

26. *P.Coll.Youtie* II 81 = *P.Oxy.* XLV 3265 (326 CE); for a similar report, see *BGU* IV 1028 (II CE), submitted by an official of a bronzesmiths' association.
27. *P.Got.* 7 (225–75 CE).

herders and donkey drivers, complete with officials who interacted with the estate on behalf of the group.[28]

Evidence from the Apion estate, one of the largest and best-documented late Roman estates that included holdings in the Oxyrhynchite and Cynopolite nomes, also indicates that groups of some sort worked for or held leases from the estate.[29] Sixth-century accounts prepared by stewards employed by the family and documenting the estate's expenses and incomes derived from holdings in and around Oxyrhynchus mention groups described as *koina* of farmers and of vinedressers.[30] In the context of the estate accounts, the term *koina* may refer to groups of farmers who had pooled their resources to manage their leaseholds or to agricultural employees working collaboratively. These *koina* do appear to have acted as corporate groups, and the estate stewards interacted with them as such. One detailed mid-sixth-century account of the Apion estate attests that the estate had a relationship with nineteen different *koina* of farmers and vinedressers, each with roughly ten members.[31]

Even when dealing with well-documented estates, the picture remains fragmentary. The accounts on which we have to rely for our understanding of these groups on the Appianus and Apion estates provide a relatively sparse amount of information about them. Heroninus or the stewards employed by the Apion family may have had a clear idea of who belonged to these groups, their needs, and how they functioned. Unfortunately, a single entry recorded in an account book reveals very little about how these groups may have been organized, their composition, or the full range of their activities.

Associations of oil workers also worked with estates.[32] Connections between estates and oil workers, who relied on the agricultural production of an estate and its tenants for their business, are not entirely unexpected. Estate owners also had to protect their fields, livestock, and physical improvements to the land (irrigation machinery), from damage and theft. In Aphrodito during the sixth century, the landowners employed an association of shepherds to act as field guards and address these problems.[33] Entries in estate accounts for payments made to brick makers show that landowners (or their stewards) hired

28. *P.Lond.* III 1170v (259 CE), lines 70 (*sunodos* of Deidas), 72 and 119 (*sunodos* of herdsmen), 122 (*sunodos* of Sotas); Rathbone 1991: 146–47.
29. For the Apion archive, see Mazza 2001; on the estate, Hickey 2012.
30. *SB* XXIV 16324 (557 CE), line 31; *P.Oxy.* XVI 1911 (557 CE), line 42; LV 3804 (566 CE), lines 34, 47.
31. *P.Oxy.* LV 3804 (566 CE); on the average size of *koina*, see Ruffini 2008b: 110–11.
32. See Mitthof and Papathomas 1994; Gascou and Worp 1990.
33. *P. Cair.Masp.* I 67001 (514 CE); see Keenan 1985: 254–56.

groups of craftsmen to complete construction and repairs of buildings owned by the estate.[34] Some payments to groups of brick makers included additional expenses for builders who partnered with them.[35] Individual contracts confirm what is found in the accounts. An early sixth-century text from Oxyrhynchus, for instance, records a transaction between an Apion estate steward and three individuals acting on behalf of a group of brick makers and builders.[36] These brick makers and builders may have organized themselves as associations that helped coordinate their activities and work for the estate, but that is unclear.

This evidence does not mean that the brick makers worked exclusively for or held leases on the estate. Cisterns, irrigation works, and other structures on estate property required maintenance and upkeep, and estates hired groups of craftsmen to perform the work. Another contract from the Apion estate mentions a certain John, "head of the stonecutters," who agreed to provide two hundred large stones to the estate.[37] That the text describes him as the head of a group of stonecutters alludes to the likelihood that he coordinated the production and paid employees or colleagues. Such coordination points toward the sort of work expected from the head of an association.

These *koina* of farmers and vinedressers, *sunodoi* of cattle herders, and groups of craftsmen transacting business with estates may have operated like other associations. If that was the case, membership in these groups would have helped individuals establish bonds of trust, gain access to information (market or otherwise), and maintain a reputation (with other groups and the estates) that lowered transaction costs and provided access to reliable business partners and labor when necessary. The estates and their stewards apparently found these individuals and their groups reliable enough to enter into contracts with them. Combining economic resources and manpower as these *koina* and *sunodoi* did also increased the options for dealing with risk and uncertainty in any enterprise—be it the risks of weather, soil conditions, drought, excessive flood, illness, or injury, along with personal and economic pitfalls covered in association charters. Landlords typically placed the burden of dealing with the risks of the market on the tenant, especially in the case of a late Roman estate like that

---

34. *P.Oxy.* LV 3804 (566 CE), line 151; see also XVI 1912 (566 CE), col. 3, lines 127–28.
35. *P.Oxy.* LV 3804, line 151; XVIII 2195 (576/7 CE), line 92.
36. *P.Oxy.* XVI 2007 (early VI CE) is a receipt addressed to a *pronoetēs* from three individuals apparently acting on behalf of a group of brick makers and builders.
37. *P.Oxy.* I 134 (569 CE). At line 15, the papyrus reads *kephal/ tōn laotomōn*, where the editor has restored *kephal(ē)*; he similarly restores *keph/* on the verso. *Kephal/* might also be an abbreviation of *kephalaiōtēs*, a term used for association officials during the sixth century.

owned by the Apion family, who relied on long-term, fixed-rent leases payable in cash.[38] Associations provided members access to economic and social capital, which offered an additional means of dealing with the particular circumstances in which many tenants found themselves.

Association Ties and Individual Activities

The Kronion Archive and First-Century Tebtunis

Access to trust networks and information—about not only colleagues but also the costs and availability of labor and materials—helped craftsmen and merchants coordinate the work required to complete contracts for public officials, estate managers, and others. The individuals named in these documents probably benefited from the institutional framework that associations provided. The degree to which the ties forged within an association carried over into the private economic activities of members is an important but difficult question to answer. In many ways, the picture of activities undertaken by individual members is no less fragmentary than what the documents tell us about actions coordinated by associations as a group. Nevertheless, a number of texts do reveal economic and social connections between members outside of a specific association context, to the extent that anything would happen outside of an association framework, given that members shared common bonds and the obligations to the group.

The evidence from Tebtunis contained in the Kronion archive once again offers a starting point. These texts indicate that association members did rely on and undertake business with colleagues in private transactions. Besides the charters considered in the previous chapter, the archive includes other texts related to associations in Tebtunis. One document preserved a list of contributions made by members of a group associated with the god Harpocrates (*P.Mich.* V 246). Two others preserve membership rolls: *P.Mich.* V 247 lists the names, ages, and defining physical characteristics of sixteen members ranging in age from twenty-two to fifty-two, and *P.Mich.* V 248 contains the names of nine members ranging in age from twenty-nine to sixty. There is no indication, however, of either group's name. Both lists were the product of several hands and

38. On late Roman estate management, see Hickey 2007, 2012.

were intended to be appended to each group's charter, which would have contained the missing information.

Combined with the association charters contained in the archive (*P.Mich.* V 243–45), these texts provide a sample of eighty-one people who lived, worked, and belonged to associations in Tebtunis in the early to middle parts of the first century CE. Yet this data also presents certain obstacles to interpretation. Patterns of nomenclature and repeated use of common names (such as Harmiusis, Orseus, and Herakles) make it difficult to track individuals. The same issues make uncovering the familial relations between individuals daunting.[39] Even in the small sample provided by the salt merchants represented in *P.Mich.* V 245, deciphering the relationships between people like Orseus and Apynchis proves challenging. Thankfully, reliance on an association network or on a family network enhanced by association membership can be tentatively identified in other texts preserving transactions conducted between individuals.

A man named Eutuchos and his five sons, including three named after their father (Eutuchos the elder, Eutuchos II, and Eutuchos III), are well attested in Kronion's archive. Some of his sons also belonged to associations active in Tebtunis during the early first century CE. Two sons, Sisoeis the carpenter and Eutuchos II, belonged to the *apolusimoi* of *P.Mich.* V 244. Eutuchos III belonged to the unspecified group whose membership list has been preserved as *P.Mich.* V 248. Given that more than half of his sons belonged to some sort of association, Eutuchos and his family were doubtless familiar with this social and economic milieu.

Not surprisingly, Eutuchos' sons worked with each other to manage property that they had inherited from their father. They sold some of this property to Chrates, son of Akousilaos.[40] Chrates was no stranger to the family. He belonged to the same association as Eutuchos III, the unspecified association of *P.Mich.* V 248.[41] The connection that Eutuchos III and Chrates shared may have factored into this property purchase. Since associations facilitated the exchange of information about members and sought to establish trust, their relationship might have reduced the transaction costs associated with finding a buyer for the sons of Eutuchos. Since Eutuchos III knew Chrates through their association membership, he and, presumably, his family had access to

39. For Egyptian onomastics, see Fikhman 1996; see also Hobson 1989. On family relations within groups, see Venticinque 2010: 277–79.

40. *P.Mich.* V 305 (I CE).

41. *P.Mich.* V 248 (early I CE), lines 3–4.

information about Chrates' needs, resources, and reputation for following through on contracts.

Further details provided in the contract indicate that this was not the only transaction between Eutuchos' family and Chrates and his family. Eutuchos' sons had previously sold other vacant lots and a house to Chrates and his brother Herakles.[42] Shared connections and prior successful interactions might have assured buyer and seller alike that the contract would be honored. Since a portion of the vacant lots purchased by Chrates bordered property that Eutuchos' sons would have continued to own and use after this transaction, both families might have sought ways to protect themselves from incursions, improper use, or attempts to reclaim the property. With this in mind, the families of Eutuchos and Chrates might have considered dealing with known individuals a suitable strategy to reduce risks, including heirs trying to restore the property to the family of Eutuchos through legal action. Although many contracts contain clauses that the sellers and their families "agree not to proceed against it forever and not to bring any claim, and that no one else shall on their behalf," reliance on association ties and the resulting desire of all parties to preserve a trustworthy reputation might have made this promise seem more secure for Chrates and Herakles.[43]

Connections also reduced less ominous legal problems, including day-to-day issues associated with shared use of entrances and exits. The sons of Eutuchos and the brothers Chrates and Herakles found themselves in such a situation as a result of the purchase of the vacant lots. Part of the agreement called for Chrates' brother Herakles to craft an additional entrance in the property that Chrates and Herakles owned.[44] The new door opened onto a common entrance used by Eutuchos III, his brothers Sisichales and Sisois and their families, and Chrates and Herakles. Sharing entrances and exits that passed through the property in question offered opportunities for the families to come into contact and conflict with each other over use of and access to the space. Having an established relationship underpinned by association connections would hopefully mitigate potential difficulties.

An established relationship did not help only the sellers. Chrates' connections to Eutuchos' family lessened the transaction costs he incurred as the buyer. Buyers rarely have as much information as sellers. That Chrates knew

42. *P.Mich.* V 305, lines 18–19.
43. *P.Mich.* V 305, lines 17, 21, 25, trans. Boak.
44. *P.Mich.* V 305, lines 14–15.

Eutuchos III leaves open the possibility that his access to additional information facilitated the decision to purchase the lots. Transactions between the family of Eutuchos and Chrates and his brother Herakles also reveal the ways in which family and association ties overlapped and reinforced each other.

Another of Eutuchos' sons, Eutuchos the elder, was part of a transaction that involved Tebtunis' associations. Eutuchos the elder served as the scribe for a property purchase that involved a member of an association.[45] The property in question was a courtyard located between plots owned by the buyer, Labesis, son of Labesis, and the seller, Psenobastis, son of Thebaios. Psenobastis does not appear to have belonged to any of the associations known from *P.Mich.* V 243–48. Labesis, however, belonged to the *apolusimoi* (*P.Mich.* V 244). Eutuchos the elder, although not a member of this group, was part of the larger network of the *apolusimoi,* thanks to his two brothers who did belong to the association.

Strictly speaking, membership in an association might not have been pivotal in this transaction. Labesis and Psenobastis were neighbors and may have had some knowledge of each other, although perhaps not as detailed as the financial information that could be obtained from membership in an association, thanks to internal record keeping regarding contributions, loans requested, or money owed. What motivated Psenobastis to make the sale is unclear. Perhaps Psenobastis had fallen on hard times and needed money but was unable to find or had no access to credit. Without an association to turn to, Psenobastis could have decided to sell some possessions to acquire the resources he needed. That Labesis belonged to an association may, however, have factored into his decision to purchase the courtyard. The particulars of Labesis' own situation are unknown, but membership in an association might have enabled him to act more quickly or in an opportunistic manner, even on a large expenditure, knowing that association membership offered a financial safety net should he find himself in difficult straits later. His affiliation with a group might also have made him appear more trustworthy to Psenobastis; whether Labesis was actually reliable is another question.

There is some indication that connections across professional, family, and neighborhood networks may have played a part in the transaction. Eutuchos the elder acted as a scribe on behalf of both men, suggesting a link to both Labesis and Psenobastis. Eutuchos was probably known by Labesis through his

45. *P.Mich.* V 306 (I CE); Eutuchos the elder acted as the scribe in several other documents: *P.Mich.* V 249 (18 CE), 291 (I CE), and 296 (I CE).

brothers who belonged to the same association as Labesis. A neighbor of Psenobastis, Papnebtunis, son of Paanouphis, also belonged to an association, but not to the *apolusimoi;* he was instead a member of the group affiliated with Harpocrates (*P.Mich.* V 246). Although there is no evidence that Psenobastis belonged to an association, perhaps access to association networks through Eutuchos or Papnebtunis provided Labesis and Psenobastis the security and information they needed to complete the transaction and even reduced the transaction costs related to finding witnesses and a scribe. Regardless of the exact scenario, that Eutuchos acted as a scribe does seem significant. His presence as a scribe points to the fact that members of associations turned to their colleagues and relatives of their colleagues to act as witnesses, draw up contracts, and facilitate transactions.

There might have been other connections between Eutuchos the elder and Labesis. The same Eutuchos purchased vacant lots from a man named Pyrrhos who was identified as the son of Labesis in a bilingual Demotic and Greek contract.[46] This Pyrrhos was probably the son of the Labesis mentioned in the property purchase discussed above. Labesis was not a common name. According to the Trismegistos onomastic database, Labesis is attested in only eleven texts prior to 48 CE. All of those examples originate from Tebtunis and the Arsinoite nome.[47] Provided that the family connection did exist, this signals another economic connection between the two families and between Eutuchos and Labesis, by way of his son. Since the precise dates of these two texts are unclear, it is difficult to determine which transaction occurred first and the impact one transaction had on the other. In any event, the texts stand as examples of repeated interaction in which links between families and associations might have played a role.

More texts in the Kronion archive indicate economic links between association members in Tebtunis. For instance, *P.Mich.* V 299 (I CE) records that Harmiusis and his son Mieus sold Harmiusis' half of a two-level house and courtyard to Horus, the son of another man named Harmiusis. It is possible that Horus may have been the son of Harmiusis by a different mother and that this was an effort to make an arrangement between sons. But Harmiusis is a common name, and we may just be dealing with a different man. In the association texts contained in the Kronion archive alone (*P.Mich.* V 243–48), there

46. *P.Mich.* V 308 (I CE).
47. http://www.trismegistos.org/name/3806 (accessed June 3, 2015).

are several different people named Harmiusis. For the first century CE, the Trismegistos database cites eighteen different texts for a Harmiusis and 664 total individual references to that name, not counting all variant spellings in Greek or Demotic Egyptian.[48] This is a higher frequency than what is observed for the name Labesis. It is significant, however, that both the buyer and the sellers belonged to an association. Harmiusis and his son Mieus were members of the association of sheep and cattle herders whose charter was preserved as *P.Mich.* V 243, and Horos belonged to the *apolusimoi.* It was probably not a viable strategy to eschew business from those outside the group. This may have increased the risk of opportunistic behavior, compared to the supposed security in dealing with a colleague from within the same group, but developing overlapping connections allowed groups to gather information on other community members that could be shared during a regular meeting. The very fact that someone belonged to any association might have provided more security than dealing with someone who was not an association member. Given the similarities in organization and charters between groups, individuals might have understood that members of other associations were essentially playing by the same rules, so to speak.

In a roughly contemporary *paramone* contract that also belongs to the Kronion archive, a forty-year-old man named Pabelleous placed his daughter in the service of a twenty-six-year-old man named Harmiusis, son of Onnophris.[49] A *paramone* contract was a particular type of labor contract for unspecified work and services, usually associated with interest-free loans. In this case, Pabelleous' daughter lived and worked for one year in the home of Harmiusis and agreed to follow him wherever he went throughout Egypt. In exchange, Harmiusis provided food, clothing, and housing. The daughter's services were provided in lieu of the interest charges that Pabelleous would have incurred from a loan of forty-eight drachmas that Harmiusis had given him.

Long-term connections between members of associations in Tebtunis may have factored into this loan and contract. A Harmiusis who was the son of Onnophris belonged to the group represented by the membership list that survives as *P.Mich.* V 247. This text identifies Harmiusis as forty-two years old, suggesting that sixteen years have passed between the *paramone* contract and the composition of the membership list. The same list contains no mention of a person

48. http://www.trismegistos.org/name/274 (accessed June 3, 2015).
49. *P.Mich.* X 587 (24/25 CE).

named Pabelleous, who would have been around fifty-six years old by now, but four men listed, ranging in ages between twenty-six and thirty-nine, identified themselves as the sons of a man named Pabelleous. Pabelleous is not a common name and is only referenced in the two documents in question, *P.Mich.* X 587 and V 247.[50] If these were sons of the same Pabelleous, that means that the oldest son was born when Pabelleous himself was seventeen or eighteen, which is possible. It also was not uncommon for fathers and sons to belong to the same association or for sons to take their father's place within an association. Besides the sons of Pabelleous, one finds the sons of Marres, Onnophris, and Paeus in this same group, indicating that family ties were strong within this association. With this in mind, the fact that not Pabelleous but the sons of Pabelleous are mentioned in the membership list does not rule out the possibility that Pabelleous belonged to the group at some point. If this was the case, his membership may even have overlapped with that of the man who had loaned him a significant amount of money sixteen years earlier, Harmiusis, son of Onnophris. That Harmiusis and the sons of Pabelleous remained in the same association may point to the fact that the relationship between the two families had continued beyond the scope of the initial loan and *paramone* contract.

It is not surprising to see what was essentially an interest free loan within an association context. Interest-free loans might have been given out less frequently, if at all, to unknown individuals. In some sense, hiring out a son or daughter in lieu of interest would seem riskier and present higher stakes than accepting a traditional loan. Slander, corruption of a household, or breaking an agreement—the sorts of action that charters advised against—would have had greater fallout for all involved here, besides the monetary amount of the loan.

Association members were not only supposed to provide loans to each other; they could fall back on trust networks to mitigate risks involved in transactions that would have been riskier for others who were not in a similar position of strength, including arrangements like a *paramone* contract. Normally, association members are regarded as being on relatively firm financial footing. Providing the labor of one's daughter in exchange for a loan suggests that it was a decision made out of something less than a position of strength. But even association members might have needed money at times. The contract does not necessarily tell us anything about Pabelleous' circumstances. As detailed as the papyri can be, the evidence needed to be sure is lacking. Pabelleous' finances

50. http://www.trismegistos.org/name/19586 (accessed June 3, 2015).

might not have been exceedingly bad for too long, if his sons were able to sustain membership in an association themselves. Although it seems that he was in a powerless position, association connections may have provided Pabelleous access to capital when he needed it in the first place and may have offered the security of knowing that his daughter would not be mistreated.

The penalty clauses that the contract contained may also reveal a link with association membership, because they mirror strategies that groups adopted to monitor economic activities. The contract stated that should Pabelleous, his daughter, or any family member violate the agreement, they would be liable for payment of the forty-eight drachmas plus interest to Harmiusis. Violation of the contract also called for paying an extra one hundred drachmas to the public treasury. This stipulation, which calls to mind the penalties that the salt merchants in Tebtunis adopted, seems aimed at damaging the offending party's reputation in the community.

Family ties between craftsmen and merchants mattered not only in *paramone* agreements but in apprenticeship contracts as well. According to contracts from Egypt, an apprenticeship was a long-term commitment that ranged between one and five years.[51] During that time, the apprentice essentially became a member of the household of the master craftsman, who provided room and board, clothing, and money. If the associations of weavers, dyers, builders, or goldsmiths in Tebtunis operated like craftsmen elsewhere, certain conventions probably governed how they arranged apprenticeships. Weavers in Oxyrhynchus typically sent their children to the home and workshop of another weaver to learn the trade. Craftsmen did not regularly train their own children or their slaves. Exchanges of apprentices (sons, daughters, or slaves) thus extended networks and, depending on the circumstances, solidified bonds already in place.[52]

No less than in regard to other contractual arrangements, association membership and the access it gave to trusted partners and information regarding individual reputations provided members a means to deal with the complexities present in apprenticeships. Such ties between family members and associations present in both *paramone* and apprenticeship contracts add further import to the ethical regulations that these groups devised and to the norms that members were expected to follow. Failing to honor contracts and slandering

51. On apprenticeship, see Bradley 1991.
52. Venticinque 2010: 289–91.

other members damaged more than the immediate business venture. If these connections lasted over the course of many years (as seems to be standard with apprenticeships), such ties could become a source of strength. Given the delicacy of a contract that necessitates one member of a family living and working with another family for some time, these relationships between individuals, family members, and association members could be equally tenuous. A dispute relating to slander by a third party—the sort of behavior that associations tried to limit according to their charters—could quickly involve other members of the network. Vital in such an environment were establishing and relying on trust and reputation, as well as knowing who would abide by the rules and cultivating ties with those individuals. Rather than making up for a deficiency in a member's family network, associations provided a means (unavailable to nonmembers) to protect and support a member's own interests and those of his extended family network.

Aurelius Leonides and Fourth-Century Oxyrhynchus

A fourth-century archive of texts from Oxyrhynchus that relate the economic activities of Aurelius Leonides, son of Theon, provides another perspective that details how association members managed their affairs. Leonides was a merchant who dealt in flax, an important cash crop in Egypt.[53] Flax seeds could be processed for oil, and its fibers provided raw materials used not only for clothes but for making things like fishing nets.[54] Leonides was not just a flax merchant, however, he also belonged to an association of tow workers.

The archive of Leonides contains thirteen texts that span just over twenty years (312–34 CE), including time he spent as the monthly president (*mēniarchēs*) of the association of tow workers. Twelve of these texts are documentary—letters, leases, and receipts. The majority of the texts deal with different aspects of work involved in flax production and distribution, undertaken by Leonides alone and in collaboration with partners. Others deal with requests sent from local officials to Leonides and his fellow monthly presidents of the association. A single documentary text pertains not to Leonides but to a partner named Aurelius Dioscorus, with whom Leonides collaborated through the years.[55] In an excellent study, AnneMarie Luijendijk recently assigned a fragment (as-

53. On flax production, see Mayerson 1997.
54. Mayerson 1997: 202.
55. *P.Oxy.* XLV 3255 (315 CE) = *P.Coll.Youtie* II 80.

sumed to have been a writing exercise) of Paul's letter to the Romans (*P.Oxy.* II 209) to the archive of Leonides, who, if we judge on the basis of the letter's inclusion, was apparently a Christian.[56] Grenfell and Hunt, the excavators and original editors of the text, claimed that the fragment of Paul's letter "was found tied up with a contract dated in the year 316 A.D., and other documents of the same period," which detailed the affairs of Leonides. This suggests that the texts had been collected and bundled as an archive in antiquity.

Leonides followed what appears to be common practice and identified himself as a member of the association only in official documents, with the exception of one damaged and fragmentary receipt he wrote himself.[57] Thanks to these few references to his membership and status as an official, however, more is known about the business endeavors of Aurelius Leonides than about those of many other association members in Egypt or anywhere else. This provides a unique window into the strategies that association members employed to manage production, the market, and, as the case may be here (when dealing with flax production), the agricultural year.

The texts indicate that Leonides operated primarily in two villages located in the Oxyrhynchite nome, Ision Panga and Antipera Pela. One text reveals that Leonides also purchased flax from a resident of a village named Teis.[58] Leonides was not just a merchant buying crops from farmers and selling them to craftsmen in the city. He apparently participated in all aspects of cultivating, processing, and distributing flax crops. Several of the texts specifically mention the production process needed to prepare the flax to be used for other goods.

Leonides sometimes worked in partnership with other flax merchants. In 316 CE, Leonides and a merchant named Aurelius Dioscorus, son of Ammonios, began what appears to have been a lengthy partnership. In that year, the two men leased a single aroura of land in the village of Ision Panga, land owned by someone who had served as a gymnasiarch and prytanis.[59] Dioscorus himself, like Leonides, was already active in and around Oxyrhynchus. In the previous year, Dioscorus had leased six and three-eighths arouras of land for sowing with flax on his own initiative.[60]

That both men belonged to an association related to flax production and

---

56. Luijendijk 2010.
57. *P.Oxy.* XLV 3262 (328 CE).
58. *P.Oxy.* XLV 3254 (312–15 CE).
59. *P.Oxy.* I 103 (316 CE).
60. *P.Oxy.* XLV 3255 (315 CE) = *P.Coll. Youtie* II 80.

distribution can be inferred from the lease of 316 CE (*P.Oxy.* I 103). On the verso of the document, both men were styled *stippotimētai*, measurers or valuers of tow, flax that had been processed and spun and used for ropes, cords, and other items. This suggests that both Leonides and Dioscorus may have shared long-standing ties to the association that would later elect Leonides as an officer.

Perhaps coming off a successful initial arrangement, Leonides and Dioscorus decided that it was a good idea to continue the business relationship. The two men partnered again in the following year, 317 CE, when they increased their stakes and interests in flax production. In this case, the two men leased thirteen arouras of land in Antipera Pela; the land was owned by another former gymnasiarch and prytanis of Oxyrhynchus, Aurelius Heron.[61] Leonides and Dioscorus agreed to do all the work (or to hire others to do it) and to return the proceeds of seven of the thirteen arouras as rent.

Dioscorus was not Leonides' only partner. In the next year, 318 CE, Leonides and Aurelius Ammonios, son of Copres, leased five arouras of land owned by a group of heirs in Ision Panga, through the heirs' agent Matrinus.[62] Leonides did not have to go far to find another reliable colleague; Ammonios was probably the father of Leonides' partner Dioscorus.

Leonides may also have sought to spread out his risk and resources by taking leaseholds in different villages in alternate years. For instance, in 319 CE, he again leased an uncertain amount of land in Antipera Pela, without partners.[63] The terms of the contracts varied, which suggests that Leonides and his partners used different strategies when crafting agreements, to suit the particular demands of a situation. Instead of paying rent in kind, for instance, Leonides and Ammonios paid three talents and one thousand drachmas per aroura and avoided payment of taxes. The landholder apparently would continue to assume the tax burden.

Leonides might have been taking advantage of the economic difficulties of others, although it is difficult to know the circumstances that motivated the transactions. On one occasion, Leonides subleased a portion of the land that a man named Gaianus had leased for one-third of the resulting crop.[64] In another arrangement, several years earlier, Leonides had avoided sowing the land and had purchased harvested crops but had assumed the burden of processing, sell-

61. *P.Oxy.* XLV 3256 (317/18 CE).
62. *P.Oxy.* XLV 3257 (318 CE).
63. *P.Oxy.* XLV 3258–59 (319 CE).
64. *P.Oxy.* XLV 3260 (323 CE).

ing, and paying the taxes on the produce.[65] With access to trusted partners like Dioscorus and Ammonios and to connections through the association, Leonides might have been in a better position to bear the risk of production and the market than someone like Gaianus (about whom comparatively little is known). The decision Leonides made to enter into these contracts without a partner may suggest a more cavalier attitude toward economic activity, but managing leaseholds on his own allowed Leonides to spread his resources out and secure additional profits. It also enabled him to make connections with more elite landlords, connections that, in the long run, may have helped him and, by extension, his association. Given the nature of the evidence, it could suggest that Leonides entered into these agreements after he had already made arrangements for other leases with his partners. That he subleased and bought produce from land that had already been sown may even allude to the fact that these were exceptional situations.

It is also difficult to judge whether Leonides' activities were similar to the entrepreneurial endeavors of Aurelius Phoibammon in Aphrodito during the early sixth century; thanks to James Keenan's analysis, Phoibammon has become something of a benchmark.[66] Phoibammon took advantage of the neglected or failed agricultural efforts of others. In one case in particular, Phoibammon was able to act in an opportunistic manner to exploit the difficulties that the soldier Flavius Samuel had with his property and to prey on Samuel's apparent need for money and grain.[67] Over the span of two years, Samuel went further into debt and ultimately mortgaged the property to Phoibammon, whose ability to lease twenty-eight arouras of land and provide Samuel, up front, with substantial loans approaching eighteen gold solidi and fifty-eight artabae of grain suggests that he was operating at a different scale than Leonides. With only one exception, Leonides and his partners paid rent, cash or otherwise, at the conclusion of the lease.[68] In any case, Leonides' position as an association official, his connections with former council members, and the large sums of money that he was able to pay for rent indicate that he would have been a man of some means. Business relationships with council members suggest that at least in their eyes or the eyes of their estate managers and agents, Leonides represented a reliable partner who would make good on the terms of a lease agreement.

---

65. *P.Oxy.* XLV 3254 (312–15 CE).
66. Keenan 1980.
67. *P.Michael* 37 (526 CE), 44 (527 CE); *P.Mich.* XIII 670 (527 CE).
68. *P.Oxy.* XLV 3254 (312–15 CE).

The documents of the Leonides archive reflect the complexity of Roman and Late Roman social and economic relationships. Leonides and his partners transacted business with tenants, landowners, groups of heirs, and women. Contractually, it seems that the leaseholders took on the risks of agricultural production and of marketing the goods, although the landowners did provide Leonides with seed.[69] The landowners might have provided irrigation and access to water, too. Rents in kind were more favorable to leaseholders than forcing them to pay a fixed cash rent up front. Unlike fixed cash rents, rents paid in kind would not have lessened the economic stake for the landowners necessarily, as the output depended on a number of variables throughout the year and on the tenant's ability to manage the land. Even in this situation, the landowners still saved themselves the expense of working the land and processing the flax, responsibilities that Leonides and his partners assumed.

Coptic hagiographical works suggest that ties between merchants and landowners could be quite strong. The Coptic *Martyrdom of Paese and Thecla* describes the amicable and personal relationship between Paese, a wealthy landowner who sowed flax, and his kinsman Paul, the merchant who purchased the goods produced on Paese's land and that of other estates throughout the Hermopolite nome. Paul would later bring the flax to Alexandria and sell it.

> There was a man in the city of Shmoun who was a great merchant in his family, being a kinsman (of theirs). And this man had much wealth; and it was he who bought the flax fiber of that whole nome; and the name of that man was Paul. . . . And that man was friendly with Paese, since the latter sowed a great plantation of flax. And Paese was noble and rich and famous in that whole nome. He would load the camels for the (goods for) disposal, and arise and go to the city of Shmoun to Paul the merchant; and Paul was glad whenever he saw Paese, and he would keep him with him for a month at a time, while they ate and drank together, rejoicing exceedingly and conversing together upon the word of God.[70]

Cooperation, rather than conflict, seems to have been the order of the day in these relationships. Unfortunately, the picture provided by the documentary papyri and by the *Martyrdom of Paese and Thecla* remains fragmentary. Con-

69. For parallels, see *P.Cair.Masp.* I 67116 (548 CE), II 67128 (547 CE), II 67129 (549 CE).
70. Trans. Reymond and Barns (1973: 153).

tracts, leases, and agreements between merchants and landlords were only part of a more complex set of business arrangements that would have been negotiated and renegotiated each year.

As illuminating as the documents and anecdotal evidence provided by hagiographical texts can be, they represent a fraction of what may have been recorded by others involved in these transactions. How Leonides and his partners managed the land is unclear. We do not know about the arrangements that Leonides made regarding the sale of the flax crop he was left with after making rent payments. If Leonides, like Phoibammon, had taken advantage of the economic circumstances of others, those relationships might not have been as amicable as the one that existed between Paese and Paul, although a Christian text touting the virtue of both Paese and Paul would show their relationship in nothing but a positive light. As the leases contained in the Leonides archive represent the start of an economic relationship and the flax production process, it is difficult to say whether market or environmental conditions played out in a way that allowed Leonides to meet his rent payment and still derive enough profit to make the endeavor sustainable. His eventual appearance as one of the leading officials of his association a decade after the first lease in his archive implies that he met with more success than failure.

Conflict and Violence within Associations

Public Complaints in Late Roman Oxyrhynchus

In an ideal world, close ties supported by trust between individuals and by their repeated successful interactions would reduce transaction costs and benefit the economic, social, legal, and political activities of association members. Such was the case for many of the members of associations that were active in first-century Tebtunis and for Leonides in Oxyrhynchus and his partners. These individuals forged long-lasting and apparently stable ties that factored into a number of social and economic transactions, from providing scribal services in Tebtunis to executing more secure partnerships in agricultural and commercial endeavors. This is certainly the economic and social world that association charters responded to and sought to create.

Yet these same ties could lead to conflict. Charters contain prohibitions against slander and other breaches of decorum and trust, acknowledgment that violence directed at the person or the reputation of a member and his family was a real possibility. Overlapping or multiplex ties, such as those discussed in the preceding section of this chapter, strengthened relationships and supported economic undertakings. This did not preclude the possibility that an errant word or action could complicate relationships between family members and business associates. The structure provided by charters, the trust that developed between individuals, and association members' access to information about colleagues—including the likelihood that someone would follow through on a contract versus initiating legal action against a colleague—probably could not always prevent discord.

Association attempts to enforce regulations and punish rule breakers did not prevent individual members from taking matters into their own hands at times. Charters encouraged internal dispute settlement, but this was not the only avenue available. Going to the authorities remained a possibility, presumably after weighing the various options available. Association members might have viewed turning to the legal authorities as a last resort. But promises of surety, loans, and mutual aid from each other may have helped support legal action initiated by colleagues who had not violated the group's norms.

A number of texts mention disagreements between individual craftsmen and merchants who probably belonged to associations. During the last quarter of the fifth century, the tow workers of Oxyrhynchus took legal action against someone named Menas and filed a petition against him.[71] In their complaint, the tow workers described Menas as a "fellow worker" or "colleague" (*homoergos*), likely indicating that he belonged to their association. The association of bleachers in Oxyrhynchus used the same term when nominating a colleague for a public position during the sixth century.[72] An association of carpet weavers in Oxyrhynchus used the term to refer to a member as well.[73] The tow workers maintained that Menas had broken a written contract "that had been agreed upon."[74] It is not clear what this contract might have been. The complaint may have arisen from different scenarios. Menas could have broken an agreement between himself and the corporate group. He might also have violated an agreement with another member, like the contract Aurelius Iohannes and Aurelius Pseeis, two members of the association of tow workers, entered upon in 557 CE

71. *P.Oxy.* XVI 1943 (late V CE).
72. *P.Oxy.* LIX 3987 (532 CE).
73. *SB* XX 15134 (483 CE).
74. *P.Oxy.* XVI 1943 (late V CE), lines 5–6.

for a year's service.[75] That the association is seeking redress as a collective does not imply that it would not take action on behalf of a member the group felt that Menas had wronged.

The allegation might also refer to a failure on Menas' part to contribute his share of taxes, follow through on the group's nomination to a public post, or fulfill some responsibility he held. Perhaps Menas had neglected to pay back a loan from the group. Associations and their individual members continued to provide loans and credit into the late Roman period, as indicated by a loan that an official of the Oxyrhynchus sausage makers' association made to a member.[76] It is also possible that the group took action against Menas for not fulfilling his portion of a larger contract that the group had taken on to supply processed flax for a public obligation. The salt merchants in first-century Tebtunis reserved the right to punish members that failed to satisfy public obligations.[77] All of these scenarios presuppose, however, that Menas had been expected to cooperate and collaborate with the group and the other association members. That the petition was directed at restitution of a broken contract or partnership agreement further indicates that individuals relied, in their undertakings, on association colleagues and on the association as a corporate group. A breakdown of normal procedure precipitated this complaint.

In any event, the tow workers exposed Menas as a less-than-reliable colleague in a public suit, the sort of action that associations normally sought to prevent members from taking against each other. Initiating action against Menas might have been an important strategic decision on the association's part. If the activity involved was a public undertaking that impacted the group's standing, the stakes would have been high and would have justified collective action, motivated by a desire not just to punish rule breakers but to protect the group's standing in the community.

Factional Strife, Conflict, and Competition

There is another side to strong trust networks, close ties, and collective action. Ties that sought to protect colleagues could sometimes be directed toward harming other members and those outside of the group. Such a case is evidenced by a group of papyri from Aphrodito. A village of perhaps seven thou-

75. *P.Oxy.* XVI 1980 (557 CE); see Gonis 2004: 200.
76. *P.Oxy.* LXXII 4903 (417 CE).
77. *P.Mich.* V 245 (47 CE), lines 37–41.

sand people in the Antaeopolite nome, Aphrodito was home to a number of associations.[78] Payments by eleven associations listed in an expense account prepared in 532 CE provide a sense of the variety of groups active in the village, including, among others, fullers, shipbuilders, cobblers, masons, smiths, tailors, weavers, carpenters, bakers, barbers, and oil workers.[79] Some of these groups were prominent and influential. A famous petition addressed to the empress Theodora and defending the village's right to collect its own taxes was signed by the leading landowners, ecclesiastical officials, and the officers (*kephalaiōtai*) of six associations, representing the cloak weavers, shipbuilders, wine merchants, fullers, bronzesmiths, and carpenters.[80]

Thanks largely to the documents preserved in the archive of a prominent lawyer, landowner, public official, and poet, Flavius Dioscorus, the life of the community and its inhabitants is more readily recovered for Aphrodito than for many locations at any other time period, save for Oxyrhynchus and the Fayum.[81] In this substantial collection of over 550 texts, several document acts of violence and theft apparently perpetrated in Aphrodito in the sixth century by craftsmen, merchants, and association members. One document that may have been written by Dioscorus himself lists a number of people who had stolen from him.[82] Dioscorus included different craftsmen among the alleged perpetrators: four goldsmiths, a carpenter, and a shipwright. In the list of thieves, Dioscorus also named several shepherds, who had organized themselves as an association in Aphrodito.[83] Besides a list of animals and property that the victim alleges these people had taken, the exact details of the caper are murky; what motivated the theft and the nature of the conflict between Dioscorus and the accused also remain unclear. Given the extent of the theft, it might be more complicated than a dispute over rent and taxation with a landlord, and, as Keenan has pointed out, Dioscorus had experienced problems in the past with shepherds trampling crops in fields under his management.[84]

Also unclear is the role that association ties within or between groups may have played in the execution of the theft by the individuals mentioned. That the *kephalaiōtai* of both the carpenters and the shipbuilders signed the petition to

78. On Aphrodito, see Keenan 1984; MacCoull 1984; Bagnall 2005b, 2008.
79. *P.Cair.Masp.* II 67147 (532 CE).
80. *P.Cair.Masp.* III 67283 (before 547 CE).
81. On Dioscorus, see MacCoull 1988; Fournet 1999; 2008: 307–43.
82. *P.Cair.Masp.* II 67143 (538–47 CE).
83. *P.Cair.Masp.* I 67001 (514 CE), line 4; 67090 (VI CE), line 2.
84. Keenan 1985.

Theodora alludes to the fact that those groups had shared interests and may have belonged to the same faction at some point. Although evidence exists for an association of bronzesmiths, who also signed the same petition, there is no clear identification of an association of goldsmiths in Aphrodito. Associations of goldsmiths did exist in other, though larger, communities; Oxyrhynchus and Antinoopolis both had associations of goldsmiths.[85] The goldsmiths in Aphrodito, a relatively large village, may have organized themselves along these lines as well.

Conflict and competition that manifested itself as violence and theft was not limited to Aphrodito. A headman of a village in the Oxyrhynchite nome was also the victim of a significant theft, considering the long list of people he implicated and attempted to hold financially responsible for the loss.[86] A cross section of the community took part in the theft or thefts, including landowners, craftsmen, merchants, entire families, and individuals identified as *presbuteroi* and deacons. Four builders, three merchants, and two oil makers were among those people the headman accused by name. The dyers were implicated as a group; the text mentions not individual craftsmen but designates only the *bapheis*, which can imply a group or an active association.[87] It would seem that these dyers had collaborated somehow to carry out the theft and that they might have relied on association ties in the process. The scale of the theft and the number of people implicated in the Oxyrhynchite village went far beyond that attested in the account from Dioscorus' archive, although that also involved a substantial number of people. In both situations, the victim either knew or gave the appearance that he knew who was involved in the robberies. These incidents were not random but were targeted at specific individuals for reasons that, while uncertain, might speak to larger factional strife between everyone involved.

Associations and the "Aphrodito Murder Mystery"

Two texts recording the proceedings of a hearing before a military official (*comes militaris*), now in the University of Michigan's collection, invite a closer look at the dynamics of conflict and competition in communities and at the

85. *PSI* XII 1265 (426 or 441 CE); *P.Ant.* II 109 (VI CE).
86. *P.Oxy.* XVI 2058 (VI CE).
87. *P.Oxy.* XVI 2058, line 151.

participation of associations in the process.[88] Many people were involved in this conflict in some way, shape, or form, but the state of the texts makes it difficult to determine every detail. The murders of two men, Herakleios and a priest named Victor, were at the heart of the matter. Supposedly orchestrating the murders were two men of comparatively high standing: a soldier named Flavius Menas and Flavius Sarapammon, who may have been the *praeses* of the Thebaid province. Leslie MacCoull originally dubbed this episode the "Aphrodito murder mystery" and argued that the violence revolved around a religious dispute between Monophysites and Chalcedonians.[89] James Keenan rightly questioned these claims and MacCoull's emendations; he suggested that there need not be anything regarding a religious dispute in the text.[90] The texts and the curious circumstances surrounding the deaths of Herakleios and Victor call for continued examination. The interpretation of the episode can be pushed even further by setting it within an association context, and the language and terminology used in the account of the proceedings invite such an approach.

Herakleios' widow, Maria, and Victor's brother Theodorus made the accusations. According to the description of events provided by Maria and Theodorus, Menas delivered the deathblows to Victor and helped round up the additional muscle that did away with Herakleios. Theodorus singled out Menas as the man who apparently beat Victor to death with a piece of wood, described as a *xulon mēchanikon*, which probably means a part from irrigation equipment (as the editor suggested).[91] Such a beating, one that Theodorus asserted had lasted "from the fifth hour until the evening," would account for the abscess that Menas claimed actually caused the priest's death.[92] Menas, however, denied any involvement in Herakleios' death and claimed that he had not even known the man at all.

Maria maintained that a group of unnamed men acting on orders from Menas and Sarapammon seized her husband, murdered him, and disposed of his remains.

> The *kephalaiōtai* of my village Aphrodito together with others who are in their service after having arrested my husband Herakleios put him in the

---

88. *P.Mich.* XIII 660–61 (first half of VI CE).
89. MacCoull 1990.
90. Keenan 1995.
91. *P.Mich.* XIII 660 (first half of VI CE), lines 10–11.
92. *P.Mich.* XIII 660, lines 7–8.

> watch-house of my village Aphrodito and after having taken wine to the same watch-house they drank with him. And when evening came, after beating my same husband Herakleios they killed him with their swords and after that they gave his remains to the fire. They did these things to him on the eighth of the month Phaophi of the passed sixth indiction at the setting of the sun. Being asked why they murdered my husband they said: "The most illustrious Sarapammon and Menas wrote us to kill him," and I reserve against them the law filing suit regarding the death of my wretched husband. When my wretched husband Herakleios had been killed and his remains had been given to the fire so that they may be burned, they poured again water on the same remains and they threw his bones in a basket and I do not know where they buried them. I ask, therefore, that they are given to me so that I can bury them. For concerning just this matter I approached already the most illustrious Sarapammon and it was agreed to arrange that they would be given to me, but they were not given.[93]

Herakleios' widow referred to the men who carried out her husband's murder as *kephalaiōtai*, a term commonly used to describe officials of late Roman associations. Sarapammon and Menas seem to have used these association officials to do their dirty work; in turn, to coordinate this dastardly deed, the officials relied on close ties with each other and people who worked with them.

Herakleios was targeted for an uncertain reason, but he seemingly knew his attackers, with whom, according to his wife's account, he willingly went to a secondary location. An additional text from Aphrodito indicates that the ties between the victim and his attackers might have been more than that of a passing acquaintance. Although his wife makes no mention of it, Herakleios himself may have been an association official. An account dating to 541–46 CE lists a payment made by a man named Herakleios who is identified as a *kephalaiōtēs*.[94] In his prosopography of Aphrodito, Giovanni Ruffini maintained that the texts refer to the same person.[95] If Ruffini is correct, some of the particulars of Herakleios' murder, the way it was carried out, and the role that connections between association members played become apparent.

It is possible that Herakleios and his attackers even belonged to the same group. Some associations had multiple officials, but such a connection is un-

93. *P.Mich.* XIII 660, lines 13–19, trans. Sijpesteijn (adapted).
94. *P.Cair.Masp.* II 67139, fol. 5v, line 21; the text refers to the man as Herakleios, *keph (alaiōtēs)*.
95. Ruffini 2011: 209; see also Ruffini 2008b: 183–84.

clear in this case, as nothing in the account of Herakleios' murder specifies an occupation for him or his attackers. Even if they were not plying the same trade, the heads of the village associations probably were known to each other and worked with each other periodically. Herakleios' attackers may have preyed on these ties to help lure him into a fatal trap.

It is unclear what Herakleios or Victor did to make themselves the object of targeted violence. Ruffini pointed out that Herakleios was identified as a "denouncer" in the proceedings.[96] Such an accusation may indicate that Herakleios had violated an agreement with the association members or had fallen afoul of influential individuals like Sarapammon and Menas. Perhaps he had alerted those outside the group of nefarious activities being carried out by the *kephalaiōtai* at the instigation of Menas and Sarapammon. At the end of the day, Sarapammon profited from large sums of gold changing hands in the background of the murder mystery. Maybe Herakleios followed these men willingly to work out their differences and trusted that no real harm would come to him, even if he was, as they claimed, a denouncer. Repeated interactions and shared celebrations and rituals would have left Herakleios with no reason to suspect that foul play awaited him in the future. Sarapammon, Menas, and the *kephalaiōtai* took advantage of this.

Conclusions

Association members relied in many ways on bonds of trust fostered by their groups. Professional networks supported by association membership helped individuals and groups coordinate and complete larger orders and construction projects. Such collaborations depended on the cooperation of all members, as any defectors could endanger the success of the group as a whole. Membership also facilitated members' access to information about their own trades and professions, including costs of materials and labor. But as we have seen, the benefits of membership extended further into the private economic, social, political, and legal lives of members, as they sought out and relied on colleagues or people within a colleague's family network for business opportunities. Loan agreements between members, provisions to offer surety for colleagues (like the provisions of the weavers in Euhemeria), and transactions involving reliable and

96. *P.Mich.* XIII 661, line 7.

trusted business partners (such as those contained in the material from the Kronion and Leonides archives) indicate such an extension of membership benefits into the late Roman period.

Much of the evidence discussed in this chapter deals with associations and their members operating, theoretically, according to the precepts of the charters and the accepted norms of the group; but adherence to these precepts and norms must have been challenging to maintain at all times. The suit that the tow workers brought against their colleague Menas provides just one example of a failure. The exact nature of this complaint is uncertain beyond allegations that Menas violated a deal, but it encourages speculation about the tension that accompanied decisions to act against a member and to do so in a public way. Loans may have been given freely, but calling in a loan from a colleague might have caused tension between the individuals involved and might have impacted relations throughout the entire network. Despite the fact that charters stipulated a time limit for loans and surety, requests for repayment might have caused conflict.

That the framework provided by associations did not always foster peace and harmony within the group or in the community as a whole does not negate what these organizations were trying to accomplish. It also does not take away from our understanding of the approaches taken by individual craftsmen and merchants. Indeed, in the case of the Aphrodito murder mystery, a number of association members and officials were working together and relying on bonds of trust with each other—even if the collective endeavor was not a contract to repair the baths but violence.

CHAPTER 3

Reputation Management

Construction of burial monuments, oversight of commemorative activities, and participation in funerary rites for a colleague or a colleague's relatives were perhaps some of the more public acts that associations performed. Funerary rituals and commemorative practices varied over time and from region to region, but some sort of participation by associations in burial, mourning, and commemoration appears to have been standard practice throughout the ancient Mediterranean. Although focused on the group and its membership, funerals and the commemorative activities that associations conducted were also orientated outward. Whether associations and their members participated in funeral rites provided by the group itself, in separate supplemental feasts for the bereaved, or in the suite of rituals and celebrations carried out for the deceased by the family, their participation was at once public and private, and the ways in which associations and their members handled funerary activities betray an understanding of this fact. The association of sheep and cattle herders active during the early first century in Tebtunis, for example, expected members to attend a colleague's funeral, to contribute one drachma and two loaves of bread toward a feast held by the group, and to place a wreath at the tomb.[1] The sheep and cattle herders were also supposed to shave their beards and cut their hair to show grief. Adopting a specific mourning posture allowed members to display to the community their participation in the rituals, their piety toward the group, and their observance of social norms, even if in a temporary way.[2]

1. *P.Mich.* V 243 (14–37 CE).
2. *P.Mich.* V 243, lines 9–12.

A funeral thus also provided an association and its membership a platform on which to play a specific role in a social drama, with the association, members' families, those affiliated with the group, and the community providing the audience. Diodorus' description of an Egyptian funeral emphasizes the communal as well as the social performative element of the rituals.

> But not least will a man marvel at the peculiarity of the customs of the Egyptians when he learns of their usages with respect to the dead. For whenever anyone dies among them, all his relatives and friends, plastering their heads with mud, roam about the city lamenting, until the body receives burial. Nay more, during that time they indulge in neither baths, nor wine, nor in any other food worth mentioning, nor do they put on bright clothing.[3]

Though Diodorus visited Egypt during the late Ptolemaic period, continuity into the Roman period in terms of ritual practice, burial, and mortuary texts suggests that the scene in a Fayum village might have been similar.[4] For groups in Asia Minor and Greece that oversaw tombs or burial plots and were charged with ongoing commemorative activities—such as the coppersmiths[5] in Alexandria Troas; the builders[6] in Aphrodisias, to whom fines would be paid for violation of graves; or the donkey drivers in Thessalonike, who paid for a burial and monument out of their common fund[7]—participation in the public social drama continued long after the funeral had ended, as did their ability to accrue social capital. In addition to participating in a funeral, any activities that associations undertook to look after a particular burial plot, individual tomb, or *columbarium* enabled a group not only to evaluate its own membership's adherence to group norms and to display continued connections with a member or wealthy benefactor but also to cultivate a positive reputation in the eyes of the community.

Onno van Nijf and Philip Harland, among others, have argued convincingly that associations helped craftsmen and merchants articulate a place in the social, religious, and political fabric of daily life in Asia Minor and throughout the Roman Empire in a number of ways. Funerary monuments and commemo-

3. Diodorus, I.91.1, trans. Oldfather (Loeb).
4. On funerals and burial in Roman Egypt, see Riggs 2005; Montserrat 1997.
5. *I.Alex.Troas.* 122 (II CE).
6. *SEG* XLVIII 1326 (212–25 CE).
7. *AGRW* 54 = *NewDocs* IV 17 (159/60 CE).

rative epitaphs citing membership or affiliation with an association were an important part of the way groups accomplished these aims. Maureen Carroll astutely pointed out that commemoration provided an opportunity for not only identity formation but identity correction, what could also be characterized as efforts at reputation management by individuals and groups. Participating in funerals and providing for monuments and commemorative activities were not the only ways that associations relayed information about themselves, their undertakings, or their connections with key constituencies to the community. In addition to funerary monuments, possession of designated seating, market stalls, construction or use of meeting places (*scholae* or *oikoi*) embedded within the community, and erection of honorary monuments and decrees saluting members or benefactors in public spaces communicated specific information about an association and its members and provided opportunities for an association to manage its reputation or that of its membership.

Public monuments also reveal, at least in part, the strategic ways that associations, individual members, and a group's benefactors sought to present themselves to the community in everyday life, to borrow noted sociologist Erving Goffman's formulation. In his *Presentation of the Self in Everyday Life*, Goffman employed a dramaturgical framework for assessing the ways individuals conduct themselves in society. Goffman focused largely on face-to-face contact between individuals, unmediated by texts, inscriptions, or monuments such as those through which ancient association activities must be parsed. Yet Goffman's inquiry can inform our consideration of the strategic interactions between associations and communities and of the messages groups communicated to various constituencies within the community that provided the audience for their actions—their performances, as it were. Goffman was keenly aware of the social performative aspect of life and claimed, "All the world is not, of course, a stage, but the crucial ways in which it isn't are not easy to specify."[8] For Goffman, face-to-face interactions between individuals and groups amounted to a conversation with (and performance of) social norms and expectations incumbent upon the parties involved. This chapter will probe to what extent this is true of Egyptian associations and the information they com-

8. Goffman 1959: 72. The dramaturgical metaphor that Goffman employed has drawn no small amount of comments and critiques, even prompting elaboration by Goffman himself. He remained interested in the performative and ritual aspects of social interaction throughout his career, although he did qualify his remarks somewhat. Philip Manning pointed out that Goffman later tried to limit his definition of "performance" to indicate discrete moments or interactions and not necessarily perpetual or ongoing actions; see Manning 1991: 81.

municated about their groups in different venues, not necessarily with regard to individual face-to-face interactions, but by focusing on an association's strategic, public communications during members' own "performances" on the social stage of their community.

Given that the evidence for association activities in Egypt is primarily derived not from inscriptions but from papyrological records (often of transactions or contracts), the public face of associations is not easy to recover in all respects. In this chapter, therefore, some attempt will be made to place the papyri, inscriptions, and archaeological evidence that Egypt offers into a wider context, by resorting to comparisons with material documenting association activities beyond the confines of Egypt—in particular, in Ostia, Delos, and Asia Minor. Despite taking into account appropriate caveats that should accompany such comparisons, the efforts that Egyptian associations made in the realm of reputation management compare well with how groups operated elsewhere. Our ability to couple the public and private face of association activities, thanks to the presence of papyrological documents, provides added nuance and clarity to questions of how associations interacted with the community and sought to develop a specific reputation and amass social capital within the community, questions for which answers are not always readily apparent in other contexts.

Associations in the Community

Associations helped to shape public spaces in the Roman world, with investment in and construction of their own properties, with use of civic and religious spaces, and with the monuments such groups erected outside their meeting places and displayed for the community to see. Many groups owned houses and meeting places, most often referred to as *scholae* in the Roman west or *oikoi* in the east.[9] Clubhouses provided groups with honorific spaces for their own use, where associations exhibited the statues, portraits, and decrees erected in honor of members and patrons who had supported the group. In this respect, Egypt is no different. Associations most likely paid for structures out of their own funds, accumulated from dues payments, entrance fees, or fines. In some cases, individual members or patrons who donated land or

9. Bollmann 1998; see also Waltzing 1895–1900, vol. 4: 437–44, 653–61; van Nijf 1997: 107–9; Ascough, Harland, and Kloppenborg 2012: 221–40.

made additional contributions to the group also provided funds and resources necessary for *scholae* or *oikoi*. In those situations, the buildings became a monument to the benefactor.

The areas where associations located *scholae* or *oikoi* probably reveal something about the groups, their relationship with the community, and, in some cases, the image the associations wanted to project. Some meeting places were in prominent locations. The house of the builders (*fabri tignarii*) in Ostia, for instance, occupied prime space on the *decumanus*, across from the forum.[10] Built during Hadrian's reign and used into the third century, the builders' *schola* was a large structure, with space for meetings, dining rooms, a kitchen, and a central courtyard. In the courtyard, a membership list containing roughly 350 names and dating to 198 CE was found inscribed on a base supporting a statue of Septimius Severus that was dedicated to the emperor.[11]

The builders also owned a temple dedicated to Pertinax, built toward the end of the second century CE, according to the dedicatory inscription.[12] The builders may have paid for the temple with dues, donations, rents from *tabernae* that lined their *schola*, or some combination of those resources, and they may have used the temple for meetings, feasts, and the ceremonial life of the association. Hermansen suggested that the temple, with its dedication to Pertinax, allowed the builders to signal loyalty and devotion to the ruling authorities, at a time when succession following the death of Commodus was a contested issue. This may have been the case. Egyptian groups did include activities focused on the emperor and his family. For instance, the *apolusimoi* of Tebtunis pledged to celebrate the "day of the god Augustus" with a feast each month. That the builders might have marked these occasions and thus displayed loyalty provides further insight into the image and reputation that they hoped to assert and maintain. If not actual loyalty to Rome, such measures at least indicated an association's attempt to show their sensitivity to current social and political norms. Whether or not the builders' actual intent was to exhibit loyalty to ruling powers at Rome, the temple communicated a message about how the builders saw themselves to the rest of Ostia's community, which was their immediate audience. The temple's prominent position along the *decumanus*, elevated above street level, with a monumental entrance measuring roughly 3.5 meters wide, signaled the builders' substantial wealth. The temple also may have of-

10. On the *schola* of the builders, see Bollmann 1998: 287–88; Meiggs 1973: 324.
11. *CIL* XIV 4569 (198 CE).
12. Hermansen 1982: 64; Bollmann 1998: 340–48.

fered a showpiece for their own architectural skills, an equally important aspect of the image they sought to craft. Combined, their *schola* and the temple gave the builders a significant architectural presence commensurate with the reputation and esteem they intended to project to the community (and probably felt that they enjoyed), as Emanuel Mayer suggested.[13]

It could be said that Ostia's builders' association was unique in size, scale of investment in property, and audacity in trumpeting its wealth and success. Different groups might not have been in a position to rival such an association. A number of associations in Ostia did possess *scholae,* however; many of these buildings also happened to be located along the *decumanus.*[14] Although identification of structures as *scholae* is fraught with difficulty, nineteen buildings have been tentatively identified as structures used by associations in Ostia.[15] Hermansen suggested that the association of ferrymen (*lenuncularii*) used the basilica located across from the builders' *schola,* during the mid-third century.[16] If Hermansen's identification of the *schola* of the ship caulkers (*stuppatores*) in Ostia is correct, this association occupied a prominent position to the south of the forum, across from the Tempio Rotondo, and may have owned a row of shops adjoining that property on the north.[17] The builders were also not the only group to maintain a temple in Ostia. During the late second century, the shipbuilders (*fabri navales*) apparently owned a temple constructed on a location along the *decumanus* that once housed a fullery.[18]

In her survey of the spaces used by associations of traders doing business on Delos, Monika Trümper argued that groups used their buildings and clubhouses not only for internal celebrations but also in ways that projected outward to the community.[19] Trümper emphasized that the meeting places occupied by groups were embedded in the architectural fabric of their neighborhoods, an example being the building located near the sanctuary of Apollo and used by the traders known as the *koinon* of Poseidoniastai from Berytus. The *schola* the Poseidoniastai used from the mid-second century BCE was relatively large: it occupied space totaling roughly fifteen hundred

---

13. Mayer 2012: 94–96.
14. For Ostia and its *scholae,* see Meiggs 1973: 324-25; Hermansen 1982: 57–89, 111–20; Bollmann 1998: 195–99.
15. Bollmann 1998: 47–57.
16. Hermansen 1982: 115–19; Bollmann 1998: 275–78.
17. Hermansen 1982: 61–62, 119–20. See also Bollmann 1998: 278–82; Meiggs 1973: 329.
18. Hermansen 1982: 63; Bollmann 1998: 304–7.
19. Trümper 2011.

square meters, contained rooms with dining couches for sixty-eight people, and had a courtyard that housed statues and honorary monuments.[20] The architectural footprint and decoration of the Poseidoniastai's clubhouse "testified to the commercial power and high social standing of the association" (according to Trümper)—or, if nothing else, to the image they wished to assert to the community.[21] Such a building also put on display the social capital that the group had stored up through interactions with and benefactions received from patrons, for an audience consisting of members, patrons, and guests who might be invited to functions held within the *schola*.

Egyptian Associations, Meeting Places, and Use of Space

In contrast to Ostia or Delos, where the physical remains of *scholae* and other structures owned or used by groups remain more evident, the physical reality of the spaces used by associations in Egypt and the ways in which such spaces contributed to efforts of reputation management must be inferred largely on the basis of papyri and inscriptions. Egypt does not provide archaeological and architectural analogues to what can be observed in Ostia or Delos. Since Ostia and Delos were major commercial centers where trade helped support and called for the construction and maintenance of houses, warehouses, and gathering spaces that associations used (such as Ostia's Square of Corporations), it is difficult to compare them with most other places. Nevertheless, what can be inferred from papyri and inscriptions that mention possession or use of spaces by Egyptian associations suggests a parallel on some level. Not unlike the builders in Ostia or the Poseidoniastai in Delos, Egyptian groups used their structures to communicate to the community. The comparison is thus useful not so much in search of a one-to-one correspondence between disparate areas of the ancient world but to help focus on the sorts of questions that could and should be asked of the Egyptian evidence with regard to the physical presence of groups in communities and their use of space.

Honorific stelai and inscriptions dedicating construction or refurbishing of structures, as well as papyri, indicate that trade-based and religious groups either had their own houses in cities and villages or used other buildings for their

20. Trümper 2011: 53–58, 82–84. See also Trümper 2006; Bollmann 1998: 14, 158.
21. Trümper 2011: 57.

events and activities. At a meeting held in their meeting place, referred to as the house (*oikos*) of the *sunodos*, an association affiliated with the imperial cult active in Alexandria voted to honor their officers with crowns and preferential treatment at banquets.[22] The decree is recorded on papyrus and may have been kept by the officers in the group's archive, but it probably was meant to be inscribed and displayed in their meetinghouse, alongside other honorific statues and monuments.

An association of carpenters (*tektones*) active in Ptolemais Hormou during the first century CE designated their meeting space as a *topos*; according to the inscription, it was a space that the group's officials (*presbuteroi*) had refurbished and embellished.[23] The term *topos* referred to places, spaces, and structures associated with religious, economic, and domestic contexts.[24] Some *topoi* in Asia Minor as well as Egypt were places where merchants sold goods. The salt merchants in Karanis, for example, had a *topos* around the temple, according to a short text inscribed on the outside of the temple's enclosure wall.[25] But the term *topos* also indicates a particular place or structure used by associations, seemingly as a synonym for *oikos*. A late first-century CE *stele* refers to the reconstruction of a *topos* affiliated with an association of Isis at Theadelphia, carried out by the group's presiding officer (*prostatēs*) and recorded by another member of the group, who probably served as scribe.[26] A third-century CE *stele* erected by a group of weavers under the direction of their official Hierax also designated a *topos* at Abydos. Like the carpenters or the association of Isis, the weavers presumably used the space for meetings and other activities.[27]

Groups also possessed or used spaces owned by temples or by the community and not necessarily designated as *oikoi* or *topoi*. An association of weavers in Theadelphia in the early second century CE used or possessed a space for their banquets and meetings that was designated as a dining room (*deipnētērion*), according to an inscription that was found *in situ* in a wall of the room.[28] The weavers' officials (*presbuteroi*) apparently contributed the funds necessary to purchase, lease, or maintain the space. A fragmentary inscription dating to the time of Vespasian also identifies a room in the temple

22. *SB* XXII 15460 (5 BCE) = *AGRW* 280.
23. *IGR* I 1155 (45 CE) = *SB* I 996. See also *IGR* I 1151 (80/81 CE); on this text, see Bernand 1993: 108.
24. On the term, see Bernand 1993.
25. *I.Fayum* I 96 (III CE); see also 95 (III CE).
26. *I.Fayum* II 121 (93 CE).
27. *I.Varsovie* 66 (257 CE) = *SB* IV 7290.
28. *I.Fayum* II 122 (109 CE).

of Pnepheros and Petesouchos in Karanis as a *deipnētērion*.[29] That text's reference to a *hēgoumenos*, a common title for association officials, may point to the use of the room by or affiliation with an association. Excavations in Tebtunis have uncovered numerous single-room structures identified as *deipnētēria* and positioned along the *dromos* leading to the temple of Soknebtunis, the central feature of the village's architectural landscape. These rooms date to the Roman period and may have been used not only by priests and temple personnel but also by the associations of Tebtunis, including the salt merchants, the cattle herders, the association of Harpocrates, and many others.[30] Similar structures used by associations and temple priests have been identified in Karanis, suggesting that what is seen at Tebtunis and in the epigraphic record might have been relatively common elsewhere.

Evidence from the final decades of the Ptolemaic period reveals that associations possessed property and meeting spaces at this time as well. A *sunodos* of goose herders possessed a *topos* (potentially affiliated with a temple) in Theadelphia.[31] In Euhemeria, another *sunodos* of farmers appears to have had a *topos*.[32] The physical description of one *topos* suggests a structure used by another *sunodos* associated with Isis in the Fayum.[33] In the first of two honorary decrees passed for a man named Paris, a group of fellow farmers active around Alexandria in the middle of the first century BCE referred to property they possessed in the village of Psenamosis.[34] The group, composed of twenty-nine members, also appears to have owned (or was closely associated with) a gymnasium and a clubhouse, described as an *oikos*. The association constructed these buildings on land that the same Paris had donated to the group; according to the decrees, this was among the first of what appear to be continued benefactions he provided.

Texts indicate that groups used *scholae* and meeting places not only to mark out symbolic claims to participation in the community or to showcase wealth or standing. Egyptian inscriptions attest to the decisions associations made to use their *scholae* as billboards to broadcast specifics about the group and its membership to the community. The decrees honoring Paris erected by the fel-

29. *I.Fayum* I 87 (69–79 CE).
30. Rondot 2004: 150–52, 158–59.
31. *I.Fayum* II 109 (106 BCE). This inscription is dated to the reign of Cleopatra by some; see Bernand 1993: 107n43.
32. *I.Fayum* II 134 (79 BCE).
33. *I.Fayum* III 204 (68 BCE); see also III 205 (51 BCE), for another example.
34. *I.Prose* 40 (67 and 64 BCE) = *SEG* VIII 529 = *SB* IV 7457 = *AGRW* 287.

low farmers from Psenamosis provide a case in point. For his work on behalf of the group, Paris received the full range of honors that groups awarded. The group displayed statues of Paris in the *oikos*, awarded him special seating at banquets, held celebrations in his honor during the year, and gave him the right to extend memberships to three people; additionally, those Paris chose would not be assessed the entry or membership fees common to nearly all associations. Two years later, the fellow farmers awarded Paris extra honors following more donations and goodwill: the group held additional banquets in Psenamosis and Alexandria in honor of Paris, he received immunity from paying dues and special collections, and he received double portions at feasts—even if he did not attend.

Perhaps more important for our purposes here, the association also intended that decrees citing Paris' devotion to the group be posted not only within the clubhouse but in public. Like the *schola* of various *collegia* in Ostia or the Poseidoniastai in Delos, the fellow farmers from Psenamosis used their *oikos* for more than internal functions, such as meetings, banquets, and displaying statues. The group planned to inscribe and display the first decree, which recorded Paris' donation of the place (*topos*) to the *sunodos,* over the entrance to the *oikos.*[35] The second monument summarized his accomplishments and all the honors bestowed on him and was supposed to be displayed at the entrance of a sanctuary that the group apparently used.

> And when he dies in old age, the *sunodos* will yearly observe for him the customary rites of the dead at the tomb and will crown him from common funds with a special crown at the toasts. The *sunodos* will inscribe a decree on a plaque regarding all the aforementioned things, and erect it at the gate of the sanctuary [*temenos*], concerning the three days that are held yearly in his honor and the three statues, in accordance with the decrees.[36]

Public displays of a decree signal adherence to norms and participation in the common language of honorific exchange, so important at elite and nonelite levels. Combined with the group's affiliation with a *gymnasium*, the language of the decree may perhaps show a group aligning itself with a particularly Greek identity. Regardless, mounting the decree in a public place allowed this associa-

35. *I.Prose* 40, lines 13–14.
36. *I.Prose* 40, lines 42–47, trans. Ascough, Harland, and Kloppenborg (2012).

tion to signal to the community their attention to developing social capital and honoring benefactors. The fellow farmers' decisions regarding the honors awarded to Paris and regarding their use of the *oikos* remind us that associations remained ever orientated outward.

Another association of fellow farmers (*sungeouchoi*) provides an example from the early Roman period.[37] This *sunodos* of fellow farmers had a house or meeting place that had fallen into disrepair in the village of Psenemphaia in the Delta. The reconstruction of the house was among many good deeds performed on the group's behalf by their *prostatēs* Apollonius and prompted them to bestow honors saluting his *aretē*.[38] The decree outlining the honors states that Apollonius and his son received portraits that were displayed in their meeting place and crowned celebrations.[39] Like the group in Psenamosis, the fellow farmers also displayed an inscription on the house itself and inscribed the text on the meeting hall's entryway.[40] The decree posted allowed the group to showcase Apollonius' generosity and the group's adherence to norms of honorific exchange and to announce an expectation that the group would recognize and celebrate excellence, piety, and goodwill.

Such displays also provided the fellow farmers a means of competing with other groups, an endeavor related no less intimately to the exchange of honor and honorifics. Posting the decrees and displaying the statue of Paris in the gymnasium, for instance, allowed the group from Psenamosis to trumpet their ties with Paris (who was perhaps an influential member of the community) and to distinguish themselves from other associations. That the second monument was intended to be erected following Paris' death speaks no less to the fellow farmers' efforts at reputation management. The group likely would have wished to maintain close ties with his family. Given the timing of the monument's installation, the group's actions may speak just as much, if not more so, about the specific image that the fellow farmers wished to communicate to the community, the image of an association that follows through on pledges, honors its members and benefactors, and can be expected to do so in the future.

Groups could use the arrangement of internal space and the display of statues and decrees within their *scholae* or other structures to establish and reinforce their own internal hierarchies. The honors voted to Paris included a spot

---

37. *I.Prose* 49 (5 BCE) = *SB* V 8267 = *I.Delta* 899–913, no. 2.
38. *I.Prose* 49, line 33.
39. *I.Prose* 49, lines 34–37.
40. *I.Prose* 49, lines 40–41.

at the most important banquet table, and the contribution list of the association of Harpocrates indicates that they seated individuals in a deliberate way, though this arrangement likely changed based on current officers and member contributions.[41] This is a reminder that hierarchies within groups were not static; they were negotiated at different times based on a number of factors, including changing contributions and the economic profile of membership. Clubhouses also provided a locus for and, in some cases, were a product of benefactions. Donations of land by men like Paris and efforts of the officers to refurbish *deipnētēria* in Theadelphia and Karanis or to rebuild a dilapidated *topos* enabled groups to acquire and sustain not just a meeting place but a physical location embedded in a neighborhood. Where that location can be ascertained for Egypt, it was often a space located in the proximity of a temple or on the main *dromos* of a village or city. Although associations are often considered marginalized in social and economic terms, the placement of their buildings and meeting places in their communities argues otherwise.

Honorific Activities, Monuments, and Dedications

The fact that the meeting place of the Poseidoniastai in Delos contained thirty-three inscriptions, coupled with evidence of Egyptian honorary decrees that provided for erecting portrait statues and decorating them during banquets, suggests that the *scholae* that Hellenistic and Roman associations used were not an insignificant venue for honorific exchange. Statues and decrees displayed within their own buildings speak to the image that groups attempted to construct for largely internal audiences. These monuments could fulfill a variety of functions: to reinforce a group's own internal hierarchies and values, to solidify ties with members of the elite or those outside the group, to reward individuals who acted in accordance with group norms, to disseminate information about individuals, and to encourage approved behavior in the future.

Not all of an association's honorific activity took place within the group's own clubhouses. Associations also strategically communicated and displayed their accumulated social capital beyond the confines of their own structures or, in some cases, on the actual facade. Statues and other honorific monuments paid for by associations and erected in public buildings, along streets and pro-

41. *P.Mich.* V 246 (I CE).

cessional ways, or in temple precincts allowed groups to share information about individual members, their relationships with benefactors, their organization, and the qualities they valued (so often highlighted in monuments and inscriptions): *eunoia, philotimia,* and *aretē.*

In the Hellenistic and Roman world, monuments, statues, and decrees constructed in honor of prominent members of the local community were a common feature of public colonnades, marketplaces, civic council buildings and their facades, and theaters.[42] Honorific monuments were also part and parcel of local political maneuvering and euergetism. Not only the actual award but the display of honors in public played a role in elite identity formation and lent support to the place of primacy occupied by elites, who were the main recipients of such distinctions and commemorations. Looking at the detailed evidence of Termessos as a case study, van Nijf viewed honorary activity as part of a local "monumental celebrity culture" that allowed elites to express and solidify their power and influence on the local level.[43] To put it another way, as Zuiderhoek maintained, euergetism and its trappings "constituted precisely the sort of symbolic statement needed to affirm the legitimacy and naturalness of the existing socio-political order."[44]

In discussing the acquisition, bestowal, and representation of public honors, R. R. R. Smith asserted that "public statues were the highest denomination in the currency of euergetic politics" in which local elites engaged.[45] Associations participated in the symbolic economy of praise and honor Smith described by trading in the currency, so to speak, of honorific statues, monuments, and decrees. Usually with their officers taking the lead, associations dedicated public monuments honoring individuals (sometimes members but also patrons) who had aided the group; some groups, like the dyers of Hierapolis, even honored the council itself with a statue.[46] In many cases, associations received the local council's or governing body's approval to erect monuments saluting the good works of patrons, local magistrates, or their own officials. Through monuments, associations emphasized their relationships (not only actual connections, but also perceived ones) with influential members of the community and, in some cases, their families, in officially sanctioned ways.

42. On honorific activity, see Smith 1998; Ma 2007; van Nijf 2011.
43. Van Nijf 2011: 216.
44. Zuiderhoek 2007: 200.
45. Smith 1998: 63.
46. *SEG* XLI 1201 (II CE) = *AGRW* 147. On honorific activity by associations, see van Nijf 1997: 73–128; Harland 2003: 137–60. See also Arnaoutoglou 2011.

Following Alcock, van Nijf viewed honorific activities undertaken by associations as part of a process in which both elite and nonelite groups used the architectural landscape of their communities to "clarify their role in society and to define their relationships with their social superiors."[47] The evidence of honorific activities in general, then, provides a map of the different constituencies in a given community and offers information about the relationships that individuals, groups, and civic bodies maintained among themselves in the Hellenistic and Roman world.[48] Dedications honoring donors and patrons certainly indicate participation by associations in a common civic activity. Taking part in the exchange of honors also provided associations, not unlike other groups, an established and accepted method to assert their place in the social and political world of their communities, as has been convincingly argued by both van Nijf and Harland with reference to Asia Minor. Monuments placed in prominent locations would have been particularly effective in achieving this outcome.[49] Both participation in the process and the fact that councils awarded groups the privilege to erect monuments also point to elite acknowledgment of the place that associations occupied in communities.

That being said, the dedications that associations made were strategic and coordinated acts by the group and its leadership, aimed at achieving a number of ends. Public monuments and participation in honorific exchange on any level allowed groups to display their accumulated social capital in a public way, to broadcast to a wider audience their relationships (real or perceived) with specific individuals and families, and to jockey for position with other constituencies honoring the same (or other) benefactors. For instance, the temple-building craftsmen (*tektones*) of Ephesos who honored P. Vedius Antoninus, a civic benefactor, with a statue may have been competing with other groups, as well as marking out their niche in the community, when they referred to him as their own *euergetēs*.[50] The wool workers (*lanarioi*) sought to stake a claim to Vedius when they honored him with a portrait statue, whose base was found near the council building.[51] A similar dynamic might have been in place in the third century, when different Ephesian associations honored M. Fulvius Publicianus Nikephorus, a former asiarch, *prytanis*, and civic secretary. Numerous

47. Van Nijf 1997: 73.
48. Ma 2007: 205.
49. Van Nijf 1997: 114; see also van Nijf 2011: 221–22.
50. *I.Eph.* 3075 (150 CE).
51. *I.Eph.* 727 (160–69 CE).

associations documented their connections and debt to Nikephorus for his efforts in securing them market stalls with columns marking their spaces.[52] The garment merchants, on the other hand, might have been trying to distinguish themselves when they honored Nikephorus with a portrait statue on account of his goodwill (*eunoia*) toward Ephesos.[53]

Associations presumably believed that displaying ties with prominent individuals or local magistrates through honorific monuments enhanced a group's reputation in the eyes of the community's elites and nonelites. Public displays may also have had some positive impact on the reputation of the honoree. Local officials and their families included information about affiliation with or donations made to associations in biographical inscriptions. The inscription crafted by T. Flavius Alexandros' daughters, for example, began the description of his career with the honors voted to him by the association of leather workers in Thyatira, because of his diligence when he served as a market overseer (*agoranomos*), among other offices.

> The leather cutters honored T. Flacius Alexandros son of Metrophanes of the tribe of Quirina, who was market overseer in vigorous and extravagant manner for six months, curator of the association [*conventus*] of Romans, ambassador to the emperor in Rome three times, legal representative in the laborious cases concerning the Attaleians [?] at his own expense, and priest of Artemis in a manner displaying piety and love of honor. This was set up on behalf of Flavia Alexandra and Flavia Glykinne, his daughters.[54]

The prominent position of the leather workers in the text comes from the fact that they actually dedicated the monument on behalf of Alexandros' daughters.

Egyptian officials also were concerned with displaying ties to groups. It is unclear who dedicated a statue commemorating a man named Aurelius Apollonius in Dendera.

> A statue of Aurelius Apollonius also known as Masculinus, the son of Besarion, the son of Chairemon, former *exēgētēs*, councilor [*bouleutēs*], and *prostatēs*.[55]

52. *I.Eph.* 2076–82 (222–35 CE).
53. *I.Eph.* 3065 (222–35 CE).
54. *TAM* V.2 1002 (late I CE) = *IGR* IV 1169 = *AGRW* 131, trans. Harland.
55. *I.Portes* 38 (III CE) = *SEG* XXXIV 1619.

The statue is missing, and the base bears no indication of who paid for the monument. It may have been put up by Masculinus, his family, or the community he had served as an official and as a council member. The group he served as *prostatēs*—if that designation indicates here, as in other contexts, belonging to and being a presiding officer of an association—is also a candidate for erecting the monument. André Bernand suggested this as a possibility but also acknowledged that the term could refer to a position in a temple hierarchy; however, membership in an association and the temple hierarchy need not be mutually exclusive.[56] Local officials and their families apparently considered association membership meaningful and displayed it along with their genealogies and the local offices that they had held. This indicates that both the local official and the association benefited from the process. Not only did associations accumulate social capital for their organization through this process, but honors bestowed by the groups augmented the social capital of benefactors as well; at least, an individual's family or community members assumed so.

Honorific Activities, Associations, and Temples in Egypt

Admittedly, the evidence of honorific activities in Egypt is much sparser. But papyri and inscriptions suggest that similar dynamics operated in Egyptian communities. Inscriptions saluting local elites for good deeds, monetary contributions, and construction indicate adherence to and employment of familiar technical language when explaining the reason for granting honors, usually the excellence (*aretē*), piety (*eusebeia*), or love of honor (*philotimia*) displayed by an individual.[57] The family of a councilor from Alexandria, for instance, touted his excellence (*aretē*) and honor-loving ways (*philotimia*) in an inscription that accompanied an honorific monument dated to the early third century CE.[58] Honorific activity extended beyond the social and political milieu of Alexandria. A former *agoranomos, exēgētēs,* and *neokoros* of a shrine for divine Hadrian was honored by his community (perhaps Antinoopolis) for *philotimia.*[59] Decrees passed in honor of local gymnasiarchs in Naukratis also cited their *philotimia.*[60]

56. For example, see *I.Portes* 58 (32 CE), 59 (14–37 CE), and 60 (14–37 CE), a series of dedications (two of which are bilingual Greek and Egyptian hieroglyphs) made by a man identified as a *prostatēs* of Isis.

57. For Egypt in general, see van Minnen 2000.

58. *SEG* XII 557 (212 CE).

59. *I.Portes* 75 (138–99 CE); see also 76 (II CE, Coptos).

60. *P.Oxy.* III 473 (138–60 CE).

Honorific exchanges exhibited by papyri and inscriptions may be part and parcel of a process of municipalization taking place in Roman Egypt, as Alan Bowman and Dominic Rathbone suggested. In their study of civic administration, Bowman and Rathbone claimed that communities of local landowning elites were "increasingly allowed and encouraged to behave and function like the older Greek cities in other provinces," contrary to the usual assertions of Egypt's exceptional position in the Roman world.[61] Peter van Minnen similarly concluded that euergetism had become a "routine phenomenon" and that the actions of benefactors and local elites compare favorably to what is observed elsewhere in the empire.[62]

Amid this process of municipalization, or perhaps operating alongside what was taking place in the *metropoleis*, Egyptian temples remained a focal point of life in large and small communities. Roman rule changed the economic nature of temples and the status of the land they owned, but not their position as a focus of community activities and individual piety.[63] Donations, votive dedications, *proskunemata* carved into temple walls, and festivals centered on temple cults throughout Egypt offer evidence of the continued vitality of temples as a locus of piety during the first three centuries CE.[64] Temples also continued to serve as a hub of social and economic life. The temple of Serapis at Oxyrhynchus, for example, housed what appears to have been one of the city's primary markets.[65] Marketplaces were associated with temples elsewhere in Egypt too.[66] Based on archaeological evidence that points to abandonment and on epigraphic evidence that suggests a decline in dedications and cult, the situation with respect to temples began to change toward the end of the third century.[67] Papyri, however, suggest that traditional cults and priesthoods continued to function into the fourth century, even under Constantine.[68]

Many public activities that were undertaken by Egyptian associations and that could be categorized as honorific in nature or that have left traces in the epigraphic record were focused on or intertwined with temples. Local temples provided a location for dedications of monuments, statues, and *stelai* recording honors and benefactions, written in Greek, demotic, hieroglyphs, or a combi-

61. Bowman and Rathbone 1992: 108.
62. Van Minnen 2000: 453.
63. For discussion, see Monson 2012: 131–41.
64. Frankfurter 1998: 37–82. See also Finnestad 1997; Alston 2002: 196–218.
65. *SB* XVI 12695 (143 CE), XX 14996 (238–44 CE); *P.Koln*.V 228 (176 CE); Parsons 2007: 103–4.
66. Alston 2002: 207–8.
67. Bagnall 1993: 260–64.
68. Bagnall 1993: 264–66.

nation of the three. Given that temples were a focus of social, religious, and economic life, it is unsurprising to see associations making dedications within or near temple precincts. For some time, temples had been an appropriate location where individuals and groups could display devotion to the gods and the community. As such, temples also provided a fitting place to display ties with prominent community members and to salute the actions of group members and benefactors, with dedications made in a more public way than decrees and monuments erected within a *schola*.

In some cases, Egyptian associations used temples as meeting places, in lieu of or in addition to their own buildings. Using temples gave groups a place to meet but also cemented ties with temples and priesthoods. According to its charter, for instance, the *sunodos* of Zeus Hypsistos in Philadelphia held meetings and banquets in the temple of Zeus.[69] Prior to rebuilding their clubhouse, Psenemphaia's fellow farmers had been holding their meetings at a temple, as recorded in an honorific decree that the group posted.[70] Groups centered on craft and merchant activities also used temples in this way. The ironsmiths from Hermonthis continued to meet at the temple of Hatshepsut in Deir el-Bahri (on the Theban west bank) during the fourth century, even after it had fallen into disuse.[71]

As elsewhere, placement of monuments was critical to the efforts of association members to assert their place in the community, to craft a public image, and to communicate information about their group, its membership, and the individuals with whom they associated. In Egypt, the location of a monument (where find spots can be discerned) also emphasized connections with specific temples and provides another perspective on the prominent position that groups occupied in the community. When a *prostatēs* acting on behalf of a *sunodos* dedicated a portrait statue of a man named Herakleides early in the Roman period, he did so in a familiar way that also signaled a connection with a temple. The text that accompanied the statue described Herakleides as the patron (*patrōn*) and benefactor (*euergetēs*) of the group.[72] The statue base was found in or near the temple of Ptah in Memphis, which may suggest that it had been housed within the temple precinct. If this is the case, the *sunodos* not only honored its patron but also signaled its desire to participate in the life of the

69. *P.Lond.* VII 2193 (69–58 BCE), lines 7–8.
70. *I.Prose* 49 (5 BCE).
71. Łajtar 1991.
72. *IGR* I 1114 (17 BCE), lines 4–5 = *SB* I 983.

temple and the community, adapting Greek honorific language to a traditional Egyptian context.

Associations showed devotion to particular deities and ties to temples with more than honorific monuments, particularly early in the Roman period. Temples also stood as a recipient of an association's largesse (or that of a member or patron). During the first decades of Roman rule, an unspecified association dedicated or constructed a building—perhaps a refectory, according to Vleeming's reading of the demotic—affiliated with a chapel of Isis at Dendera.[73] The man named, along with the association, as a dedicator of the refectory, Ptolemaios, son of Pana, also had a relationship with the temple of Hathor in Dendera, according to a series of demotic sandstone votive stelai.[74] One trilingual limestone stele dating to 12 BCE records Ptolemaios' donation of vacant land to the temple.[75] Ptolemaios' titles (*stratēgos* and *sungenes*) indicate that he was a man of some standing in the area, beyond his role in the association. Other associations had ties to temples in Dendera and to Ptolemaios as well (or at least hoped to communicate that message in the dedications they made), such as the so-called great association of Harsomteus, which erected demotic votive sandstone stelai in 10 and 6 BCE.[76]

> The great Association of Harsomteus [Tꜣ sn.t ꜥꜣ.t n Ḥr-smꜣ-tꜣ.wi] which is established in the sight of Isis of the House of Eternity, towards the east side, by [(n)-ḏr(.t)] Ptolemaios son of Pana, the *stratēgos*, and also Pachompshenihy, son of Pachomnemeskos, the *lesonis*, with the Association members [irm nꜣ rmt.w sn.t] in one time. Year 24 [?] under Caesar, 1st month of the pr.t season, day 15.[77]

The association of Harsomteus was still operating almost a decade later, when they erected another votive, although the major players had changed. A man named Tryphon, not Ptolemaios, was now the *stratēgos*.[78] The great association of Hathor, who recorded their piety at some point during the reign of Augustus, perhaps also had a connection with Ptolemaios. The members of the association of Hathor attempted to signal a tie with Ptolemaios in the inscription that

73. *Stud.Demotica* V 159 (19 BCE).
74. *Stud.Demotica* V 161 and 162 (13 BCE).
75. *Stud.Demotica* V 163 (12 BCE). See *I.Portes* 24 for the Greek inscription. See also *Stud.Demotica* V 164 (10 BCE).
76. *Stud.Demotica* V 165 (10 BCE), 166 (6 BCE).
77. *Stud.Demotica* V 166 (6 BCE), trans. Vleeming (2001).
78. *Stud.Demotica* V 170 (2 CE).

named him along with the *lesonis*, the village scribe, and other association members, in a similar fashion.[79]

It is possible that men serving as *stratēgoi* actually belonged to several associations. Vleeming takes the demotic n-ḏr(.t) to designate a dedication made by or from the persons or groups named. A dedication from another association was apparently made by (n-ḏr(.t)) the *stratēgos* Tryphon and his associates. Though formulaic, the phrase "made by" (n-ḏr(.t)) might suggest more personal involvement—not only in the dedication, but also in the association's affairs—than descriptions of dedications as set up "before" or "in the presence of" (m-bꜣḥ) a particular public or cult official and "from" (n-ḏr(.t)) others. Dedications made "before" Tryphon by other associations or individuals could indicate proper deference to his position as an official but not signal direct involvement.[80] A bilingual stele that documents repair work completed by the town scribe of Abydos and his family in 31 CE suggests a similar distinction.

> [Demotic:] In the time [?] of Tiberius Caes[ar] Sebastos, by Ap[oll]onios, son of Kolluthion, the town scribe of Abydos with his wife, with his children, here before [m-bꜣḥ] Osiris, Horus & Isis, and the gods of the temple of Abydos, with the gods who rest with them, because he is the one to have completed the repair of the portico within the temple of Abydos. In writing in the year 17 under Tiberius Caesar, who has been deified, 1st month of the pr.t season, day 18, of the Greek which makes 2nd month of the pr.t season, day 1 of the Egyptian.[81]

> [Greek:] On behalf of Tiberius Caesar Augustus, Apollonius the village scribe on behalf of his wife and all his children, made/dedicated this building. Year 17 under Tiberius Caesar Augustus, Tyb[i 18.][82]

It follows, then, that Ptolemaios might have been affiliated either with the associations of Harsomteus and Hathor or with the temple itself. The lines blurred between Ptolemaios' many different functions and responsibilities, which makes it difficult to unravel the implications of the texts. It is also possible that groups like the associations of Harsmoteus and Hathor were commemorating

79. *Stud.Demotica* V 167; see also 168 (30 BCE–14 CE).
80. *Stud.Demotica* V 170 (2 CE), 171 (3 CE), 173 (5 CE).
81. *Stud.Demotica* V 175 (31 CE), trans. Vleeming (2001).
82. *SB* I 684 (31 CE), trans. Vleeming (2001, adapted).

benefactions and signaling ties (no matter how tenuous) with influential individuals like Ptolemaios and Tryphon when making dedications. The use of the phrase m-bḥ in this context would be a nod to Tryphon's or Ptolemaios' own elevated political position. In either case, the votive stelai function as monuments that display to the community, the temple, and its priesthood the social capital a connection with an official brought (or was perceived to bring) to the association.

Sponsoring the construction of temple buildings was not only the purview of local officials. An association of sheep and cattle herders (*probatoktēnotrophoi*) along with their wives and their children dedicated and paid for the construction of a wall (*peribolos*) surrounding a temple at Soknopaiou Nesos shortly after the Romans began to rule.[83] If Paola Davoli's suggestion that the *peribolos* paid for by this group could be the sanctuary's *temenos* is correct, this would be a significant dedication.[84] The text and the decoration of the stele recording the herders' donation present a number of interesting aspects of the image that the association attempted to craft for itself. The text begins with the typical formula indicating that the herders made the dedication on behalf of Augustus, following previous Ptolemaic paradigms. The stele on which the Greek dedication was recorded depicts Egyptian motifs, including a sun disk and *uraeus*, and what Milne took to be a representation of the group (what appears to be a shepherd depicted with a ram's head) before a god with a crocodile body and falcon head. If this is the case, it might imply that the group viewed themselves as "tending" to the god and its cult. As another association of sheep or cattle herders in Tebtunis made clear in their charter, public appearances and fulfilling obligations were important.[85] Displaying ties with the community's primary temple and deity in this way makes a powerful statement.

In other dedications, not commemorating any specific person, associations offered a votive or dedicated a monumental stele displayed within or near a temple. Such monuments ultimately highlighted the collective piety of the group and their adherence to the association's (and community's) norms and indicated a connection to influential individuals named in texts, as might have been the case with *stratēgoi* named in first-century dedications at Dendera. For example, piety could be shown with dedications of ritual objects at a temple. A demotic inscription on a bronze drinking cup records that it was a votive of an

83. *I.Fayum* I 73 (24 BCE); on the sanctuary and its enclosure, see Davoli 2007.
84. Davoli 2007: 107.
85. *P.Mich.* V 243 (14–37 CE).

association (sn.t) and was offered by the group's official along with the other association members (irm nꜣ rmt.w (n) sn.t).[86] The cup's provenance is uncertain. The mention of Isis may suggest a temple context, but it also may have emanated from any number of associations affiliated with Isis or from a craft or merchant group. At some point in the first or second century CE, two *sunodoi* dedicated statues to Anubis and Apollo that occupied places along the processional way leading toward the temple in the Fayum village of Narmouthis.[87] It is not apparent which associations dedicated and paid for the statues. Perhaps other texts or monuments would have made this clear in antiquity, but the identity of the associations cannot be ascertained on the basis of the inscriptions (which are no longer visible).

At times, groups spell out the reasons for their donations more clearly and use language familiar from other honorific monuments and dedications dating to the first three centuries CE. According to a text inscribed on a statue base that dates to the first century CE, an Alexandrian association identified only as a *kollēgion* in Greek (Latin *collegium*) made a dedication on account of piety (*eusebeia*).[88] The high priest of a *sunodos* of Ammon, along with all his fellow members (*sunodeitai*), declared a dedication on account of *eusebeia* on a second-century stele found in Edfu.[89] An early third-century stele decorated with a sphinx wearing a pharonic crown and with a praying man records another offering made to Ammon on account of piety (*eusebeia*), by a *sunodos* associated with Tutu (Tithoes).[90]

Given the close ties that existed between associations and local temples, it is worth considering whether the associations considered here, priestly or otherwise, helped support Egyptian temples when financial support from the state was withdrawn during the Roman period. Referring chiefly to religious associations composed of priests and temple personnel, David Frankfurter has suggested that such groups "offered a measure of continuing religious solidarity to villages already involved to varying degrees in the functioning of the temple."[91] This very well might have been the case. Frankfurter is right to have pointed out the role these groups likely played in popular defense of temples in the face of Roman administrative reorganization that significantly changed the privileged

86. *Stud.Demotica* V 60 (73 CE).
87. *I.Fayum* III 171 (I/II CE) = *SB* V 8133 and *I.Fayum* III 172 (I/II CE) = *SB* V 8135.
88. *IGR* I 1314 (I CE) = *SB* I 1013.
89. *I.Portes* 111 (150–60 CE).
90. *I.Portes* 83 (209/10 CE).
91. Frankfurter 1998: 72.

economic position of temples and their priesthoods.[92] Donations and contributions made by groups during this period also evidence temple support from craft and merchant associations. In this context, the type of piety exhibited by Egyptian associations suggests that affiliation with temples accomplished more than helping groups assert a place in the community and its hierarchy. The contributions that associations made had an increasingly important economic impact on traditional temple cult in Egyptian communities. By emphasizing their inclusion in the community in this manner, associations not only responded to and acted in accordance with social and religious norms but also participated in the process of creating and perpetuating those norms.

The offerings that associations made and the public monuments that they erected worked in a variety of linguistic and visual idioms and sent signals out to different audiences in their communities. To the priesthood supervising the cult activities in the temple—which, during the Roman period, still numbered over one hundred at the temple of Soknopaiou Nesos or fifty at the temple in Tebtunis, for example—donations affirmed continued support of the temple and adherence to established practices of individual and group piety. To those outside the group, including influential members of the community, monuments and the language used in the accompanying inscriptions indicated recognition of the importance placed on a certain set of civic virtues by an association and its members. Dedications and monuments also functioned as orchestrated social performances that allowed associations to make a claim for a specific reputation in the community and to display accumulated social capital based on ties (real or imagined) with local officials. Demonstrating allegiance to the Roman authorities and local officials and signaling submission to a dominant social order might have been part of the social performance but were not its only purposes.

Festival Participation

Onno van Nijf and Richard Alston asserted that public festivals, processions, and ceremonies fulfilled a similar function as the exchange and display of honorifics in the Roman world.

92. Frankfurter 1998: 65–73; for the impact of Roman reorganization on temples, see Monson 2012: 218–27.

> Public ceremonial in the imperial Greek city served as a symbolic expression of civic order and was used to reinforce a conception of society that was rooted in a hierarchy of status groups. These groups were as effectively and symbolically integrated into both the urban and imperial framework.[93]

Citing public distributions, the presence of associations at processions, and festival participation, van Nijf contended that these settings offered associations (and other constituencies) an opportunity to assert yet another manifestation of their position within communities in the Roman east.[94] With regard to public ceremonies and processions in particular, van Nijf claimed that "inclusion or exclusion could be read as a potent symbol of the degree of integration and involvement (or lack of it) of specific groups in the city."[95] It is perhaps easier to envision ceremonies, festivals, and processions as social performances than to see dedications, votives, and monuments as such. Participation in festivals and rituals, organized and funded mostly by local elites, provided community members a chance to display their rank and privileges and to further articulate their place in the community's social, economic, and political hierarchies.[96] As a part of these performances, the individuals and groups who participated (including associations) were expected to play particular roles in accordance with social, political, religious, and economic norms. Not unlike when a council granted an association permission to honor an official or patron in a public place, inclusion of associations in festivals and ceremonies amounted to an acknowledgment of the influence that certain constituencies possessed. Proper participation in the suite of activities involved in a public festival or ceremony allowed associations to send a powerful message to the community. Language commonly included in association charters makes it clear that members understood the importance of acting publicly in accordance with social norms and expectations set by the group and by the community, as well as the impact that participation in public activities had on the community's perceptions of the group.

Though the evidence is not plentiful, Egyptian associations, craftsmen, and merchants appear to have taken advantage of these occasions to accrue social capital and manage their reputations. A sandstone stele recording the rules of a

93. Van Nijf and Alston 2011: 12.
94. Van Nijf 1997: 131–46, 191–206; see also van Nijf 1999.
95. Van Nijf 2011
96. For elite participation, see Perpillou-Thomas 1993: 226–37; see also Alston 2002: 245–47.

weavers' association operating around Coptos included provisions—for taking part in festivals and other rituals centered on the temple of Geb—that display a desire to participate in the community in a traditional way.[97] Dating to the first year of Roman rule, the charter was inscribed in demotic and used typical Egyptian religious and visual motifs to depict the pharaoh making an offering before deities. In addition to the familiar ethical and behavioral rules, the charter specifically stipulated that members and their families would pay and provide for the burial of animal mummies each year and would take part in the ritual and festival life of the temple. Participation in this manner allowed the weavers to develop and perpetuate relationships with the priesthood, as well as with local officials and leading community members who may have had a connection to a temple and its cult, like Ptolemaios or Tryphon. Provided that the weavers followed through on promises to contribute for festival celebrations, the stele monumentalized these connections and displayed their piety to priests, local officials, current and future association members, and the community. In the process, their presence at ceremonies and processions gave the weavers an additional venue in which to reinforce bonds of trust and build social capital within their own network.

A second-century account of contributions for a festival in honor of the Dioscouri may have been compiled by an association; at least, that is the suggestion made by the editor.[98] The document is labeled as an account of a feast related to the adornment of cult statues of the Dioscouri. The text, possibly from Bakhias in the Fayum, was laid out in two columns. The first column contained twenty-six lines of text and listed the items that had been assembled for the occasion, as well as their costs. Among other things, the list included two linen garments at 119 drachmas; honey in an amount worth 29 drachmas; two types of oil, at 60 drachmas total; and spices, grain, food, and lamps. The second column listed the contributions made by twenty individuals who presumably belonged to this group. The association's membership composition is interesting: it included seven veterans, one oil maker, and others identified only by a patronymic (although the state of the text might obscure details originally supplied by the scribe). Parallels in the way the contributions were reported—they were apparently ranked according to the monetary amount given (between 20 and 100 drachmas)—suggested to Perpillou-Thomas that the text belonged to

97. *Stud.Demotica* V 158 (30 BCE).
98. *P.Lund.* IV 11 (169/70 CE).

an association.[99] The list of contributions made by the association of Harpocrates in first-century Tebtunis provides an obvious analogue, although that text's scribe organized individuals by contribution and seating order.[100] Other texts document festivals and celebrations of the Dioscouri that took place in the Fayum from the first three centuries of Roman rule and that were attended by associations and community members, making Perpillou-Thomas' identification more secure.[101]

A late third-century text from Oxyrhynchus also reveals that craftsmen, merchants, and associations continued to participate in public festivals and made financial contributions toward their celebration.[102] The text recorded contributions made to a *sunodos* of sacred victors (*hieronikai*) for a festival—possibly the inaugural celebration of the Capitoline games at Oxyrhynchus, according to the editor. Unfortunately, the state of the papyrus obscures many details. It is unclear whether the contributions were made by members of this *sunodos*, friends of the group, or patrons. Based on the names and trades of the contributors, membership or affiliation with the group cut across elite and non-elite lines and extended beyond the community of Oxyrhynchus. The text lists several individuals who might not have been residents of Oxyrhynchus and who stayed in someone else's home, another indication that the membership reflected a more complex social, political, and economic network.[103] Some of the men listed were apparently of councilor rank and active in local political life: two individuals were described as *exēgētai*.[104] A majority of the men listed, however, were craftsmen and merchants practicing different trades, such as Ammonius the dyer, Neilus the tapestry weaver, Pammenes the spice merchant, and Philosarapis the goldsmith.[105]

Given this mix of councilor elite, merchants, craftsmen, locals, and those from other communities, it is worth considering the nature of a sunodos of *hieronikai*, associations of sacred victors commonly affiliated with athletic and artistic competitions. Members celebrated their affiliation with associations of *hieronikai*, and individuals who belonged to such groups were often among the

99. Perpillou-Thomas 1993: 84.
100. *P.Mich.* V 246 (I CE).
101. Perpillou-Thomas 1993: 82–87.
102. *P.Oslo* III 144 (270–75 CE).
103. *P.Oslo* III 144, lines 16–17, 21–22.
104. *P.Oslo* III 144, lines 31, 36.
105. The text also lists Ammonios, son of Sarapamon the dyer (lines 9–10); Sarapamon the bronzesmith (line 12); Heras the oil merchant (line 13); the sons of Suros the baker (line 16); Papontos the carpenter (line 18); and the sons of Demeios the wine merchant (lines 19–20).

local political elite. For instance, one of the five officials with whom the *euthēniarchēs* Sarapion had coordinated production and provision of bread at the end of the second century CE, Tiberius Claudius Didymus, was affiliated with a group of *hieronikai*. Like the other men mentioned, Didymus was serving as a gymnasiarch and *euthēniarchēs*; some of his fellow officials had also previously served as *exēgētai*. In the letter to his colleagues, Sarapion further described Didymus as a sacred victor (who was free from taxation) and as a member of the Dionyseum and the sacred club of *hieronikai*.[106]

A member of the Alexandrian elite honored for his service as gymnasiarch and *agonothetēs*, Marcus Aurelius Mikkalon, also counted affiliation with the *hieronikai* among his accomplishments.[107] According to the inscription, Mikkalon came from a family that had ties with an organization of *hieronikai* over two generations. Although details of his involvement in the group go unmentioned, his affiliation could have arisen out of his duties as gymnasiarch and *agonothetēs*. Since the aforementioned group of *hieronikai* from Oxyrhynchus had ties with craftsmen and merchants, a similar situation might have existed for Mikkalon's group in Alexandria. Cicero the philosopher would not have encouraged Mikkalon to keep company with dishonest spice merchants, goldsmiths, and dyers; but Cicero the politician might have. In reality, local elites benefited from relationships with craftsmen and merchants who had expendable resources and could help elites fulfill the obligations associated with the official posts they held.

The Oslo *hieronikai* text invites further comment. Within the established idioms of euergetism and patronage, we have grown accustomed to seeing craftsmen, merchants, and associations as the recipients of donations and benefactions. In this case, however, craftsmen and merchants may have supported this group and its activities and shared ties with the councilor elite in doing so.[108] Apparently, in the social and economic setting of late third-century Oxyrhynchus, making contributions to the *hieronikai* held some significance for craftsmen and merchants (and for members of the elite). Taking part in the festivals and celebrations in which the *hieronikai* contributed offered another opportunity for craftsmen and merchants to accrue social capital and partici-

106. *P.Oxy.* VI 908 (199 CE), lines 8–10.
107. *OGIS* II 713 = *SB* V 8915 = *I.Cair.Milne* 9223 = *IGR* I 1083 (III CE); for discussion of the text, see van Minnen 2000: 45.
108. For professionals as patrons, see Verboven 2007: 884–85; for patronage in general, Waltzing 1895–1900, vol. 1: 425–66.

pate in the community, by cultivating relationships with traditional cults and temples and through affiliation with groups more closely aligned with Greek or Roman practices, such as the *hieronikai.*

Forging ties with an association of *hieronikai* and participating in their activities likely contributed to identity formation for these individuals. Operating in this manner also gave craftsmen and merchants another means to manage their reputation strategically, provided they had the necessary resources available to do so. Accumulating social capital in this way came at a cost—just as it did within their own associations, in the form of regular contributions for banquets, dues payments, and extra fees. But affiliation with a group that participated in a public festival allowed craftsmen and merchants to highlight ties with members of the councilor elite and to express them to a wider community; such display also helped craftsmen and merchants reinforce or confirm their own position in a local hierarchy and separate themselves from other members of the nonelite. Certain individuals did so under the auspices of an association like the *hieronikai,* which might send a different message than the weavers in Coptos sent several centuries earlier. Although the different merchants and craftsmen listed in *P.Oslo* III 144 would not have been considered members of the elite, such texts suggest that the social and economic distance between them and councilors was not as exaggerated as often supposed, something that Laurens Tacoma and Arjan Zuiderhoek maintained in their discussions of elites in Egypt and the Roman east.[109]

Craftsmen and merchants derived additional benefits from forging ties with a group of *hieronikai* and spending their personal and financial capital in this manner. Affiliation with the *hieronikai* also gave these craftsmen and merchants an opportunity to connect with wealthy and influential individuals in a more concrete manner than through honorific exchanges. Association with these groups suggests that the success of group activities was linked to the contributions of people from a variety of professional, social, economic, and political backgrounds. The end result of such an investment was a wider social network beyond an individual's own craft or merchant group. Craftsmen and merchants tended to seek out and rely on each other to protect their interests, but if the Oslo text is any indication, the most successful and wealthy among them seem to have sought out additional ways to participate in the community, to solidify their position, and to access multiple networks. Ties with a group

109. Zuiderhoek 2011; Tacoma 2006.

like the *hieronikai* might have also mediated differences of political status and established trust between seemingly disparate groups. In the process, such ties might have enhanced an individual's reputation or that of an entire craft or merchant association.

Conclusions

Exchanging honors with benefactors and patrons, making donations to temples, displaying traditional piety through votive offerings, and taking part in public celebrations and festivals allowed associations to do more than claim a place in their community. Association use of *scholae* to display their wealth and standing (or perceptions of their standing) and reliance on a combination of activities orientated outward beyond those *scholae* were part of a group's approach to interacting with the community and communicating information about the group, their individual members, and their ties to members of the elite. The concern for public perception of the reputation and esteem of the group and its membership present in association charters corresponds to what can be observed in the ways associations engaged their communities. Each votive placed within a temple, honorific monument erected in public, and inscription displayed on the gateway of a *schola* transmitted specific messages about the individuals mentioned in a text and their adherence to norms of *eusebeia, philotimia, eunoia*, and *aretē*. These monuments and texts sent a similar message about the entire group and its officials, as did their participation in public ceremonies and festivals.

More specifically, monuments provided information about the types of values, characteristics, and traits that guided the actions of and were rewarded by associations of merchants, craftsmen, or "fellow farmers." Besides claiming status or defending a place that groups had successfully carved out for themselves, public monuments allowed associations and their members to indicate that they had acted in accord with a larger set of the community's social, political, and religious norms; that they honored patrons; that they did not violate agreements; and, perhaps more important, that they could be expected and trusted to continue to do so. By managing their reputation in this way, associations were able to establish themselves as the type of group—and to establish their members as the type of individuals—who could be trusted to act in a predictable manner. Inclusion in public processions and distributions, designated seating in theaters, and permission to set up honorific monuments in public communicated that specific associations already occupied a trusted position—perhaps something not lost on others that had been excluded.

The approaches of non-Egyptian associations bring what can be observed in Egypt into focus. A *koinon* active in Ephesos during the second century BCE saluted an individual named Damoteles for *eusebeia* toward the gods and for *eunoia* and *philotimia* toward the group. The Ephesian group voted him a crown and a portrait that would be displayed in a conspicuous place. It also promised to read his honorary decrees at feasts. The *koinon* saluted Damoteles' efforts not only because he had performed admirably but also because the group wanted to communicate this information to all who attended its events, viewed the portrait, or saw the decree.

> Therefore, in order that the association [*koinon*] of Aphrodisiasts may demonstrate the noble and good qualities of men by giving out appropriate favors and, not neglecting to return favor, may invite others to choose to do good things in addressing common concerns in return for glorious honors, it was resolved by the association of Aphrodisiasts to praise Damoteles son of Hippostratos because of his piety towards the gods and his goodwill and pursuit of honor in relation to the association, and to crown him along with the following proclamation by the association of Aphrodisiasts: "The association of Aphrodisiasts crowned with the crown of the god Damoteles son of Hippostratos on account of his piety and his goodwill towards the association." This will be proclaimed during all the days of the rites, which . . . the manager and the secretary at the time are to take care of his proclamation and crown, . . . and of placing a painted portrait in a very conspicuous place in the shrine with the following inscribed on a plaque: "The association of Aphrodisiasts honored Damoteles son of Hippostratos, who pursues honor [*philotimos*] in relation to the *sunodos* of the praiseworthy goddess Aphrodite." In order that everyone may know all the good qualities of the whole *sunodos*, let the decree be inscribed . . . [110]

The group desired to use this opportunity to share details about their own reputation for piety and to encourage others to follow suit. The final line of the dedication, though fragmentary, indicates the group's own understanding that a successful strategy of reputation management included being honorable and

110. *SEG* XLIII 773 (II BCE), trans. Harland (adapted slightly).

demonstrating the "noble" and "good" (*kalos* and *agathos*) qualities that the association honored here and sought to encourage in others.

It is important to communicate this information widely, and associations helped in that process. From the association's perspective in Damoteles' case, the group's interest extended beyond simply honoring Damoteles. The association sought to communicate information about reputation and esteem and to cultivate similar behavior in members. The approach to honorific activity taken by the Aphrodisiasts displayed an awareness of social capital's importance in establishing trust between members and patrons. Perhaps more important, the association also used honorific activity to confirm to the community that they were a group that could be trusted to act like Damoteles in the future and to honor those who acted likewise.

The actions of Egyptian associations reinforce what groups elucidated in their charters, and their attention to public monuments and honorific decrees reveals an understanding of the social performative aspect of their activities for establishing trust. Following the rules and showing piety toward colleagues and the gods—whether through participation in a colleague's funeral, helping someone in need, or contributing to a temple—were important steps toward developing a trustworthy reputation within the group and the community. After establishing this sense of trust (even if only the perception of it), broadcasting to a wider audience information about themselves, their members, and those affiliated with the group was crucial in order for associations and their members to accomplish their aims.

That associations managed their reputation by participating in the community and adhering to a set of social norms and expectations should be expected. Goffman maintained that in public, with community members serving as an audience for an individual's performance (or that of a group like an association) on the social stage, behavior reflects "common official values of the society in which it [the performance] occurs"; he concluded that "when the individual presents himself before others, his performance will tend to incorporate and exemplify the officially accredited values of the society, more so, in fact, than does his behavior as a whole."[111] A willingness to participate in a larger social, political, and religious system and to align themselves with community values, norms, and institutions was, of course, the ideal message that associations sought to communicate. Alston and van Nijf have each made sim-

111. Goffman 1959: 35.

ilar claims regarding associations in Egypt and Asia Minor. For van Nijf, associations expressed their participation by conforming to and adopting the ideals that the elite expressed through the rhetoric, language, and mechanisms of euergetism.

> It is obvious that they [associations] used their honorific inscriptions not as public declarations of autonomy, separating themselves from the general populace, but rather as demonstrations of conformity, consciously adopting public models of euergetism.[112]

Alston believed that Egyptian associations indicated their conformity to community values through their relationships with temples. The evidence does indicate that temples occupied a central place in the world of Egyptian associations and played a role in crafting their identity, one that used Greek and Egyptian idioms to signal piety and participation in the community.

That does not necessarily mean that associations in Egypt or elsewhere were not also emphasizing their autonomy in some sense or that their conformity was any less strategic. Associations tried to set themselves apart or to distinguish themselves from the rest of the community. Goffman would say that making strategic decisions to conform or not and to communicate this fact could be part of the social drama, although he was also interested in "unintentional" actions.

> Regardless of the particular objective which the individual has in mind and of his motive for having this objective, it will be in his interests to control the conduct of others, especially their responsive treatment of him. This control is achieved largely by influencing the definition of the situation which the others come to formulate, and he can influence this definition by expressing himself in such a way as to give them the kind of impression that will lead them to act voluntarily in accordance with his own plans. Thus, when an individual appears in the presence of others, there will usually be some reason for him to mobilize his activity so that it will convey an impression to others that it is in his interests to convey.[113]

---

112. Van Nijf 1997: 128.
113. Goffman 1959: 3–4.

The decisions that associations made to act in a particular manner while adopting their public persona, so to speak, was no less a part of a strategy by which individuals and their groups could attempt to control or influence the reactions of others. Groups like the builders in Ostia or the Poseidoniastai in Delos apparently sought to convey to the community an impression of their reputation and their place in society. Communities participated in this process and confirmed the standing of many associations through the use of designated seating, market stalls, and the exchange of honors.[114]

Although participation in rituals (public and private), celebrations, and dedications emphasized group solidarity and enabled association members to signal continued observance of group norms (not unlike any other activity described within a charter), that does not mean that groups were not contentious. Each votive or monument documenting the good work of a member or patron reinforced economic and status hierarchies within the group as well as in the community. The public aspect of these rituals—such as the participation of the weavers from Coptos—raised the stakes. It follows, then, that decisions to deviate from the norm, to make a conscious turn away from expectations imposed on members by the group or the community, would be no less strategic and meaningful. Breaks with expectations, though, could also be a source of conflict between associations, local officials, and the Roman authorities. The following chapters explore how associations managed such breaks while at the same time defending their somewhat privileged position and continuing their participation in the community.

114. Van Nijf 1997: 210–40, 257–59; see also Harland 2003: 108–12. For a discussion of reserved seats for goldsmiths in Aphrodisias, see Roueché 1995 ;1993: 88–89. For seats in the Latin west, see Verboven 2007: 882.

CHAPTER 4

Reputation, Rhetoric, and Participation

A "well-to-do man" from Alexandria named Isidorus, who claimed to be a weaver, found himself in what he perceived to be a difficult position toward the end of the second century CE.[1] Epimachus, another wealthy man and a current deputy *stratēgos*, had nominated Isidorus, whom he identified not as a weaver but as a spice merchant, for the same post, and now Isidorus was trying to do what many people in antiquity attempted: avoid service any way he could. No shortage of petitions and appeals for relief from public duties on various grounds have survived from the seven centuries of Roman rule in Egypt.[2] Based on transcripts of formal hearings and written petitions submitted to seek relief, how individuals framed their situation and discussed their personal status was of the utmost importance. In these situations, the nominee often bemoaned his poverty (real or imagined) and claimed that there must be someone wealthier to assume the post.[3] Others asserted special privileges, exemptions, past precedent, or a combination of the three to avoid obligations, which is the strategy Isidorus and his advocate employed.[4]

Roman imperial administration typically relied on the wealthier segments of local communities to shoulder obligations and public duties. Egypt was no different. Referred to under the general heading of liturgies, these services included major metropolitan offices (*archai* such as the gymnasiarch, *agorano-*

1. *P.Oxy.* XXII 2340 (192 CE).
2. *BGU* I 180 (172 CE), IV 1022 (196 CE); *P.Oxy.* XXII 2130 (267 CE).
3. *P.Lond.* III 846 (140 CE); *SB* VIII 10196 (ca. 180 CE). *P.Fay.* I 106 (140 CE) asserted poverty and exemptions for physicians.
4. *P.Panop.* 29 and 30 (both 332 CE) refer to exemption based on age; *P.Wisc.* I 3 (256–59 CE) deals with exemptions based on age and past service.

mos, or *exēgētēs*). The holders of these offices were entitled to an honor guard and distinctive marks of office and enjoyed a certain amount of esteem in exchange for their service. Other unpaid and compulsory positions at the metropolitan and village levels carried less esteem but were no less necessary and also fell under the heading of liturgies. These posts included tax collection, oversight of the water supply, or arranging grain transport, to name only a few.

Nominations submitted by local officials mention two qualifications for holding these offices: a man must be wealthy (*euporos*) and suitable (*epitēdeios*). Certain levels of wealth were a threshold for service, and officials noted a person's wealth in nomination lists.[5] Census records registered estimates of wealth, and rolls of property owners were cataloged at local and provincial levels, which ultimately made this information accessible and verifiable to community members (and Roman officials).[6] Enormous wealth probably made anyone seem suitable. Suitability was perhaps also related to other personal qualities, skills, or a reputation as being trustworthy and reliable. The associations to which someone belonged likely also factored into a sense of an individual's reputation.

Local officials highlighted qualities like trust (*pistis*) and care (*epimeleia*) in letters informing wealthy and suitable individuals of an appointment.[7] Mettius Rufus, Egypt's prefect from 89 to 91 CE, emphasized qualities beyond wealth for officeholders. According to the nomination instructions sent by Rufus to the *stratēgoi*, officials that administered the regional districts (nomes), suitable (*epitēdeios*) individuals had to be of a certain age and display appropriate personal conduct commensurate with the responsibility of holding office, in addition to wealth.[8]

In whatever way these qualities were measured, Isidorus seemed suitable enough in the minds of his opponents and the officials who had initially approved his nomination. For Epimachus and his representative Hippias, the facts and Isidorus' eligibility for office were clear. They asserted that Isidorus was a spice merchant and a "well-to-do man" (*euschēmōn anthropos*), perhaps referring to the sorts of qualities that Mettius Rufus was looking for a century or so earlier. Apparently, Isidorus possessed substantial wealth, and his wealth assessment (*poros*) would have been recorded like that of any other potential officeholder. One's reputation as "well-to-do" was probably also known among

5. Lewis 1997.
6. For example, see *Sel.Pap.* II 342 (169 CE) = *BGU* I 18; *Sel.Pap.* II 343 (early III CE) = *P.Ryl.* I 90.
7. *Sel.Pap.* II 340 (215 CE) = *BGU* II 362, lines 7–8; *BGU* I 18 (169 CE), lines 14–16.
8. *SB* VI 9050 (117–27 CE), col. 4, lines 9–13.

possible candidates for liturgies and community members and may have been just as important when nominations were made.

The appeal for relief that Isidorus made through his advocate Eudaemon disputed neither his "well-to-do" status nor his wealth. Instead, Eudaemon contended that Isidorus was not a spice merchant but a weaver and that Isidorus' trade entitled him to special consideration.

> On the petition of Isidorus, Eudaemon, his advocate, said: "Epimachus son of Gaius, assistant *strategos* of the fourth district, has nominated my client in place of himself. My client is a foreman weaver who has many workmen in his factory, and men in his position have in the past been exempted because they are useful to the Treasury and now I urge you to order Epimachus to nominate someone else in place of himself and I will now read a report of Macrinus dated to the 22nd year, Pharmouthi." Hippias the advocate said: "Epimachus asserts that Isidorus is not a weaver but a spice merchant and a well-to-do man." Julianus said: "According to decisions given in similar cases if he is a foreman weaver he can use the same precedent and in turn nominate someone else instead of himself."[9]

Eudaemon claimed not only that Isidorus was a weaver but that he was an influential one who employed multiple weavers in his workshop. It is unclear whether Isidorus belonged to an association, though he might have. Weavers' associations were rather common in Egypt.[10] Spice merchants' associations also existed, and different merchant associations were active in villages and cities across Egypt.[11] A statue dedicated by a spice merchant to a *sunodos* of which he had served as the *prostatēs* indicates that spice merchants belonged to associations in Alexandria as early as the reign of Augustus; it is also possible that this was specifically a group of spice merchants, though it is not clear.[12] Identifying a practitioner of a specific trade as an association member is difficult because members are rarely described as such outside of official declarations on behalf of the group, honorary inscriptions, charters, or internal documents. It is pos-

9. *P.Oxy.* XXII 2340, lines 3–24 (*BL* V, 81 and VII, 148), trans. Roberts (adapted according to suggestions in Youtie 1964: 316–18).
10. For examples, see, for Tebtunis, *P.Mich.* II 121 R (42 CE), col. IV, vi; for Euhemeria, *P.Ryl.* II 94 (14–37 CE) = *Sel.Pap.* II 255; for Oxyrhynchus, *P.Oxy.* LXXVI 5097 (62 CE); for Theadelphia, *I.Fay.* II 122 (109 CE); for Abydos, *I.Varsovie* 66 (257 CE).
11. *P.Oxy.* XLV 3731 (310/11 CE), 3733 (312 CE), 3766 (329 CE); LXXV 5063 (392 CE).
12. *I.Alex.Imp.* 96 (30 BCE–14 CE) = *AGRW* 279.

sible that Isidorus' affiliation with an association, if he had one, might have been known to the parties involved. Isidorus does, however, fit the profile of a member: he managed his own workshop, had multiple people working for him, and possessed significant financial capital. In any event, Isidorus was not an anonymous and marginalized craftsman or merchant, whether he was a weaver or not. Isidorus was known to the local officials involved and to Epimachus. That Isidorus was able to obtain representation, like his opponent, and to challenge the nomination indicates that he was not an oppressed member of society.[13] He either had financial means himself for an advocate or belonged to a network, like an association, that linked him to such resources.

When Eudaemon asserted that being a weaver entitled Isidorus to exemptions because of usefulness (*chrēsimos*) to the state, he made a claim based on precedent and on the reputation that weavers like Isidorus had earned through previous work. Roman jurists, who dedicated entire volumes to public duties, invoked utility (*utilitas*) when discussing exemptions from service enjoyed by certain individuals and groups.[14] Inscriptions also celebrated the quality of utility or usefulness (*chrēsimos*).[15] All of this suggests that a reputation for utility and a sense of trust that individuals would follow through on contracts based on past transactions (and successful reputation management) was meaningful beyond its use in public display.

Isidorus' nomination and subsequent petition bring up many questions related to the participation by craftsmen, merchants, and associations in the economic and political life of their communities, how they negotiated their place in that society, and how they interacted with local officials. The language reportedly used in the proceedings before the *iuridicus* also forces us to examine the reality and the rhetoric of how elites and nonelites alike viewed and interpreted this participation. In this way, Isidorus' petition provides a glimpse into the operation of trust and reputation at the level of local politics, beyond an association network, and how officials, craftsmen, and merchants tried to use reputation and trust to their advantage, alongside economic, political, and legal influence.

This chapter will unpack Isidorus' petition and the issues it raises, to understand better what was at stake in the dispute and what it reveals about interactions between elite and nonelite groups at the local level. To begin to under-

13. Harries 1999: 81–83.
14. In general, see Millar 1983.
15. *TAM* V 980 (120 CE), 991 (II/III CE).

stand the dynamics at work here, it is important to set associations and leading craftsmen and merchants in the larger economic and political context of their communities. By looking at contractual relationships between associations and local officials and at evidence of office holding by craftsmen and merchants, we can clearly see that these groups were an important constituency. The remainder of the chapter examines the rhetoric of participation used in this petition and other papyrological and epigraphic texts. Of particular concern are both what descriptors such as "well-to-do" and "useful" tell us about Isidorus' perceived reputation in the community and how concepts of reputation and esteem factored into the political machinations of members of the elite and non-elite. The evidence suggests that being a craftsman or merchant did not preclude participation in an official capacity in Egyptian communities. Some people, like Isidorus, asserted their usefulness to the community and the state based on their own efforts and the work of other craftsmen and merchants as a group and may even have been considered trustworthy and reliable to undertake certain obligations; membership in or asserting an affiliation with a group could be a key part of the strategy. Craftsmen and merchants understood their position and made efforts to perpetuate such a reputation in official documents, to maintain their influence and procure additional benefits for themselves. Acting in such a manner, however, may have ultimately placed them at odds with other local elites, who were themselves vying and competing for exemptions and privileges from the Roman authorities.

Communities and Constituencies in Egypt

Egyptian communities, large and small, handled their own administration both before and after Septimius Severus' grant of councils to capital cities (*metropoleis*) in administrative districts around 200 CE.[16] Much of the work and responsibility actually fell to members of the local elite, like Epimachus. This would not have been very different from the situation in the rest of the Roman world, although the history and civic traditions of each municipal and village administration in the provinces were unique in certain ways.[17] Egypt's own civic history was complicated. The Romans might not have known an exact parallel for

16. For Roman Egypt in the first four centuries CE, see Lewis 1983; Bowman 1986; Bagnall 1993; Capponi 2005. On community administration, see Bowman 1971; Bowman and Rathbone 1992.
17. Garnsey and Saller 1987: 32; Lendon 1997: 3–6.

the traditional dominance of temples in the economy of Egyptian communities, although temple institutions throughout the ancient world could be powerful economic forces and sources of credit.[18]

Three "Greek" cities—Naukratis, Ptolemais, and Alexandria—possessed civic status and were organized along the lines of a traditional Greek *polis,* with familiar institutions, assemblies, and offices. In the second century, Hadrian added a fourth city to this list, Antinoopolis. Prior to Severus, only these cities had a council (*boulē*), with the exception of Alexandria. Citizenship in one of these communities carried with it certain tax breaks and immunities, creating a privileged position for these individuals, relative to the rest of Egypt. Traditional administrative geography also divided Egypt into roughly forty nomes, each under the oversight of a Roman official called the *stratēgos*, who was normally a member of the Egyptian elite, serving in a district other than his own. Each nome's wealthy elite resided primarily in its metropolis but may also have owned land in surrounding villages, and it filled liturgical offices and managed taxation and financial concerns throughout the district.[19]

The Roman administrative structure in Egypt, as in other provinces, was lean. Roman officials charged with interpreting and enforcing law, keeping the peace, and managing income for the imperial treasury were few in number. Initially, Egypt was a single province, governed by a prefect that came from the ranks of Roman equestrians, since Augustus limited the influence of the senate in Egyptian affairs.[20] Later administrative reorganizations under Diocletian and his successors would see Egypt divided into six provinces and standing as its own diocese.

If the case of Flaccus and the difficulties he encountered in Alexandria as prefect during the first century CE can serve as any indication, Egypt presented a difficult mix of constituencies, defined in ethnic, religious, political, legal, social, and economic terms.[21] Although the unrest Flaccus saw was not typical, the complexities he faced might have been similar to what other officials encountered. A governor and his staff had to manage and negotiate relations between powerful elites (some with ties to Rome) and vocal constituencies (in-

18. For the social and economic history of Egypt prior to Ptolemaic rule, see Trigger, Kemp, O'Connor, and Lloyd 1983: 279–348; for Ptolemaic Egypt, Manning 2010; for the transition from Ptolemaic to Roman rule, Monson 2012.
19. For office holding, see Hagedorn 2007.
20. On the prefect, see Capponi 2005: 29–31.
21. The details of Flaccus' time in Egypt and the unrest in Alexandria is well documented in ancient sources and has been treated extensively in modern discussions: see Alston 1997; Harker 2008: 9–47.

cluding associations), as well as conflicts between different population groups. Besides the prefect, the administration of Egypt included a small number of important officials appointed by the emperor (all Roman citizens)—who dealt with matters of civil law (the *iuridicus*) and managed financial concerns and the affairs of the temples (the *idios logos*)—and regional administrators overseeing a number of nomes (*epistratēgoi*).[22] Roger Bagnall estimated that the imperial presence during the fourth century, when Egypt was divided into four provinces, would have been close to four hundred individuals, roughly one hundred people on each governor's staff. That translates into one member of the imperial bureaucracy for every five or ten thousand people, depending on the estimates.[23] As the Roman administrative structure of Egypt changed over several centuries, the number of these officials increased, and others were added, such as the *logistai* (officials chosen from the councilor ranks to oversee the financial operations of councils not their own).[24] Even with increases, however, imperial officials comprised a very small percentage of the total population.

Regardless of the particularities of the systems in place, the administration of villages and *metropoleis* depended on the financial and social capital possessed by a community's leading members. It has been assumed that local elites ascribed to or tried to conform to the elite ideology predicated on an aversion to commercial activity and preference for agriculture espoused by their elite Roman social superiors.[25] Local notables in a metropolis served on a council or some similar body that existed before Severus' grant of councils, such as the *koinon of archontes* in Oxyrhynchus, and also held civic offices involved in running the community on a day-to-day basis.[26] Leading individuals at the village level, some of whom might also have been players in metropolitan politics, held posts on boards of *presbuteroi* like those found in Fayum villages and shouldered other obligations. Operating individually or as part of larger boards or groups, local officials and members of the council helped manage the food supply, markets, baths, and temples; additionally, they oversaw the intricacies of tax collection. In fulfilling these duties, officeholders maintained contact with

22. For a summary of the Roman administration of Egypt, see Capponi 2005: 25–42.
23. Bagnall 1993: 66. Lendon (1997: 2–3) suggested that the imperial administration consisted of "somewhat over thirty thousand functionaries," which results in a ratio of one imperial official for every two thousand people. A more recent estimate for Egypt by Palme (2007: 251) places the number of imperial officials at one for every twenty-four hundred Egyptian inhabitants, given a population estimate of 4.75 million.
24. For the *logistēs*, see Rees 1954.
25. Garnsey and Saller 1987: 115.
26. For discussion, see Lewis 1997. For further remarks, see Lewis 1983: 177–84; Bowman 1986: 65–73.

and relied on craftsmen, merchants, and associations. Dependence on this segment of the population placed people who were considered negligible from an elite ideological perspective in a somewhat more than marginal position. The influence that associations, merchants, and craftsmen possessed added complexity to interactions between local elite and nonelite groups, unequal though the power relations may have been.

This has not been the standard view. Where craftsmen, merchants, and the associations to which they belonged fit into this picture of political and economic life in communities has been hotly debated. Essentially, so the story goes, they did not fit; at best, they played a marginal role in the society and economy of their communities. The growth and spread of associations throughout the Roman world, as well as their adoption of structures that mirrored *polis* organization, including rotation of elected offices and passing honorary decrees for members and patrons, have been viewed as a response to this exclusion and an attempt to reclaim control over their own lives. With no chance to hold a public office—thus being precluded from accumulating the symbolic currency on which the empire supposedly operated, honor (in the elite sense of the word)—they turned inward.[27] This seems as much a statement about the impact that status hierarchies and elite ideology had on ancient economic activity, seen as a constraint on development and growth, as about ideas concerning the role that clubs and voluntary associations have been assumed to play in modern society, as an anchor providing conviviality and camaraderie in an increasingly fractured and disconnected social world.[28] Several assumptions have led to this view: the idea that associations were not economic organizations, the notion that craft and merchant activities were insignificant in the face of overwhelming reliance on agriculture, and the ideological preference, on the part of elites, for land-based wealth over commerce. A marginal economic and social position thus corresponded to a marginal political one.

A weaver or spice merchant like Isidorus, his opponent Epimachus, and the others involved in the dispute might have thought otherwise. Beyond compensation for perceived exclusion, supposedly expressed in any number of honorific or symbolic ways, association membership provided individuals and groups additional means to engage with the society and the economy of their local communities, in ways not offered to the truly poor and marginalized. More

27. Seland 1996: 112; see also Burford 1972: 159.
28. Putnam 2000.

than this, associations offered craftsmen and merchants a means to defend collective interests, manage interactions with local elites and other nonelite constituencies, and amass and use social capital for economic gains—not necessarily because it was to the advantage of the public at large, but because it helped associations solidify and maintain their own position within the community. By virtue of their membership, individuals added to and invested in a position of relative strength.

Cooperation and Negotiation

Papyri provide a less monumental perspective on the contractual relationships and exchanges resulting in the public monuments that have often been the focus of association studies. Councils hired associations of craftsmen who coordinated a group's work on construction projects, building repair and maintenance, and supplying linen and garments for local or imperial use, among other concerns.[29] People like Epimachus, Hippias, Isidorus, and Eudaemon were aware that much of the work administering to the needs of a community was undertaken on a contractual basis. Resources and labor were not forcibly extracted, or were not supposed to be.[30] Edicts from prefects, imperial officials, and emperors consistently decry this type of abuse; yet coercion and abuse of power remained a potential threat and a reality, even with edicts in hand.[31] Visits by dignitaries and officials may have given cause for abuse, as goods, supplies, and materials had to be provisioned.[32] Tax collection—and there were many taxes for local communities to manage—was unwelcome for everyone.[33]

Repeated public and private transactions between officeholders, craftsmen, merchants, and associations presumably helped individuals like Epimachus and Isidorus or associations as collectives cement reputations as useful and, in some cases, "well-to-do." Although craftsmen or merchants tended to work on their own, associations did coordinate some of their activities by gathering

29. *P.Oxy.* XLIV 3185 (III CE), 3173 (222 CE), 3176 (222 CE); *P.Laur.* IV 155 (283–92 CE); *P.Oxy.* I 84; *P.Coll.Youtie* II 81 (326 CE) = *P.Oxy.* XLV 3265; *P.Oxy.* XII 1414 (271-72 CE); *BGU* VII 1564 (138 CE), 1572 (139 CE).
30. See, for example, *FIRA* I 21 *(lex coloniae Genetivae)*, XCVIII.
31. *Sel.Pap.* II 211 (19 CE); *P.Lond.* III 1171 (42 CE); *Sel.Pap.* II 221 (133–38 CE). See also Lewis 1983: 173–74. For abuse outside of Egypt, see Sherk 1988: no. 29.
32. See, for example, *P.Panop.Beatty* 1–2; see also Sijpesteijn 1969.
33. Lewis 1983: 178.

information related to their trade, managing a common fund, and coordinating work across workshops. Associations also helped maintain and manage the public persona of groups, through honorific activities, public monuments, and religious dedications displayed within the community.

Association officers generally took the lead in interactions with public officials, whether that entailed filing a petition on the group's behalf or dealing with the particulars of a contract. Individuals bearing the title of *proestōs* of the bronzesmiths and the locksmiths, for instance, received payment for construction work in the Arsinoite nome in the second century CE.[34] A man named Ninnos, mentioned in the same text as that payment, appears to have acted on behalf of a group of nailsmiths, although he was not referred to as a *proestōs*.[35] Documents suggest that craftsmen and merchants relied on associations not only to coordinate larger contracts across individual workshops but also to negotiate with the authorities when concerns arose during the completion of work for local administrative bodies, councils, and provincial officials. A group of four alabaster workers, for example, were contracted by the local authorities in Antinoopolis to work on an imperial temple, for which they requested payment.

> To Nikippos, nomarch of Antinoopolis, from Didymos son of Hermaios, Tothes son of Onnophris, Papentos son of Kilikas, and Psenosiris son of Sarapion, all four of the number of alabaster workers for the ornamentation [?]of the Caesareum constructed in Antinoopolis by Antonios Dios. We ask to be sent salary for the month Phamenoth at the rate of eight silver drachmas for each month in accordance with the orders of Marianus, formerly procurator of our lord Caesar, all together thirty-two silver drachmas, total 32 silver drachmas, if it pleases you to send to us. Year 17 of the Emperor Caesar Titus Aelius Hadrianus Antoninus Augustus Pius.[36]

Such was also the case for the linen merchants and weavers who petitioned the local council in Oxyrhynchus and negotiated alterations to the financial arrangements in their initial contracts.[37]

Construction projects and building maintenance were constant concerns

34. *BGU* IV 1028 (II CE), lines 8, 25.
35. *BGU* IV 1028, line 19.
36. *SB* VIII 9904 (154 CE), trans. Lewis.
37. *P.Oxy.* XII 1414 (271–72 CE).

for local officials. Throughout the Roman period, officials arranged for the upkeep of public baths, *gymnasia*, fountains, public structures, thoroughfares, and much else. A second-century account of expenses related to the fountains and the water supply in Ptolemais Euergetis, for example, details the responsibilities and costs assumed by four officials: an *exēgētēs*, a *kosmētēs*, and two gymnasiarchs.[38] Individual contracts between officials, on the one hand, and craftsmen and merchants, on the other, provide more information about specific projects and expenditures. The agreement between a gymnasiarch from Hermopolis and the two men he hired to heat the baths adjacent to the gymnasium in the mid-first century CE offers an early example of interaction.[39] Letters, requests for payment, and receipts from third- and fourth-century Oxyrhynchus reveal the associations involved in construction projects: lead workers, glass makers, iron workers, and bronzesmiths. Association officials typically estimated initial costs and submitted these to the council, which suggests that negotiations took place at multiple stages of a project.[40] Craftsmen worked on buildings like the public baths repeatedly, as indicated by the payment requests submitted to Oxyrhynchus' officials by two men who had worked on the baths in different months.[41] When an association was involved, councils and officials seem to have made payment to the group's common fund and not to the individual craftsmen.[42] The aforementioned payment requests from alabaster workers and requests from three glass workers who sought payment from the council of Panopolis for work on the baths indicate that the evidence from Oxyrhynchus was not exceptional.[43]

At other times, officials serving in executive capacities, such as the *prytanis* or the *logistēs*, relied on associations and specialized craftsmen to investigate matters related to complaints and petitions. For instance, officials needed specialized craftsmen to inspect buildings involved in disputes. In response to a fourth-century petition regarding the condition of a property, the *logistēs* of Oxyrhynchus asked the two monthly presidents of the builders (*oikodomoi*) to investigate.[44] This does not imply control over the craftsmen or their groups but does speak to the importance of associations to help officials perform their duties.

38. *P.Lond.* III 1177 (131/2 CE) = *W.Chr.* 193.
39. *P.Lond.* III 1166 (42 CE).
40. *P.Coll.Youtie* II 81 (326 CE) = *P.Oxy.* XLV 3265.
41. *P.Oxy.* XLIV 3173, 3176 (222 CE).
42. *P.Oxy.* I 84 (316 CE).
43. *P.Got.* 7 (225–75 CE).
44. *P.Oxy.* XLIV 3195 (331 CE).

Even managing the food supply required negotiation.[45] Bread was not requisitioned, even if cooperation on the part of craftsmen and merchants might have been more than expected, especially in a crisis. One text from the late second century preserves a copy of an agreement between six officials charged with managing the food supply in Oxyrhynchus, the *euthēniarchai*.[46] According to the contract, each official assumed the costs for one month for a mill (as well as the animals necessary to grind twenty artabae of wheat each day) and a bakery. Though this text lacks the perspective of the craftsmen and merchants themselves, it details the intricacies of food production in a metropolis. The agreement by six officials to outfit six bakeries and six mills to process thirty-six hundred artabae of wheat (as well as providing for the draft animals needed for milling) would have produced numerous monthly contracts with merchants, millers, bakers, farmers, and assorted middlemen. A declaration of bakers who had agreed to bake bread with grain supplied by an *agoranomos* and sell it in the market with the "usual sellers" suggests similar iterative arrangements.[47] Making all this happen called for an official's charisma and wealth, or, as Naphtali Lewis remarked, his "persuasive tongue" and "fat wallet."[48] But even having both qualities might not have made the whole process run smoothly. Officials fulfilled compulsory obligations with the help of knowledge and information about the reputations of those involved (gained from repeated interactions with craftsmen and merchants) and reliance on previously established trust.

Construction on streets, colonnades, and monumental embellishment of thoroughfares also called for contracting with associations and with individual craftsmen who may or may not have been working with or belonged to associations. A report submitted by two joiners to the *prytanis* of Oxyrhynchus detailed the work they completed on a main street.

> To Aurelius Apollonius, also called Dionysius, ex-recorder, etc. ex-gymnasiarch, councilor, prytanis in office of the illustrious and most illustrious city of Oxyrhynchus, public magistrate, from Aurelius Menestheus and Aurelius Nemesianus, both sons of Dionysius, of the same illustrious city of Oxyrhynchus, kasiotic joiners. We request that orders may be given for payment to be made to us at the city's expense on account of wages due for work done by us as kasiotic

45. For a summary account, see Sharp 2007: 218–30.
46. *P.Oxy.* VI 908 (199 CE); on this text, see Sharp 2007: 223.
47. *P.Oxy.* XII 1454 (116 CE).
48. Lewis 1983: 47.

> joiners on both sides of the street built by you from the gateway of the gymnasium leading southwards to the lane of Hieracius, of the total amount due for the whole work, in accordance with the vote of the high council, namely four talents and four thousand drachmae, 4 tal. 4000 dr. And we beg you to instruct the public treasurer to pay us in full, as is usual.[49]

This text illuminates the contractual relations between local officials and craftsmen, as well as councilors' expenditure on public works projects. The last line states that payment should be made "according to the usual custom" (*kata to ethos*), revealing that this report documents one of many transactions in an ongoing relationship between the joiners and the council. The joiners have not provided a onetime service imposed on them by the council or Roman authority. On the contrary, craftsmen like these two brothers worked for the city and its officials regularly. Aurelius Apollonius and other local officials needed the cooperation of associations to bring to fruition their own building plans or those of the council.

The work done by these joiners may also have been no minor contract. Based on parallels, the gymnasium complex probably was centrally located and surrounded by colonnades, market spaces, temples, and shops. Evidence from Hermopolis indicates a close spatial relationship between shops, market spaces, the gymnasium complex, and temples dedicated to the ruler cult of the Ptolemies and the Romans. For example, shops that were used until the site was reconfigured as a church in the fifth century surrounded the Ptolemaic temple complex situated to the southeast of the tetrastylon that marked the intersection of the main axis of Hermopolis.[50] If this is any indication, the road in question in Oxyrhynchus probably was a major public street and a hub for social, economic, religious, and political life. Any construction project like this would have been significant and would have affected many elite and nonelite groups.

As a former gymnasiarch, Apollonius may have found this project particularly interesting. Construction on the street that the text tells us Apollonius had built might indicate his own ambitious undertakings as a public official. At roughly the same time, Apollonius coordinated work on the baths with two members of the bronzesmiths' association.[51] Building projects on main thor-

---

49. *P.Oxy.* I 55 (283 CE), lines 1–16, trans. Grenfell and Hunt.
50. On the shops, see Wace, Megaw, and Skeat 1959: 5. On Hermopolis in general, see Bagnall and Rathbone 2004: 162–67; Bailey 1991.
51. *P.Laur.* IV 155 (283–92 CE).

oughfares or on bath complexes had an impact beyond city beautification. Thanks to shops and market spaces that generated rental income, they would have benefited the public treasury too.

But with potential rewards for major acts of euergetism came pitfalls and obstacles. Making changes to thoroughfares could prove delicate. Negotiating with the craftsmen doing the work was only one part of the process. Councilors had to consider the interests of groups potentially impacted by a construction project. Dio Chrysostom might have advised Apollonius to be mindful of such concerns, based on Dio's own experiences in his hometown of Prusa. On many occasions, Dio recalled the opposition he faced when trying to expand and embellish a colonnade that he thought would have increased the prominence and stature of Prusa. Craftsmen about to be displaced by the project resisted Dio's efforts; so did a number of prominent local officials and council members, some of whom may have had ties with craftsmen and merchants who would have been forced to relocate.[52] In this case, the craftsmen, merchants, and opposing councilors won the day, and Dio did not let anyone forget it.

Successful completion of projects, by contrast, earned praise and esteem for officials. Completion also solidified relationships and trust between officials and the groups involved, the sorts of connections later monumentalized and projected to the public in honorary inscriptions.[53] The officials of Oxyrhynchus, the resident Alexandrian and Roman citizens, and the *dēmos* honored one successful gymnasiarch with a portrait statue and three shields for repairing the baths, supplying oil for the gymnasium, and providing funds for shows.[54] Craftsmen and merchants that could cite a connection with an influential official in a public way likely benefited from this relationship. Of course, such actions distinguished some groups from others.

There was also wealth to be gained on the part of craftsmen and merchants working with officials. It is unclear whether the two joiners contracted by Apollonius and Oxyrhynchus' council worked alone or managed larger crews. Based on the parallel with the bronzesmiths and their work on the baths for Apollonius, the joiners might have coordinated a group of craftsmen. The large sums of money involved in this transaction (four talents and four thousand drachmas) implies that if they had been working alone, they

52. Dio, *Or.* 40.8–9.
53. *I.Eph.* 443–44.
54. *P.Oxy.* III 473 (138–60 CE).

would have been very well off after material costs.[55] For work on the road, a payment of thirty thousand drachmas, over half of the estimated amount of wealth needed to hold a council seat, would have been no less significant if it was paid to an association's common fund and not to the craftsmen themselves.[56] This amount of money would have rendered someone "suitable" and "wealthy" enough to undertake liturgies.

The role that associations played in coordinating public contracts, construction, and even food production is linked to what would appear to be a position at the center of a workshop and trading network. But it also suggests many things about the preferences of craftsmen and merchants for doing business and operating in the political and economic spheres of their communities. Just as associations purposefully coordinated public interaction via honorary inscriptions and dedications, groups also sought to manage interactions and negotiations that individual members and the entire organization had with local elites. They had political and economic reasons for doing this. The actions of one craftsman or merchant impacted the work and perception of the group as a whole. First-century association charters from Egypt make this clear in their assessment of penalties for failure to fulfill public obligations.[57] Failure to follow through on public projects, as well as perceptions of unreliability asserted by councilors with whom they did business, could have negatively impacted the group, any subsequent dealings with the council, and even future private contracts that an association and its members expected to receive. Given the amount of money involved, gains and losses, both present and future, could be great.

Shared Administration

Other texts illustrate the sort of civic and political participation that Isidorus was trying to avoid. A number of nominations to compulsory offices and liturgies have survived from the first four centuries CE and document involvement in civic life by craftsmen and merchants. Given the influence that individual craftsmen, merchants, and associations could wield and their potential economic capital as a group and as individuals, it makes sense that people such as

55. One talent was equal to six thousand drachmas; see Bagnall 1993: 330.
56. Tacoma 2003: 130–32; see also Bowman 1971: 26–27.
57. *P.Mich.V* 245 (47 CE).

Isidorus would be nominated to official posts. Isidorus' nomination and the nomination of other leading craftsmen and merchants—who, like Isidorus, supposedly ran their own workshops and employed multiple craftsmen—reflects the economic, social, and political world of the local communities in which they lived and worked.

A fragmentary second-century list of officeholders from the Fayum village Theadelphia gives some indication of participation by craftsmen.[58] A man identified as a wool merchant with a *poros* of one thousand drachmas is included. According to the list, the merchant, named Satabas, had served as an overseer of confiscated estates at Karanis.[59] It is uncertain whether or not Satabas belonged to an association, but associations related to cloth production and distribution, including wool merchants, operated in the Fayum and elsewhere at the time.[60] The list shows signs of revision and therefore might have been drawn up in preparation for filling offices. If this is the case, it would suggest that Satabas remained liable and that his turn filling an office was not an exceptional occurrence—he was in line to be appointed again.

The wealth estimate ascribed to Satabas is revealing, too. A *poros* between one and two thousand drachmas was required to serve as a komarch, a leading position on the village level, and all entries in this list of potential officeholders have a reported *poros* of at least one thousand drachmas.[61] The list also shows that Satabas compared favorably in economic terms with and was expected to fulfill office alongside men from the metropolis who probably owned property in the village but also had wealth estimates of one or two thousand drachmas.[62] Landowners from the metropolis occupied an elevated social, political, and economic position. This text, however, suggests a more level playing field and less economic distance between those from the metropolis, on the one hand, and wealthy merchants and craftsmen, on the other.

Another nomination list from Karanis, dating to the first quarter of the third century, contains the names of no fewer than fifty-two individuals liable for the post of *sitologos* in Karanis and the neighboring village of Kerke.[63] The scribe recorded the wealth estimates for those nominated as either seven or eight hundred drachmas. Checkmarks or marginal notations appear to the left

58. *P.Fay.* 23 (150 CE).
59. *P.Fay.* 23, line 14.
60. *P.Mich.* II 124r, col. ii, line 15; 123r, col. vi, line 25; *P.Oxy.* LIV 3751 (319 CE).
61. For references, see Lewis 1997: 34–35.
62. *P.Fay.* 23 (150 CE), lines 6, 11.
63. *P.Col.* VIII 230 (200–225 CE).

of many names, suggesting that the list is a draft. In any event, the scribe included multiple craftsmen, merchants, and shepherds or cowherds (*boukoloi*) among the thirty-one people nominated in Karanis: two individuals designated as *ergatai* (lines 9, 38), possibly a baker (line 22), a barber (line 44), an oil maker (line 45), a gardener (line 21), and a shepherd (line 30). Nominated in Kerke are not only a merchant (line 67) and a money changer (line 65) but also three cowherds (lines 48, 52, 55).

A number of third-century texts produced by the council scribe of Ptolemais Euergetis, what Lewis called "lists of eligibles," indicate that craftsmen and merchants did not only hold offices at the village level.[64] More precisely, as Lewis maintained, these documents probably preserved working copies of nomination lists that included more than the number of individuals whose names were ultimately forwarded on to the *strategos*. Lewis argued that final lists usually did not include information about trades, which would suggest that the absence of a trade designation does not mean that craftsmen or merchants were not usually liable.

Some of the individual craftsmen and merchants named in these lists found themselves nominated (or included as potential candidates) alongside people identified as being "from the gymnasium."[65] Although the number of individuals that belonged to the gymnasial class in a metropolis like Oxyrhynchus may have been quite large, these individuals did possess significant wealth and received tax breaks.[66] Their status as an elite group has been challenged by van Minnen, but a portion of their number may still have belonged to what Nelson termed "an elite class within the metropolis."[67] The craftsmen and merchants listed here did not belong to the gymnasial class but may have possessed similar wealth and were considered no less viable as candidates for certain posts.

A well-preserved portion of one of these texts from Ptolemais lists candidates for oversight of the water supply and fountains in the city and well illustrates the multiple layers of administration involved in the nomination process.

---

64. *SB* XVI 12497 (first half of III CE); *P.Prag.* I 14 (first half of III CE); *SB* XVI 12498 (first half of III CE). On the composition of these lists, see Lewis 1993b: 28.
65. *P.Prag.* I 14 (first half of III CE); *SB* XVI 12497 (first half of III CE); *SB* XVI 12498 (first half of III CE); *SB* XX 14584 = *P.Lond.* III 1263 (253 CE). See also *P.Cair.Preis.* 20 (IV CE), a list of liturgists that includes more unlikely candidates: Hierax the butcher, Ammonios the donkey driver, Demetrios the carpenter, and the freedman Niketas; on this text and its date, see Bagnall 1993: 87n.264.
66. Ruffini 2006.
67. Nelson 1979: 35; see also van Minnen 2002.

For taking care of the water tower and fountains in the city [
4th Sarapammon, also called Arios, son of Nilos, grandson of Zoilos, from the [district
Sarapammon is the . . . of the new landowner
8th Isidorus, also called Herakleides, son of Heron, grandson of Sokrates,
Isidorus is a good man, a manufacturer of oil in the [
5th Theodorus, son of Isidorus, grandson of Ischyrion, from the [district
Theodorus is the son of Isidorus who lives in the [
7th Ammonios son of Magnus, also called Menouthes, from the g[ymnasium district
Ammonios is a blabbermouth, a construction worker
2nd Antonius Dioskorus, son of Horigenes from Alexandria, from the [district
Dioskorus is a Christian.[68]

This list was the product of several hands and was drawn up for internal use. From this group of individuals, a final list would have been prepared for review by the nome's *stratēgos*. Perhaps most interestingly, in addition to information identifying individuals and their residence, the text preserves the rankings assigned to candidates and comments about their trade and character as recorded by officials.[69] Ammonius the construction worker (*ergatēs*) might have been a blabbermouth, but Isidorus the oil maker was reputed to be a good man or at least a good oil maker.

Good men like Isidorus the oil maker were the sort of individuals that association members sought out. The association believed to be a group of sheep or cattle herders in Tebtunis (*P.Mich.* V 243), for example, described their officer for the year as a "good man." Inscriptions from other parts of the Hellenistic and Roman world also saluted group members for this quality. The Iobacchoi in second-century Athens even described their presiding officer as "worthy [*axios*] and suitable [*epitēdeios*]," echoing terminology used in nominations.[70] In the case of Isidorus' nomination, the additional comments might have alluded to a positive reputation within the community or within a subset of the community.

---

68. *SB* XVI 12497, lines 40–50, trans. van Minnen (1994: 75).
69. For some basic facts, figures, and costs of water management, see van Minnen 2000: 460–61, based on *P.Lond.* III 1177 = *W.Chr.* 193 (113 CE).
70. *IG* II^2 1368 (164/5 CE), line 36.

It is unclear whether these men were involved in craft or merchant organizations. An oil makers' association was operating during the first century in Tebtunis, a village in the same nome.[71] Associations of oil makers were also active in Oxyrhynchus during the fourth and fifth centuries and probably earlier.[72] The type of work the talkative *ergatēs* Ammonios would have been involved in is unknown, but groups of builders (*oikodomoi*) and carpenters (*tektones*) maintained a presence in both villages and cities.[73] Not only did the spice merchant or weaver Isidorus, like other wealthy craftsmen or merchants, find himself on one of these preliminary lists, but his reputation and wealth in the eyes of the council members made sure his name was passed along to the *stratēgos*.

Attempts to avoid service also bear witness either to participation in the administration or, if nothing else, to the possibility, acceptance, or expectation of such responsibilities, further indicating that Isidorus' situation was not out of the ordinary. Craftsmen and merchants, not unlike many others, invoked poverty to nullify a nomination. The success rate of such a defense is difficult to measure. One weaver in the second century claimed poverty so that he would not have to sit on the board of village elders (*presbuteroi*).[74] A board of elders was typically composed of four to twelve leading community members who possessed a *poros* of four to twelve hundred drachmas and who were chosen to act like a council.[75] A similar list of nominations for the *presbuteroi* for Muchis, a village in the Arsinoite nome, includes a weaver and a butcher, each with a *poros* of four hundred drachmas.[76]

This level of interaction was not a development of the second and third centuries. From the early decades of Roman rule, association members, craftsmen, and merchants played prominent roles in their communities. The scribe Kronion from Tebtunis was involved in an association, perhaps the association of Harpocrates known from *P.Mich.* V 246. As the longtime scribe of Tebtunis, Kronion occupied a position of some influence; at the very least, he was in-

---

71. *P.Mich.* II 124r, col. II, line 23.
72. *P.Oxy.* LIV 3738 (312 CE), 3760 (326? CE); *SB* XVI 12628 (329–31 CE). For an association of oil merchants in Oxyrhynchus, see *SB* XVI 12648 (338 CE).
73. *IGR* I 1155 (45 CE, carpenters); *P.Mich.* II 123r (45–47 CE), col. XVII, line 38; *P.Oxy.* I 53 (316 CE, carpenters); XLIV 3195 (331 CE, builders).
74. *P.Lond.* III 846 (140 CE).
75. For the office of village elder, see Lewis 1997: 43. See also MacMullen 1974: 14, 23–24 (suggesting that the wealth required for the office is between two and eight hundred drachmas).
76. *BGU* I 6 (157/8 CE); *P.Petaus* 66 (185 CE) lists a carpenter among the *presbuteroi*; for additional nominations and appeals with similar language, see *P.Oxy.* XXXIV 2714 (256 CE).

volved in numerous economic transactions.[77] The records and abstracts of contracts, leases, and agreements preserved in the archive show the extent of a scribe's involvement in the daily life of a community. Kronion probably was relatively wealthy, considering the costs associated with managing the *grapheion*. According to the account books, operating the *grapheion* cost approximately five hundred drachmas a year (roughly three and one-half times the cost of annual dues for associations in Tebtunis). Kronion apparently used part of his economic resources to satisfy the requirements of association membership. Entries in his private accounts record expenses related to association activities that are familiar from charters: a payment of four drachmas to an association's president (*hēgoumenos*), perhaps for dues, and additional payments to the association of Harpocrates, for oil and other items he probably contributed.[78]

During the time of Augustus, a group that identified itself as a *sunodos* of fellow farmers erected an honorific monument with a Greek inscription over fifty lines long.[79] According to the text, the association honored its president (*prostatēs*) Apollonius for his devotion and service to the group, with extra portions and other distinctions during meetings and banquets. If this group was anything like the associations in Tebtunis, members might not have been exclusively farmers or landowners. Even the *apolusimoi*, a group of tenants on an imperial estate, included craftsmen, so it is difficult to say what Apollonius did besides farm and whether he leased or owned the land he cultivated or managed. In addition to listing the offices he held within the group, the inscription identified Apollonius as a komarch, indicating that he possessed influence and standing in the community.[80] That Apollonius belonged to the group reveals that this association also was connected to administrative circles through their president.

A list of contributors to the association of *hieronikai* from late third-century Oxyrhynchus (discussed in chapter 3) reveals ties between craftsmen, merchants, and members of the local elite—in particular, the two men identified as *exēgētai*.[81] If not membership in an association, other papyri indicate that councilors and craftsmen shared professional ties that placed members of the local elite within craft or merchant networks. For instance, in the middle of the

77. For the operation of the Tebtunis *grapheion*, see Husselman 1970.
78. *P.Mich.* II 127 (45/6 CE), col. I, lines 20, 30.
79. *SB* V 8267 = *I.Prose* 49 = *I.Delta* I 899, 2 (5 BCE); see also van Minnen 2000: 449–50.
80. *SB* V 8267 = *I.Prose* 49 = *I.Delta* I 899, 2, line 5.
81. *P.Oslo* III 144 (270–75 CE), lines 31, 36.

third century CE, a former *agoranomos* in Oxyrhynchus named Aurelius Hermias apprenticed his son to a linen weaver for five years.[82] In return, Hermias received an interest-free loan of four hundred drachmas. Any number of scenarios may have led to this arrangement. Hermias might have needed money, or he could have been seeking to ensure that this son had a trade to supplement an inheritance split among several heirs. Given apprenticeship patterns, it is possible that Hermias had ties to the weaving industry or had himself been a weaver. In any case, this document further illustrates how people from different social strata forged long-lasting, trust-based connections. The apprenticeship agreement also suggests that the social and economic distance separating officeholders from a weaver with enough personal and financial capital to loan an *agoranomos* four hundred drachmas and to oversee his son's training was not necessarily so pronounced.

Nomination lists and evidence of craftsmen and merchants either holding office or fulfilling duties attests to their participation in the local community, as well as to the acceptance or perhaps even expectation that wealthier craftsmen and merchants would serve in these capacities. Patterns of office holding by craftsmen and merchants are difficult to contextualize, but evidence from elsewhere shows that craftsmen and merchants found themselves in similar positions. In a recent discussion of euergetism in the Roman east, Zuiderhoek pointed out a number of often-cited examples of office holding and council membership by craftsmen and merchants.[83] At Ephesos, a baker (*artokopos*) mentioned his membership in the *gerousia* on his tomb.[84] Wealthy merchants identified as *naukleroi* possessed seats in the Ephesian council; an example is Lucius Erastus, whose council entry fees the emperor Hadrian offered to pay, according to an inscription that would have been displayed on the council building's walls.[85] Pleket proposed that a man who identified himself as a *naukleros* in Nicomedia may have been a council member.[86] Sardis had a goldsmith on its council.[87] A purple dyer from Hierapolis identified himself as a council member on his tomb.[88] Of course, each community in Egypt, Asia Minor, or Italy and the Roman west would have had its own particular social, economic,

82. *P.Oxy.* XXXI 2586 (253 CE).
83. Zuiderhoek 2011: 191. See also van Nijf 1997: 21–22, for further discussion of this evidence.
84. *I.Eph.* 2225.
85. *I.Eph.* 1487 (128/9 CE); see also 1488 (128/9 CE).
86. *SEG* XXVII 828; Pleket 1983: 134.
87. *Nouvelles inscriptions de Sardes* 14.
88. *Altertümer von Hierapolis* 156.

and political forces at work. Someone like Lucius Erastus, the merchant whose position on the Ephesian council was supported by the emperor, operated under different constraints than a wealthy Egyptian weaver or spice merchant, whatever Isidorus may have been.

Zuiderhoek suggested that the inclusion of those from beyond the traditional councilor ranks was related partly to demographic pressures. Mortality rates and difficulties arising from partible inheritances would have made it challenging to sustain enough wealth to remain at elite, office-holding levels. Something like the aforementioned apprenticeship of the son of the *agoranomos* to Hermias the weaver might be an example of a response to such pressures. Tacoma expressed similar ideas regarding the demographic makeup of local councils in third-century Egypt. Be that as it may, inclusion of craftsmen and merchants in local capacities denoting some wealth and status reflects what Zuiderhoek maintains is a "more differentiated" and "heavily stratified" elite; similar stratification also seems likely within craft and merchant circles in cities and villages.

The Rhetoric and Reality of Reputation

Public Utility and Association Petitions

Stories of participation, interaction, and office holding by craftsmen, merchants, and associations provide context for the proceedings regarding the dispute between Epimachus and Isidorus. Groups of craftsmen and merchants were important constituencies that made their concerns known to, interacted with, and were relied on to a certain extent by local officeholders in public and private contexts. Leading craftsmen and merchants might have enjoyed a favorable reputation beyond their immediate professional circles. Associations also asserted a positive and trustworthy reputation by erecting public monuments, whether that be within a funerary context, through temple dedications and votive offerings documented on stelai (such as the stele of the weavers' association in Coptos), or honorific activity in all its forms.[89]

Epimachus may have based his decision to nominate Isidorus on knowledge of Isidorus' personal reputation; but he may have had similar experiences with other craftsmen, merchants, or association members in mind or may have drawn on reputation-based information conveyed by associations in public set-

89. *Stud.Demotica* V 158 (30 BCE).

tings. Reputation and esteem also factored into the decision-making process employed by Isidorus and his advocate Eudaemon to counter the nomination. Both Isidorus and Eudaemon felt that they could rely on a reputation for utility—one based on past service and enjoyed by Isidorus and perhaps by weavers in general—in order to avoid obligations. When making their competing claims before Julianus, both sides used technical language (and rhetoric) to describe inclusion in a privileged group. One of the main points of contention here was whether Isidorus belonged to a group that owed service and received other financial benefits or to a group, like the weavers, that enjoyed exemptions from service. Based on his alleged status as a weaver, a group whose utility had been established, Eudaemon made the case for Isidorus' exemption from service; in fact, one of Eudaemon's central claims was that Isidorus and weavers like him were "useful" (*chrēsimos*) to the treasury.

Invoking utility in this way perhaps would have meant a great deal to the officials hearing the case. Examples of honorific inscriptions dedicated by the council and *demos* of communities in Asia Minor indicate that it was common to tout certain individuals, many of whom also held offices, as being "useful" (*chrēsimos*) to a city or country.[90] The wealthy *naukleros* Lucius Erastus, for example, was also identified as being "useful [*chrēsimos*] to his country," in the inscription that documented his ties to the emperor and attested to his inclusion in the council.[91] A strategic maneuver on the part of Isidorus and his advocate to appeal to this quality (and what it signified) can be construed as an assertion of some stature, reputation, and privilege in the community.

Isidorus was not the only weaver to argue for privileges based on previous work or because of utility, and that was not a claim made strictly by individual petitioners either. It was a strategy used by associations when acting on behalf of the group. Earlier in the second century, a group of weavers from Philadelphia made similar assertions in a petition to a *stratēgos*. In seeking relief from requests placed on them to produce garments for military use, the weavers reminded the *stratēgos* of their past service. The weavers also informed the *stratēgos* that other members of their group were already performing service of some sort in Alexandria, which may reveal that these men possessed enough wealth to make them liable for obligations.[92]

Individual association members or perhaps a group's leadership also kept records of past decisions and edicts issued by officials and used them later to defend

90. *SEG* II 719, LIII 1598 (III CE); *MAMA* IX 29 (after 212 CE), IV 131 (200–50 CE).
91. *I.Eph.* 1487 (128/9 CE), line 8.
92. *BGU* VII 1572 (139 CE), lines 1–18 = *P.Phil.* 10.

their interests and privileges. For consideration as part of a legal dispute over obligations to cultivate public land in the second century CE, an association of weavers in the Fayum submitted a dossier of four texts it had collected, compiled on a single papyrus. The weavers included copies of letters from the Roman authorities to officials in the Arsinoite nome, a prefect's edict, and a record of the proceedings of a previous suit the weavers had brought against a local official.[93] The second document contained a fragmentary list of groups exempt from public obligations, extracted from an edict issued by C. Vibius Maximus, Egypt's prefect from 103 to 107 CE. Included among Maximus' list were oil makers, dyers, goldsmiths, and groups liable for the trade tax.[94] The inclusion of the text in the weavers' petition suggests that the prefect had also exempted weavers, who may have already been among the privileged groups by the time of Maximus' decision. Other weavers profited from a prefect's decision to exempt weavers with a *poros* of fifteen hundred drachmas, essentially exempting wealthy weavers from service on boards of *presbuteroi*, for instance, as well as other posts.[95]

In a dispute with the builders early in the fourth century, an association of weavers in Oxyrhynchus employed the rhetoric of utility in legal proceedings before an imperial official. The builders, it seems, had tried to co-opt a weaver named Paul into their group. The weavers, acting on Paul's behalf, sought relief. In their arguments before the *iuridicus* of Egypt, the weavers emphasized the injustice of the builders, who had dared what the weavers estimated to be a most unlawful act (*paranomōtaton*), whereas the weavers and, by extension, Paul apparently caused no trouble. Perhaps more important, Paul's advocate reminded the *iuridicus* that the weavers as a group were well known for their usefulness (*chrēsimos*) to the public.

> These men [weavers] are in their own right of no small usefulness to the public services, and you, my lord, know—for they contribute abundantly to the *anabolicum*—how very much they have to produce. But the builders think it right, in a time of such pressing need, always to discuss only their own interests. For they are bent on making my client into a builder although he is a peaceful linen weaver, daring to perpetrate a very great wrong in the process.[96]

93. *P.Phil.* 1 (103–24 CE); see also *P.Phil.* 3 (123 CE).
94. *P.Phil.* 1, line 34.
95. For exemptions, see Lewis 1997: 137; for weavers, see 142–43; for a later example, see also *C.Th.* 13.4.2 (337 CE), for exemptions from *munera* enjoyed by certain craftsmen.
96. *P.Ryl.* IV 654 (302–9 CE), *BL* X, 171 and XI, 191, trans. Youtie (1958: 401, adapted).

The language used in this argument, reminiscent of the claims that Isidorus and his advocate had made just over a century earlier about his "usefulness" to the treasury, indicates how associations tried to manage a reputation in another public setting, a legal dispute. Based on the response from the *iuridicus*, the weavers' argument seems to have carried the day: he instructed the *stratēgos* and the *logistēs* that Paul was not to be made a builder if he had already learned to be a weaver. The reliance on the rhetoric of public utility remained a successful strategy, even if the circumstances of the dispute differed from Isidorus' claims for immunity and privilege.

The Roman legal corpus refines and supports the idea of associating privileges with perceived "utility" to the administration. Callistratus, for instance, cited guidelines instituted by Antoninus Pius in his discussion of immunities from obligations for groups that provide utility (*utilitas*).[97] An edict included in the Theodosian Code extended privileges to a wide array of craftsmen and merchants beyond builders and weavers, including, among others, fullers, potters, tanners, silversmiths and goldsmiths, and masons.[98] Subsequent imperial decisions reiterated this position.[99]

A proliferation of exemptions, especially for those with enough wealth to shoulder burdens, might have caused tensions with the local elites. Conceivably, tensions also might have flared between other wealthy craftsmen, merchants, and associations not accorded similar benefits. Immunity represented imperial acknowledgment of the important place occupied by weavers and others performing similar services, carried with it a level of legal recognition beyond designated seating and access to market stalls, and set certain groups apart from others.

Exemptions and favorable tax rates formed part of Roman administrative and fiscal policies. Immunity from obligations was a complicated and contested aspect of civic administration and politics, one of many played out in Roman legal codes and commentaries. It was a particularly complicated issue for influential groups that had accumulated additional privileges. The haggling involved to acquire and defend exemptions put local council members and associations in a difficult position relative to the Roman authorities. Local officials could press craftsmen and merchants for service, as indicated by the nomination of Isidorus, the impositions on weavers, and lists of craftsmen and merchants who found

97. *Dig.* 50.6.6.12.
98. *C.Th.* 13.4.2 (337 CE).
99. *C.Th.* 14.2.1 (364 CE), 14.2.3 (397 CE); *CJ* 11.15.

themselves holding official posts. But associations defended their interests and did so strategically. Going to the Roman authorities, like Isidorus and Eudaemon decided to do, was a tactical decision that exposed a petitioner to an amount of economic, political, and legal risk and uncertainty. Precedent suggested that weavers had been able to defend their rights and privileges in the past, but Julianus may have decided not to abide by previous decisions but to set his own policy.

But Isidorus Is a "Well-to-Do" Man . . .

Hippias countered the utility argument by asserting that Isidorus was not a weaver but a spice merchant; perhaps he thought that spice merchants were not covered by precedent or were less useful. Hippias further claimed that Isidorus was not just a wealthy spice merchant but a *euschēmōn anthropos*, a term that C. H. Roberts translated as "well-to-do man." This might be a loaded phrase, however. A closer examination of papyri and inscriptions indicates that an individual described as a *euschēmōn anthropos* enjoyed some standing and fulfilled responsibilities in the community. Arguing that the term referred to the "upper crust of society," Lewis suggested that, although it was an informal description, community members knew who belonged to this group.[100] It is possible that local scribes and officials compiled lists of "well-to-do" individuals, as evidenced by copies of documents described as such (*graphai euschēmonōn*) and found in archives belonging to magistrates and *stratēgoi*.[101] The use of the phrase suggests that it had a technical sense and that it referred to individuals who possessed a reputation that deemed them suitable for service. When accusations were made against a man named Severianus for some unspecified offense, a letter was dispatched to the *archephodoi* and *euschēmones* of Karanis, where he may have absconded or resided.[102] A letter sent to Tebtunis requesting the presence of the scribe of the grain collectors in the nome capital used similar terminology.[103] The scribe had some explaining to do, and the officials in the metropolis trusted these men to act on their request. Other texts imply that individual *euschēmones* served in different offices, including posts associated with transporting grain to Alexandria, duties that members of the weavers' association in Philadelphia may have been performing.[104] A text from Oxyrhynchus, for instance, suggests that a group of

100. Lewis 1993a: 106.

101. *P.Alex.Giss.* 36 (116/17 CE) = *SB* X 10644; *BGU* I 194 (177 CE) = *W.Chr.* 84; *P.Petaus.* 87 (182–87 CE). See Lewis 1993a: 108.

102. *BGU* I 147 = *BGU* II 376 (II/III CE).

103. *P.Tebt.* II 594 (III CE), line 1; see also *P.Ryl.* II 236 (253 CE).

104. *P.Oxy.* LX 4063 (183 CE).

euschēmones arranged the particulars of transporting grain including hiring the boats and paying the crew.[105] The term thus described not just influential individuals in whom trust had been placed but those who also possessed the economic capacity necessary to full obligatory duties.

Honorary decrees from Asia Minor used the term to refer to individuals who had successfully carried out services or held positions on local councils. The family of Aurelius Attalianus Neikostratus honored him with a statue and recorded how the council, the people, and the Roman inhabitants of Pisidia saluted him in such a fashion.

> [The council and the people] and the Roman inhabitants honored Aurelius Attalianus Neikostratus, *euschēmōn* and a man of distinguished lineage, useful [*chrēsimos*] to his country having fulfilled all magistracies and liturgies. Aureilus Neikostratianos Attalus and Aurelia Tatia, his children, and Aurelius Attalianus Memnon, his brother, have erected a statue.[106]

The inscription makes a connection between holding office, a distinguished lineage, virtue, status as a "well-to-do" man (*euschēmōn*), and even "usefulness" (*chrēsimos*) to the community. Other texts show the same tendency. The council and people of Pisidia also honored a certain Artemidorus as a well-to-do man and highlighted his virtue (*aretē*).[107] A text from Magnesia used the same term to identify a former officeholder honored for his service by the council, the people, and the *gerousia*.[108] In the third century, the council and the people of Pamphylia commemorated someone described as a well-to-do man and councilor.[109]

Additional resonances can be found in the legal corpus. Scaevola included a letter exchanged between a borrower and a lender that used the term when discussing their contractual arrangements.

> Having borrowed fifty denarii from you, I asked you to accept a mortgage from me instead of a guarantor. For you know without doubt that my shop and my slaves are under obligation to no one but you, and you have trusted me as the respectable [*euschēmōn*] man I am.[110]

---

105. *P.Oxy.* LVII 3912 (266 CE). For additional references to *euschēmones*, see *P.Warr.* 5 (154 CE); *P.Meyer* 14 (159/60 CE); *P.Lond.* II 301 (138–61 CE).
106. *SEG* II 744 (III/IV CE).
107. See Sterrett, *EJ*, 402.
108. *OGIS* 485.
109. Bean-Mitford, *Journeys in Rough Cilicia 1964–1968*, 87a. See also *ibid.*, 150, 152; *IGR* III 833, a–b (140–60 CE).
110. *Dig.* 20.1.34.1 (trans. Watson).

The "well-to-do" moniker described the borrower's reputation for trustworthiness or the reputation he thought he had in the eyes of his creditor. This was not merely a rhetorical flourish. It was a statement of the likelihood that a debt would be repaid, and it suggests that *euschēmōn* also had political, legal, and economic connotations.

Returning to the Egyptian context, since service in compulsory offices essentially operated as personal obligations and contracts, the use of this term to describe Isidorus may take on greater significance. By describing Isidorus as a *euschēmōn*, Hippias (or the scribe who reported his remarks) employed technical language denoting trust, reputation, esteem, and expectation of and eligibility for service. As a well-to-do spice merchant or foreman weaver, not only did Isidorus possess enough wealth and standing to be nominated, but he may have already served in such a capacity. By using this terminology, Hippias essentially asserted that if Isidorus had not yet held office, he probably should.

The Egyptian evidence and Isidorus' complaint suggest that one's trade did not necessarily exclude people from participation in local society. At minimum, neither being a spice merchant nor being a weaver was thought to be disreputable. You could at once be a useful and well-to-do member of the community and a spice merchant or a weaver, even if the inferiority of craftsmen and merchants remained a hallmark of literary and philosophical texts.

A trustworthy reputation and the economic capacity and clout that certain craftsmen and merchants wielded in their communities were important considerations for nomination that may have outweighed membership in nonelite status groups. A craftsman or a merchant could be no less *euporos* and *epitēdeios* in this sense. This suggests that local elites may not have interpreted the political and economic world around them in precisely the same terms as a member of the Roman senatorial elite. From the perspective of those involved in the nomination process, what made someone honorable, country loving, virtuous, and suitable for service was connected to qualities or characteristics deemed necessary for running a community. Technical language used in papyri, inscriptions, and legal sources that appear to make claims for or assertions of a more elite status could also be used to refer to these particular traits.

Treatments of local administration have focused less on trust and reputation. Instead, patronage and euergetism displayed by leading figures in society and their interactions with the ruling Roman elite in their pursuit of honor have been seen as the organizing principles of government and administration.[111] Investigating this type of honor (defined in terms of *dignitas* and *timē*) and the motivations behind *philotimia*, Lendon explored how it gave meaning and structure to political, social, and economic relations. For Lendon, honor and its exchange made the empire run in the face of minimal imperial intrusion and infrastructure.[112] Lendon's treatment offers a useful starting point for a larger discussion of social and political relations among local and Roman officials. This model, however, constructs the world of local communities from the top down and emphasizes interactions between the leading local figures and members of the Roman elite. This leaves little room for associations, merchants, and craftsmen and for their interactions with local officials, and it may not completely explain the efforts of an Egyptian *prytanis* or *agoranomos*.

Honorary inscriptions, including those authored by associations, attest that the accumulation of honors, offices, and awards were not unimportant motivating factors for current and aspiring civic leaders. These texts, infused with the rhetoric of honor, reveal one aspect of the mechanisms at work. But there was another side to these interactions. The reality of the situation was perhaps never as neat and tidy as honorary inscriptions make it out to be. The language used in inscriptions glosses over the complexities of the relationships between members of the elite and other constituencies on the ground. This is not surprising, as each inscription represents the final product of repeated interactions during a local official's career. Inscriptions only provide part of the story; papyri help round out the picture and speak to the complexities in unequal political power relations between elites and nonelites. For every gymnasiarch praised for supplying the best oil, another was left to argue with a merchant or an oil maker about the quality and the price.[113]

Participation in Context

Authors frame their discussions about associations and the craftsmen and merchants that belonged to these groups in terms of trust or lack of it. The highest echelons of Roman society may have had their misgivings, and trust may have always been an issue for some. But a lack of trust does not seem to have precluded involvement of craftsmen and merchants in local politics and administration.

111. See, for example, van Minnen 2000; Zuiderhoek 2009.
112. Lendon 1997.
113. *P.Laur.* IV 187 (II CE).

Associations were involved in the exchange and economy of trust, reputation, and esteem—not only for themselves, but also for the local and Roman elites. Ties with craft and merchant groups did not detract from one's status; in a way, it seems to have augmented it. Prominent local officials were not passive receivers of honor and praise; instead, they cultivated ties and maintained relationships with these organizations. All parties involved presumably benefited.

Connections could be long lasting, too, signaling that the exchange of honors and benefits was part of a complicated relationship between associations and officials. The dyers of Thyatira, for instance, thanked an official for defraying costs of repairs on their building and for support from his family over many generations.[114] At some point in the late second century CE, the bakers of Ephesos honored an individual who held a number of positions, including *agoranomos* and superintendent of the grain distributions.[115] Associations in Ephesos seem to have had relationships with the Vedii, a powerful and influential family that included a member of the Roman senate.[116] Although each community had its own hierarchies to navigate, associations played a role in managing these relationships through honorific activities. In praising patrons and benefactors, associations used honorific language typical in Italy and the Latin west, as Elizabeth Forbis has discussed in detail.[117] Behind the rhetoric of inscriptions lies evidence of successful and repeated interactions between these groups. Associations and officials assumed that these relationships would continue as well. Some texts spelled out expectations quite explicitly, suggesting that associations entered into these arrangements not only recognizing favors already granted but also believing that they would garner further benefits.[118]

Council members and magistrates, whether charged with tax collection or with outfitting the baths, did not manage arrangements in an environment free of transaction costs. These men also encountered risk and uncertainty in their endeavors, whether that involved completing grand construction plans or supplying the gymnasium with oil. Cultivating or maintaining ties with various associations might have been in their best interests.

Furthermore, local benefactors and officeholders and the wealthiest mer-

---

114. *TAM* V.2 945 (222–35 CE) = *IGR* IV 1265.
115. *TAM* V.2 966 (late II CE).
116. On the family of Vedius, see Kalinowski 2002.
117. Forbis 1996.
118. See Forbis 1996: 51, no. 328, lines 16–18.

chants and craftsmen, who held association offices and were honored by their groups, may have had more in common with each other in economic terms than members of the municipal elite had with Roman aristocracy. The documentary evidence reveals that shared business interests and municipal obligations brought the local liturgists and leading craftsmen and merchants together. Wealthy craftsmen and merchants and the local elite also had more at stake in sustaining relationships and stood to benefit more from such bonds than their provincial and Roman counterparts. Roman prefects concerned themselves primarily with taxation, justice, and extracting vital grain—more than enough to keep a prefect and his staff busy for a typical three-year term. Managing cities and towns remained the purview of the local populations. Providing food, oversight of markets and temples, organizing public festivals, and general maintenance all proved to be complicated endeavors. As a result, the nature of municipal administration in the Roman world required cooperation between different stakeholders in the community.

The sorts of services that wealthy craftsmen and merchants provided indicate not only that they were involved in their local communities but that they enjoyed a certain amount of trust and esteem relative to the rest of the population. For some on the local level, affiliation with an association was a part of the image crafted by elites or their families, one that, according to Zuiderhoek, they relied on to solidify their place in the local hierarchy in the face of demographic pressures. In such a context, craftsmen, merchants, and associations could prove influential.

When considering the variety of their participation and the different offices held by craftsmen and merchants, it is important not to confuse obligations for providing transport of food or for the maintenance of fountains with the manual labor involved in such tasks. That individuals often considered to be of a lower status were involved in these activities makes a case against uniform marginalization of these groups on an ideological basis. The evidence indicates that a direct correlation between occupation and position within the social, political, and economic hierarchies did not always exist on the local level.

Conclusions

Isidorus took a series of risks when he brought his complaint to Julianus. Epimachus and Isidorus or groups to which they belonged may have had some history of competition and conflict that culminated in a political maneuver on

Epimachus' part. Depending on Julianus' ruling, a good deal may have hung in the balance. Julianus' decision could have impacted not only Isidorus and whether he had to serve; the outcome could complicate relations between the two men and between any support networks on which each relied. An adverse decision for either Isidorus or Epimachus also would have meant financial fallout and would have set a precedent that each wanted to avoid. In the end, Julianus appears to have followed past precedent and decided that, if a weaver, Isidorus could nominate someone else.

Whatever the situation, the text illustrates that local elites accepted and even expected that craftsmen and merchants would participate in the political life of the community. Certain individuals had developed reputations for usefulness and perhaps trust, and Epimachus had already convinced other members of the local elite and the *stratēgos* (who would have verified the appointment) that Isidorus was someone they could expect to fulfill official obligations. This text and the others discussed here illustrate that local officials, craftsmen, and merchants knew how to manipulate the rules and the rhetoric involved and that they tried to use their knowledge for their own benefit when making their cases to the Roman authorities.

Possessing exemptions and privileges granted by the Roman authorities also marked participation by men like Isidorus and different associations in the community, the society, and the Roman administrative regime. The acquisition of these exemptions probably caused some tension between local elites and wealthy craftsmen and merchants and probably even led to rivalries between groups who did not meet the utility requirement or could not successfully argue that they did. These different constituencies were vying for exemptions and privileges from the Romans. Both associations and members of the elite argued for a financially privileged position and tried to manipulate perceptions of each other's usefulness in the eyes of the Roman authorities. Honor—the dominant metaphor that, according to Lendon, gave order to the world—was a part of the process and the competitive dynamic; but it was not the only part.

Treatments of associations and their participation in their community often have assumed that they were poorly served by existing Hellenistic, Roman, and late Roman civic structures.[119] Associations supposedly offered nonelites a refuge, as Torrey Seland maintained.

119. Kloppenborg 1996: 18. For similar views, see Wilken 1984: 31–34; Meeks 1983: 77–80. For discussion of earlier phases of scholarship emphasizing the compensatory nature of association membership, see Harland 2003: 90–97.

> The internal organization of the clubs and associations, especially in the Greek cities, had the polis as its structural model; they had a structured leadership and laws regulating activities, duties, and responsibilities. In this way, people who had little influence in their polis could find a setting where they were acknowledged. Club membership gave a feeling of belonging.[120]

Based on what we have seen here and in preceding chapters, the approach of using exclusion and compensation as a starting point for understanding the activities of associations should continue to be refined in line with recent studies. Associations and individual craftsmen and merchants were engaged in the community on many levels: association leaders and wealthy craftsmen and merchants shouldered administrative responsibilities; associations carried out public contracts, participated in festivals and ceremonies, owned and rented property, and sustained relationships with temples in Egypt; and associations gained and bestowed public recognition through honorific activity.

The participation of Isidorus and other leading craftsmen and merchants does not mean, however, that there were not subtle gradations within their own groups or that all members possessed wealth that made them liable to service. That was not the case. Membership lists, internal association documents, even the election of officers and bestowal of honors within an association point toward differences of influence and economic capacity among members. Nevertheless, all members presumably would benefit from the contacts made and the reputations earned by their leaders or fostered by the group in public, the privileges individual members of specific craft and merchant groups enjoyed, and the privileges gained by their leaders in the group. All members of an association may have found a sense of self-determination by participating in a group, regardless of their individual economic capacities. But beyond self-determination or a sense of belonging (benefits that have been asserted often), they also gained much more, in ways not available to anonymous peasants or craftsmen in workshops. The anonymous laborers were actually society's marginal members, who neither enjoyed the benefits that membership offered nor were able to use similar strategies to defend their own interests.

120. Seland 1996: 112.

CHAPTER 5

Associations in Legal Thought and Practice

Not all craftsmen and merchants followed the examples of Isidorus or the weavers from Philadelphia. The ability to defend collective interests could manifest itself in more confrontational ways. For instance, as told in the Acts of the Apostles, an Ephesian silversmith named Demetrius, who, like the "well-to-do" Isidorus, also had multiple people working for him, adopted a combative stance to voice his complaints and those of his fellow craftsmen.[1] In what has become the *locus classicus* for urban disruptions sponsored by craftsmen, Demetrius and the silversmiths he led seized two Christian followers of Paul, occupied the theater, and caused what the Acts of the Apostles describes as "no small disruption [*tarachos*]."

> There was a silversmith named Demetrius who made miniature silver shrines of Artemis and provided no little work for the craftsmen, whom, having called them together along with workers plying similar trades, he addressed: "Men, you know well that our prosperity derives from this work. As you can now see and hear, not only in Ephesos but throughout most of the province of Asia this Paul has persuaded and misled a great number of people by saying that gods made by hands are not gods at all. The danger grows, not only that our business will be discredited, but also that the temple of the great goddess Artemis will be of no account, and that she whom the whole province of Asia and all the world worship will be stripped of her magnificence." When they heard this, they were filled with fury and began to shout "Great is Artemis of the Ephesians!"[2]

1. Acts 19: 23–41.
2. Acts 19: 24–28, trans. *New American Bible* (slightly adapted).

Once assembled in the theater, the crowd of craftsmen united in chanting, "Great is Artemis of the Ephesians!" With their actions, the smiths had seized a platform to voice frustrations over perceived threats to their livelihood and a supposedly concomitant decrease in their own standing and influence in the city, problems caused, as characterized by the author of Acts, by the all-too-successful efforts of Paul and his followers.

The stakes of the silversmiths' decision to occupy the theater that day may have been higher than disputes over immunities from civic obligations or tax assessment and may have been significant beyond their group. The local councilors found themselves in a precarious position, too, because of the silversmiths' actions. The council scribe (*grammateus*) made this clear in the remarks he offered when called on to address the crowd assembled in the theater. He urged them to consider their actions and how they could be perceived: further disturbances risked being labeled as *stasis*.

> Finally the town clerk [*grammateus*] restrained the crowd and said, "You Ephesians, what person is there who does not know that the city of the Ephesians is the guardian of the temple of the great Artemis and of her image that fell from the sky? Since these things are undeniable, you must calm yourselves and not do anything rash. The men you brought here are not temple robbers, nor have they insulted our goddess. If Demetrius and his fellow craftsmen have a complaint against anyone, courts are in session, and there are proconsuls. Let them bring charges against one another. If you have anything further to investigate, let the matter be settled in the lawful assembly, for, as it is, we are in danger of being charged with rioting [*stasis*] because of today's conduct. There is no cause for it. We shall [not] be able to give a reason for this demonstration."[3]

Sedition and *stasis*, claimed the *grammateus*, could incite Roman involvement, and that would not benefit the silversmiths, the council (of which he was a ranking member), or the people of Ephesos. Though Acts does not refer to Demetrius and his silversmiths specifically as an association, their occupation of the theater has been taken as an example of an association in action. Associations of silversmiths in Ephesos received designated trading spaces (*topoi*) and were active in honorific exchange with local and imperial elites, and their

3. Acts 19: 35–40, trans. *New American Bible* (slightly adapted).

ties to the shrine of Artemis were cited in a dedication.[4] All these measures essentially show the silversmiths to have been model citizens. As such, Demetrius and the silversmiths risked not only punitive measures from the Roman authorities but also the loss of any goodwill they enjoyed from the local council and the community, and they endangered the same carefully crafted reputation that they feared the Christians would impugn.

The actions of the smiths seem all the more risky given elite attitudes toward craftsmen and merchants and the connections that the Roman authorities made between sedition, riots, and associations. Staging a protest may have been bold, but any organized collective action was probably not as impromptu as the author of Acts made it appear. The decision made by Demetrius and the silversmiths was just as deliberate as a choice to file (or not file) a petition or bring complaints to the council directly or as a decision to honor local officials. Demetrius' supposed ability to rally the smiths illustrates the influence possessed by leading craftsmen (the sort that belonged to associations) or, at least, the influence that community members thought those craftsmen possessed. The choice the silversmiths made indicates the leverage that associations wielded to defend their own interests, as well as the perceptions of their influence within the community, as reflected by the author of Acts.

The resolution of the disturbance suggests that Demetrius and the silversmiths were not wrong to risk a protest. The smiths' shouts celebrating Artemis' greatness amounted to a statement of their allegiance to and participation in the community and were not a challenge; conversely, the chants posed an implicit question to the authorities regarding the place that the smiths occupied in that community.[5] Not unlike associations that assumed a certain public posture and projected a specific image through honorary inscriptions, dedications to a deity, or participation in a procession or festival, the silversmiths had made a public demonstration that sought to align them with the community's divine patron. In doing so, the silversmiths staged a social performance that professed their desire to participate in and not disrupt that community. After some time in the theater, Demetrius and the silversmiths received a response from the council, either favorable or not entirely negative. The council and the silversmiths agreed about Artemis' greatness, and the councilors affirmed the inclusion of the smiths in the community, by neither taking action against them nor

4. *I.Eph.* 547 (undated); *I.Eph.* 425 (81–96 CE) = *AGRW* 164; *I.Eph.* 636 (200–210 CE); *SEG* XXXIV 1094 (250–60 CE); *I.Eph.* 586 (138–61 CE).

5. In this sense, Harland (2003: 169) is right to have suggested that the smiths showed "civic pride."

calling in the Roman authorities. Instead, the councilors urged the smiths to petition the council or go to the law courts if their concerns persisted, two strategies that Egyptian associations employed at times.

Religious concerns and the emphasis given to Paul's success in Acts aside, the actions of the silversmiths and the resolution of the dispute as described prompt questions about what craftsmen, merchants, and association members expected from the authorities, how they understood Roman policies and responded to legal regulations, and how local authorities handled these situations. The occupation of the theater by the silversmiths provides a starting point for more detailed consideration of the application of law on associations, craftsmen, and merchants; conflicts with those in power; and the role that associations played in navigating the playing field. To assess the strategies employed by the silversmiths or any other group, it is necessary to understand what Nobel Prize–winning economist Douglass North called the "rules of the game," the formal and informal constraints that structure economic activities.[6] This chapter will thus examine incidents of conflict between associations and the authorities and the legal framework in which the disputes played out. Whereas previous chapters concentrated on the local level, this chapter will also involve the decisions that Roman officials made and the legal statutes and policies underlying their actions, to the extent those can be recovered. Egypt remains the focus, but the evidence considered will, by necessity, encompass Roman legal and juristic texts, in order to set Egyptian associations, craftsmen, and merchants in context within their communities and beyond. More than a discussion about individual strategies and decisions, this chapter is about the impact of Roman rule on the economic, social, and legal lives of association members and, more broadly, the extent to which law constrained or facilitated the work of craftsmen and merchants.

The Rules of the Game

Rules and regulations devised by the state and by the associations themselves in their charters provide formal constraints and are a part of what North referred to as the "institutional environment" in which economic activities are carried

6. North 1990: 3.

out.[7] The institutional environment also consists of informal constraints, defined variously as social norms, conventions of behavior and decorum, and beliefs. Taken together, formal and informal constraints define, according to North, "the rules of the game in a society, or more formally, . . . the humanly devised constraints that shape human interaction."[8]

Aside from the rules specified in association charters, which can be said to formalize behavioral norms and rules of decorum valued by association members, formal constraints included senatorial and imperial decrees, edicts, laws, municipal charters, and rules that spelled out contractual obligations and property rights.[9] The codification of law and legal commentaries in the fifth and sixth centuries provided a substantial legal corpus for officials to draw on at a later period.[10] Before these compilations were made, law emanated from Rome and its deputies in the provinces. Even after compiling the legal codes, the emperors remained a source of law as they made decisions and issued edicts. Customs regulations, Diocletian's price edict, and other rules concerning commerce and trade supplied further formal constraints that associations and their members would have had to manage. The *Gnomon of the Idios Logos*, a collection of regulations concerning a range of economic, social, and legal matters, compiled and used by provincial officials in Egypt, would have fallen into this category.

Informal constraints also structure economic, political, and social interactions between individuals and organizations. Based on Finley's models of ancient economic activity, informal constraints, characterized by an elite agrarian ideology and a corresponding negative appraisal of craft and merchant activity, would seem to provide the overarching structure to economic activity, perhaps more so than formal rules adopted by states or political bodies. Low regard for craftsmen, merchants, and the associations they formed can be found readily in the literary record, across a range of genres and time periods. Dishonesty on the part of craftsmen and merchants, who supposedly relied on deceit and subterfuge to sell their wares, was a common literary trope into the late antique period.[11] Larger groups of craftsmen and merchants only brought more sordid and

7. For a recent discussion, see Frier and Kehoe 2007.
8. North 1990: 3.
9. For formal constraints, see North 1990: 46–51; for commercial law and contracts, Crook 1967: 206–49.
10. On the Theodosian Code, see Matthews 2000; Harries and Wood 1993. On the Digest of Justinian, see Honoré 2010.
11. Cicero, *De officiis* 1.150–51. For summary accounts, see D'Arms 1981: 20–47, 149–71; Joshel 1992: 63–69.

untrustworthy individuals together, and no good could come of that, or so ancient authors have assured us.[12]

Admittedly, it is more difficult to make firm conclusions about the impact of social norms, ideologies, and beliefs on economic activity, even when not discussing premodern economies and societies, something Sheilagh Ogilvie maintained in her work on medieval trade.[13] Yet elite sentiments regarding work and trade, particularly Cicero's philosophical perspective, have remained important for studying the ancient economy, because Finley made these the building blocks of his economic analysis in *The Ancient Economy*. Finley supposed not only that these writings provided an accurate portrayal of economic thinking and attitudes toward economic activities but also that everyone at all levels of the social and economic pyramid shared and acted on similar views.

Since Finley set forth his status-based model of the ancient economy, which relied heavily on the idea that an elite ideology constrained activity and prevented economic development, the involvement of elites in trade and production has been a hotly contested topic. The search for elite connections and involvement in the sordid world of commerce has gone on now for more than four decades, since Finley published *The Ancient Economy*. The results of this inquiry have so far indicated that authors like Cicero (and therefore Finley) essentially provided an ideal model of elite attitudes toward economic pursuits and described what a member of the elite should be thinking, doing, and saying about a number of topics, though not necessarily what they always did. There remains no doubt about the strong philosophical and ideological aversion to commercial activity and craft production among the elites. Reality, however, was less susceptible to Cicero's philosophical categorizations. Numerous studies have revealed the extent to which Roman patricians engaged directly or indirectly in commerce. John D'Arms, for instance, detailed the involvement of Roman senatorial elites in trading and merchant enterprises during the republic and early empire.[14] Bruce Frier provided insightful analysis of the profits that elites derived from commercial rental properties in cities.[15] A glimpse at lists of association patrons throughout the Roman world also shows connections between local and imperial officeholders and numerous craft and merchant groups.[16] It may have been contemptible to be a carpenter or a cobbler,

12. Pliny, *Ep.* 10.33–34; MacMullen 1992: 173–78.
13. Ogilvie 2007: 676–79.
14. D'Arms 1981.
15. Frier 1980.
16. Waltzing 1895–1900, vol. 4: 388–417.

and fishmongers and perfume sellers may have often been the butt of jokes, but when these individuals and their associations dedicated a statue honoring a member of the elite or rented workshops owned by the elite or the community itself, that action augmented the social and economic capital of those involved.[17]

Formal Constraints in Communities

Municipal Charters and the Lex Irnitana

All politics being local, civic charters provide a good starting point for a larger discussion of the formal constraints within which associations operated. The evidence provided by municipal regulations, chartered by the emperor and senate at Rome, offer insight into the ways in which local and Roman officials approached associations. Several examples of municipal charters from the first century CE from communities in Spain have survived: the *lex Malacitana, lex Salpensana,* and *lex Irnitana.*[18] The most complete charter, the *lex Irnitana*, indicates some concern with associations, craftsmen, and merchants. Dating to 91 CE, the *lex Irnitana* was originally inscribed on ten bronze tablets and apparently was affixed to the facade of a public building in the town of Irni, as holes at the top and bottom of each tablet suggest.[19] Each tablet contained three columns of text and measured nearly three feet long and two feet wide. The ten tablets would have contained around fifteen hundred lines of text in total. Of the original ten, six relatively complete tablets, along with other fragments uncovered in excavations carried out in 1981, are now housed in museum collections in Madrid, Seville, and Huelva. The text that survives generally corresponds to the other charters, suggesting that a single municipal law—a Flavian municipal charter or a *lex Flavia municipalis*—was promulgated in Spain and elsewhere. Galsterer proposed that the slight variations between the texts reveal accommodations for the particular needs of each community.[20]

Irni was located near modern Seville, roughly thirty kilometers south of the

17. *P.Fay.* 96 (122 CE); *P.Oxy.* XII 1461 (222 CE). Although we lack a similarly detailed archaeological context in Egypt, contracts and leases suggest that craftsmen and merchants leased space from current or former local officials and from communities.
18. *FIRA* I 23 (*lex Salpensana*), 24 (*lex Malacitana*); for text and translation of the *lex Irnitana,* see Gonzalez and Crawford 1986.
19. Gonzalez and Crawford 1986: 147–48; for monumental legal documents, see Williamson 1987.
20. Galsterer 1988: 79.

colony of Urso, for which an earlier charter also has survived.[21] The town of Irni itself was unknown until the discovery of the charter, but as Galsterer maintained, the *lex Irnitana* reveals a town that would have been similar to many other communities in the Roman world, complete with a local council composed of wealthy individuals (*decuriones*) who provided administrative oversight.[22] Given the proliferation of associations from one end of the empire to the other, the craftsmen and merchants of Irni probably organized similar groups. Thanks to the repeated concerns voiced by members of the Roman elite regarding the less-than-trustworthy nature of craftsmen and merchants, one would expect municipal charters to pay close attention to associations, especially a charter that originated in Rome. Out of the *lex Irnitana*'s ninety-six chapters, however, only one concerned associations, under the heading "*De coetu sodalicio collegio*" (chapter 74).

> Rubric. Concerning assembly, society and college.
>
> No one is to take part in an assembly [*coetus*] in that *municipium* or to form a society [*sodalicium*] or a college [*collegium*] for that purpose or to conspire that it be held or to act in such a way that any of these things occur. Anyone who acts against these rules is to be condemned to pay 10,000 sesterces to the citizens of the *Municipium Flavium Irnitanum*. And the right of action, suit, and claim of that money and concerning that money is to belong to any citizen of that *municipium*.[23]

Other charters would have presumably contained similar verbiage. Although they warranted only one entry in the charter, the text does apparently prohibit groups described as *sodalicia* and *collegia* from assembling and reflects Roman sentiments regarding associations.[24] The fine incurred by offending individuals or groups, ten thousand sesterces, was a colossal sum for a craftsman or merchant and certainly was intended to discourage aberrant behavior. It dwarfed the one hundred sesterces that new members of the association of Diana and

21. On Irni, see Galsterer 1988.
22. Galsterer 1988: 83–84.
23. *Lex Irnitana*, chapter 74, trans. Gonzalez and Crawford (1986).
24. For what the text reveals about approaches to associations, see Liu 2005. On chapter 74 of the *lex Irnitana* in general, see Gonzalez and Crawford 1986: 223–24. They point out the text's implication that the ban is not so much on *sodalicia* or *collegia* as on an illegal assembly (*coetus*); see also Liu 2005: 290, for discussion of this text and for a recent summary of scholarship on these issues.

Antinous paid as an entry fee in Lanuvium in 136 CE. But it does echo the charter's penalty clauses that concerned hoarding goods and forming partnerships in order to corner the market for particular items, infractions that also carried a fine of ten thousand sesterces.

Restrictions on an assembly (*coetus*) also appeared in a fragmentary portion of the *lex Ursonensis,* where it referred specifically to conspiracies or disruptive activities.[25] The relationship established in the *lex Irnitana* between *collegia, sodalicia*, and *coetus* might imply that the Flavian municipal regulation was not concerned with associations and the normal activities of craftsmen and merchants. Instead, both the Roman authorities who authored the text and the local authorities charged with its enforcement might have been more interested in preserving order. The regulations about associations and assembly were focused on penalizing seditious or disruptive actions perpetrated by associations (or other groups) and did not aim at preventing the formation of groups outright.

As an example of the Flavian municipal law, the *lex Irnitana* (and other texts like it) originated with the emperor and the senate. This suggests that the concerns with associations, sedition, and conspiracy-laden assemblies emanated from Rome, Roman elites, and provincial officials. Any municipal charter would have reflected more the concerns of the Roman administration than lo cal concerns or policies regarding craftsmen, merchants, and their organizations. A scenario thus emerges in which a gap could develop between Roman interest in these groups and enforcement on the ground. This is precisely the observation made by Jinyu Liu, who has rightly maintained that the negotiation of these terms and the enforcement of any policy would have had a local character.[26] Dissonance between legal statutes, the reality on the ground, and local interpretation would have impacted the institutional environment and may have ultimately favored craft and merchant groups known to and trusted by local officials.

Even in light of Roman concerns, punishing disruptive and seditious behavior differs from an outright ban, and the municipal charter makes no reference to previous senatorial or imperial decisions restricting associations. A blanket prohibition may have been impractical due to the integration of associations in their communities. Both the authorities and prominent local offi-

25. FIRA I 21 (*lex coloniae Genetivae*), CVI; for a new edition, translation, and commentary, see Crawford 1996: 393–457.
26. Liu 2005.

cials, who supported groups, apparently allowed associations to operate.[27] If local notables had feared sedition sponsored by associations or had worried about Roman reprisals, it follows that they would not have affiliated themselves, literally or figuratively, with associations, yet papyri and inscriptions show that affiliation with associations was common. The *collegium* of Diana and Antinous, to offer just one example, received an endowment of fifteen thousand sesterces from a man named Lucius Caesennius Rufus, a wealthy benefactor whom the group described in their charter as a "patron of the municipality."[28]

Local officials either chose not to deal with associations according to Roman legal parameters or did not feel that these relationships significantly impaired their standing with Roman authorities. On the contrary, maintaining ties with associations seems to have been very much in keeping with social and economic norms. Although the threat remained, riots and potentially subversive gatherings like the one perpetrated by the Ephesian silversmiths were probably not prevalent. When disruptions did occur, harsh punishment need not always follow, even with steep penalties stipulated in municipal charters. Both local elites and associations benefited from making connections. Given the possible influence of some associations, though not all, it may have been riskier to adopt a confrontational stance with associations indiscriminately.

Egypt and the *Gnomon of the Idios Logos*

There is no evidence from Egypt quite like the municipal charters. Edicts issued by prefects detail Roman responses to any number of issues, but associations do not necessarily figure in these texts. Egypt does, however, offer an example of regulations that dealt with matters of law, policy, status distinctions, inheritance, and finances, in the *Gnomon of the Idios Logos*.[29] The office of the idios logos had its roots in the Ptolemaic period and was charged with managing and selling state land, including confiscated and abandoned properties. Under the Romans, the idios logos had many expanded responsibilities. In addition to overseeing state land, the office oversaw priesthoods, inheritance, and questions of status. The office was subordinate to the governor and existed into the third century CE.

27. Waltzing 1895–1900, vol. 3: 3–17.
28. *CIL* XIV 2112 = *ILS* 7212 (136 CE), lines 3, 46.
29. *BGU* V 1210 (150–61 CE). Another copy of the *Gnomon of the Idios Logos*, *P.Oxy.* XLII 3014, dates to the first century CE but preserves only sections 35–41; for the *Gnomon*, see Swarney 1970.

The text of the *Gnomon of the Idios Logos* has a complicated history. The *Gnomon* was a list of rules, decisions, and regulations deriving from the emperors, the senate, or governors and magistrates, and officials added to it over time, as situations called for innovation or clarification. It appears to have been first compiled during the reign of Augustus, although the most detailed copy that has survived is a second-century text from Theadelphia in the Fayum (*BGU* V 1210). According to the document's heading, this copy had been prepared for use by a local official as a guide when performing his administrative duties.[30] The same can probably be said for a first-century copy from Oxyrhynchus that preserves only a small portion of the text.[31]

Not unlike the Flavian municipal charter, the *Gnomon* was brief on the topic of associations. Only one of its 115 sections mentioned anything about associations. Even in this single entry, the *Gnomon* merely stated that "members of associations have been fined five hundred drachmas" and that "sometimes only the officers [*prostatai*] have been."[32] The fine of five hundred drachmas equaled the amount that the *Gnomon* assigned for violating a written agreement, perhaps suggesting that fraudulent behavior or deceit may lie behind the fines directed at associations and their officers.[33] For an individual member of the associations in Tebtunis in the first century CE, five hundred drachmas would have amounted to dues for nearly three and one-half years. In the second century, five hundred drachmas would have equaled two times the amount of the average yearly wages of an unskilled laborer.[34]

The *Gnomon* and the officials behind its development clearly intended to make a statement with the fine. Its inclusion in the *Gnomon* suggests that disputes with associations either had become an issue or had merely posed interesting legal questions for an official. It is difficult, however, to say what would have caused an association or only the officers to be fined. The text contained no mention of disruptions or *stasis* (about which the council scribe had warned the silversmiths in Ephesos) or actions akin to *coetus* (described in the municipal charter). Based on the fiscal focus of the *Gnomon*, Ilias Arnaoutoglou proposed that the fine levied against associations may have had more to do with delinquency in tax payments or other required services.[35]

30. *BGU* V 1210, lines 1–7.
31. *P.Oxy.* XLII 3014 (I CE).
32. *BGU* V 1210, section 108.
33. *BGU* V 1210, section 98.
34. Scheidel 2010: 434.
35. Cited by Liu (2005: 291).

Considering that this was a primary area in which Egyptian associations and their officers interacted with the local and provincial authorities, Arnaoutoglou may not be far off the mark.

Harsh as the fine may appear, these provisions do not indicate that sweeping punitive measures existed or that regulations prohibited association operations. A fine of five hundred drachmas was steep for an individual but perhaps less so when imposed on the group, and using the association's common fund to pay the fine may have mitigated the impact too. In whatever manner the fine was paid, it does not seem to have been meant to hinder operations of a group or its officials in a lasting way. Upon payment of the fine, the relationship between the offending group and the local authorities seems to have returned to the *status quo* that existed prior to the conflict. As an actual restriction on or attempt to monitor association activities, this measure may have been less than effective.

Formal Constraints in Juristic Thought

Unrest, Social Support, and *Homines Tenuiores*

Within the substantial body of legal, economic, and political rules that constituted Roman public and commercial law, many laws, imperial decisions, and discussions in juristic commentaries were related to associations and their operations.[36] Roman authorities at different points in time appear to have taken steps to curb association activities.[37] Tacitus reported that the Roman senate took action against *collegia* in Pompeii and imposed penalties on the individuals implicated in riots originating at a gladiatorial combat in 59 CE.[38] Earlier enactments by the senate date to the final years of the republic but were repealed in 58 BCE by Clodius, a move Cicero criticized.[39] Suetonius also reported that both Julius Caesar and Augustus attempted to impose restrictions on *collegia* or to regulate them in some fashion.[40] Augustus apparently allowed only groups approved by accepted custom and law (*antiqua et legitima*) and

36. For a summary of commercial law, see Crook 1967: 206–49.
37. On law and associations, see Cotter 1996; de Ligt 2000: 242–44; 2001: 346.
38. Tacitus, *Annales* 14.17.
39. Cotter 1996: 75–76; Cicero, *In Pisonem* 9.
40. Suetonius, *Jul.* 42.3; *Aug.* 32.1.

banned other groups. Gaius and Marcian, jurists writing in the second and third centuries respectively, referred to earlier *senatus consulta* and imperial decisions (*mandata*) regulating associations, which suggests that associations continued to prompt legal questions and responses from the highest levels of the administration.[41]

The extent to which these acts and imperial decisions demonstrate what Brent Shaw famously described as Rome's "almost morbid fear of any unofficial assembly or association" can be debated.[42] That the references spanned several centuries does not mean that legal actions taken against associations formed a coherent policy or that relations with Roman authorities were hostile at all times. Despite the supposed anxiety and suspicion with which the elite approached associations, papyrological and epigraphic records show that legislation did not hinder their proliferation. Perhaps Gaius assumed that associations were quite common, though his discussion of the provincial edict maintained that the formation of associations required some sort of oversight.[43] In his work on the Twelve Tables, for instance, Gaius claimed that individuals actually enjoyed relatively wide-ranging rights to form associations for business, religious, and social purposes, provided they violated no public laws.[44]

> Co-members [*sodales*] are those who belong to the same association, what the Greeks call a *hetaireia*. A statute gives them the power to enter into any agreement they like, so long as they do not contravene the public statute. This statute appears to have been adopted from the law of Solon which says: "If the inhabitants of a city district or precinct be in association for the purpose of holding religious feasts or of dining together or to provide for their burial or if they be members of the same club or they combine to engage in some enterprise or for profit, anything that they agree between themselves will be valid unless forbidden by public statutes."[45]

Beyond those that Suetonius reports Augustus specified, rule exceptions were as much a part of juristic discussions as were delineating acts of the senate and imperial decisions seeking to limit associations. The jurists repeatedly in-

41. *Dig.* 3.4.1 (Gaius, *On the Provincial Edict* 3), 47.22.1 (Marcian, *Institutes* 3); see De Ligt 2001: 347–48.
42. Shaw 1984: 47–48; contra Shaw, see De Ligt 2000, 2001.
43. *Dig.* 3.4.1.
44. *Dig.* 47.22.4 (Gaius, *Commentary on the XII Tables* 4).
45. *Dig.* 47.22.4, trans. Watson (1985); for discussion of this passage, see Jones 1999: 33–37, 311–20.

voked religion, burial, and support for the poor within a community (the *homines tenuiores*) as exceptions. Marcian offered further clarification in the third book of his *Institutes*, essentially concurring with Gaius on these points.

> Provincial governors are directed by imperial instructions not to tolerate secret social *collegia* and that soldiers are not to form *collegia* in camp. But the lower orders [*tenuiores*] are allowed to pay a small monthly fee, provided that they meet only once a month, lest an unlawful association be created under this guise. And the deified Severus stated in a rescript that this applies not only at Rome but also in Italy and the provinces. There is, however, no ban on assembly for religious purposes, so long as there is no contravention of the *senatus consultum* which prohibits unlawful *collegia*. It is not permitted to belong to more than one *collegium*, as was laid down by the deified brothers; and if someone belongs to more than one, it is provided by rescript that he must choose the one to which he wishes to adhere and receive from the association which he leaves the share of the common fund which is due to him.[46]

Although Marcian makes the familiar connection between associations, secret societies, and political unrest (as much a literary trope as a legal opinion) and instructs officials to treat groups with circumspection, the presence of associations seems normal. Membership of soldiers in these organizations was suspect, but membership by others, provided they only belonged to one group, fell within accepted norms.

Marcian's use of the phrase *collegia sodalicia* is curious, however, and its translation as "secret social *collegia*" is suggestive. The Latin states that the provincial governors should not allow *collegia sodalicia* to meet, but the phrase did not necessarily imply secret societies. The adjective *sodalicia* denoted any sort of collegial organization. Several texts and inscriptions refer to *collegia sodalicia*, not always with a negative connotation.[47] Other authors used similar terminology to refer to a *collegium* and specifically used *sodales* to describe members of a group without the same secret connotations, as Gaius did above.

The notion of secret or disruptive *collegia* does find support in literary evi-

46. *Dig.* 47.22.1, trans. Watson (1985).

47. For an instructive and thorough treatment of these points, see Liu 2005: 293; see also De Ligt 2001: 355–56. Liu cites specific examples, of which I name only a few: an association of fullers referred to as a *sodalicium fullonum* (*CIL* IX 5450), an association of carpenters and builders referred to as a *sodalicium fabr(orum) tig(nariorum)* (*ILS* 7241), and an association of carpenters that called themselves *sodales carpentarii* (*AE* 1927: 129).

dence. Waltzing was among the first to point out that Marcian's linguistic choice may have been a remnant of or a nod to the strife of the last days of the republic.[48] As Michael Peachin contends, the extent to which the literary tradition influenced the legal writings by the jurists and elite ideas about proper Roman literary pursuits should not be discounted.[49] Marcian's descriptions may not exactly align with a strict legal category applied to any and all *collegia* as a formal constraint to their activities, and defining such a category might not have been his aim. Marcian and the jurists based their judgments on elite ideas of acceptable public decorum and expected adherence to codes of conduct for nonelites. As fellow jurists and members of the elite were likely the main audience of their commentaries, it would make sense to describe nonelite activity in such a way. The prudent advice for governors was not to tolerate sedition or disruptions, whether perpetrated by an association or not.

Marcian, like Gaius and other authors, did assume a link between low status and association membership, which apparently gave the jurists cause for concern and may have led to the injunction that these groups should only meet once each month. The anxiety to which Marcian seems to allude and the allowances made for the lower orders (*tenuiores*) paralleled sentiments expressed in Pliny's correspondence with Trajan. When asked by the people of Amisus for permission to form an association (*eranos*), Pliny granted the request following instructions from Trajan, who assumed that the group would assist members of the lower social orders (*ad sustinendam tenuiorum inopiam utuntur*).[50]

> If the citizens of Amisus, whose petition you send with your letter, are allowed by their own laws, granted them by formal treaty, to form a benefit society [*eranos*] there is no reason why we should interfere: especially if the contributions are not used for riotous and unlawful assemblies, but to relieve cases of hardship among the poor. In all other cities which are subject to our own law these institutions must be forbidden.[51]

As far as Pliny, Trajan, and Marcian were concerned, this type of support was innocuous enough, and the citizens of Amisus had been given the right to follow their own legal statutes. That being said, the correspondence still high-

48. Waltzing 1895–1900, vol. 1: 134.
49. Peachin 2001: 119–20; see also Millar 1992: 94.
50. Pliny, *Ep.* 10.92–93.
51. Pliny, *Ep.* 10.93, trans. Radice (Loeb).

lighted familiar concerns over sedition and unlawful assemblies (*inlicitos coetus*), described using language that echoed, in part, the *lex Irnitana*.

The fact that Marcian and Pliny concentrated on *homines tenuiores* and religious groups has helped establish a link between economic hardship, social exclusion, and association membership. A closer look at Marcian's discussion in light of the papyri and inscriptions suggests that the reality of the situation for jurists, for officials on the ground, and for associations themselves was different. The notion that men of modest means belonged to associations to find financial support and proper burial in return for small monthly contributions, influential though it has been, does not match up with the economic realities of membership.[52] Membership costs were quite high, which likely provided a significant barrier for those who would have needed support.

This is not to say that the jurists were entirely wrong. In the eyes of wealthy Roman officials, most people must have appeared to be men of modest means. Within associations, there also existed a range of economic capacities. Despite assurances of equality and privilege in an association, those that held office in a group and made special contributions on top of their normal payments set themselves apart from their colleagues. Nevertheless, when placed in proper perspective, this should not make us think that ordinary members were any less financially sound. The monthly fees that members of groups paid in Egypt or anywhere else were hardly insignificant.[53] The truly downtrodden *tenuiores* in search of the support and protection that the jurists and Pliny assumed they needed were just as likely to be trod on not only by Roman officials and local elites but also by prominent and wealthy association members.

Licit and Illicit Associations

The jurists also alluded to a distinction between licit and illicit groups in different contexts.[54] Not unlike Marcian's instructions to governors, Ulpian's sixth book of his *On the Duties of the Proconsul* stipulated that "anyone instituting an unlawful association (*illicitum collegium*) will be liable to the penalty imposed upon those found guilty of occupying public places or temples with armed

52. On *collegia funeratica* as a distinct category, see Perry 2006: 23–60.
53. For discussion of this topic based primarily on non-Egyptian evidence, see van Nijf 2002: 307–11; on the term *tenuiores* as those "habitually subject to oppression by *potentiores*," see Garnsey 1970: 222–23.
54. *Dig.* 47.22.1.2

men."[55] Ulpian also reported that an imperial rescript of Septimius Severus called for prosecution of illicit associations before the urban prefect of Rome.[56] The jurist Paulus implied that associations had the right to receive legacies at least from the time of Marcus Aurelius. Paulus did attach one caveat, however: the *collegium* would inherit the legacy provided it was licit. Though legality appears to be an issue here, the affairs of an illicit group do not seem to have been impacted significantly. Paulus merely suggests that if legality were questioned, the association could not receive the inheritance, but the individual members of the group could.

> Given that during the reign of the deified Marcus the senate permitted the making of legacies to *collegia*, there is no doubt that provided the *collegium* is legal, the legacy should be delivered. If, however, the *collegium* is not legal, any legacy made to it will be invalid, unless it was made to the members individually; for in that case, they will be allowed to have the legacy not as a *collegium* but as defined individuals.[57]

Lacking the right of assembly does not seem to have impacted a group's operations significantly. Paulus' proposed solution to the problem of legality, if it was a problem, mitigates the distinction between licit and illicit, as well as the general anxiety felt by the authorities toward these groups.

Scholars still debate whether these discussions, considered with previous references to imperial and senatorial acts, implied an actual legal category or a detailed process to acquire approval, as well as how important that approval was for individual associations to attain.[58] The legal writings themselves do not show consistency, and legality does not appear to have always been a factor for receiving legacies. When considering a hypothetical situation about a bequest of a farm to a *collegium* of craftsmen (*fabri*), Scaevola did not take account of whether a *collegium* was licit or illicit.[59] In these scenarios, the possible sedition caused by associations and the uneasiness supposedly felt by the Roman elite was less the focus than legal relationships and the proper acquisition and management of economic resources. It is hard to tell to what extent not receiving

55. *Dig.* 47.22.2, trans. Watson (1985).
56. *Dig.* 1.12.1.14 (*On the Duties of the Urban Prefect*).
57. *Dig.* 34.5.20 (Paulus, *Plautius* 12), trans. Watson (1985).
58. Crook 1967: 265–66; De Ligt 2001: 349–50; Liu 2009: 97–124.
59. *Dig.* 32.93.4.

whatever passed as proper approval impeded the day-to-day operations of associations in the case of inheritances.

Gaius made no distinction between licit or illicit when discussing how the provincial edict dealt with associations, but he did suggest that groups should not be allowed to proliferate randomly.

> Partnerships, *collegia*, and bodies of this sort may not be formed by everybody at will; for this right is restricted by statutes, *senatus consulta*, and imperial *constitutiones*. In a few cases only are bodies of this sort permitted. For example, partners in tax farming, gold mines, silver mines, and salt works are allowed to form corporations (*corpora*). Likewise, there are certain *collegia* at Rome whose corporate status has been established by *senatus consulta* and imperial *constitutiones*, for example, those of the bakers and certain others and of the shipowners, who are found in the provinces too.[60]

Even with his caveat that associations cannot simply be formed by anyone, anywhere, and at any time, Gaius seems inclusive in terms of groups that could constitute themselves as associations. Public utility is the common theme for the groups he approves, particularly those associated with production and maintenance of the food supply. The way in which Gaius has framed his remarks suggests that Roman authorities had an interest in associations not necessarily because they were hotbeds of sedition but because many groups found themselves working for local and imperial authorities to provide necessary goods and services. The jurists and the evolving body of legal codes and commentaries were concerned with the structure of the relationships witnessed in the papyri and inscriptions as much as, if not more than, proper behavior.

Gaius does suggest that both the senate and emperors had set some sort of parameters for forming associations. In addition, references that Suetonius, Ulpian, Paulus, and Marcian make to acts of the senate or imperial decisions indicate attempts to monitor associations or demonstrate their opinion that attempts should have been made. Evidence of the actual legislation is often indirect, however, and the sources do not detail protocols for seeking or granting approval or rule enforcement.

Besides the literary sources and the jurists, a number of inscriptions authored by associations refer to their right to gather as a group in accordance

60. *Dig.* 3.4.1, trans. Watson (1985).

with some sort of senatorial or imperial approval. Groups asserted their rights in a variety of contexts: association charters, honorific inscriptions, dedications, and a catalog of donations and benefits given to a specific group. In all, Liu tabulated twenty-four inscriptions that mention some sort of approval and were authored by twenty-three different associations, including *centonarii* at Hispalis,[61] shipbuilders at Ostia,[62] and grain measurers at Rome.[63] Each of these inscriptions dates to the second and third centuries (save for one that can only be dated to sometime after 27 BCE, *CIL* V 2193).[64]

The association devoted to Diana and Antinous from Lanuvium is counted among this number. This group referred to previous senatorial actions in their charter, erected in the local temple associated with the cult of Antinous. After recording the endowment made by their patron Rufus, the association quoted or paraphrased a portion of a *senatus consultum,* which survives in a fragmentary portion of the charter.

> Clause from the decree of the Senate of the Roman People: These are permitted to assemble, convene, and have an association [*collegium*]: those who desire to make monthly contributions . . . may assemble in such an association, but . . . not . . . in the name of such an association except once a month for the sake of . . . , to provide burial for them when they die.[65]

Two third-century groups, an association of *dendrophori* at Rome and a group of fullers at Ostia, described themselves, using similar language, as having the right of assembly according to a *senatus consultum*: the *dendrophori* did so in a record of donations to the group, the fullers in what might be a membership list.[66] A third group, an association of *fabri tignarii,* made the same assertion in a dedication of uncertain date.[67]

How closely any group followed these instructions, what a mention of a decree might have implied for these groups, or what the impact was in economic or legal terms can be debated. The association of Diana and Antinous, for instance, would seem to have gone against the senatorial instructions it

61. *CIL* II 1167; *AE* 1987: 496 (145–61 CE).
62. *CIL* XIV 168–69 (195 CE).
63. *CIL* VI 85 (198 CE).
64. Liu 2009: 103–5.
65. *CIL* XIV 2112 = *ILS* 7212 (136 CE), lines 10–15, trans. Ascough, Harland, and Kloppenborg (2012).
66. *CIL* VI 29691 (206 CE), XIV 4573 (232 CE).
67. *AE* 1963: 17.

cited, by meeting more than once a month. The group listed two meetings in the month of August in its charter's calendar of celebrations: on August 13 to commemorate the anniversary of the association, and on August 20 to commemorate the brother of their patron Caesenius Rufus. Luuk de Ligt noted three other associations with meetings that would violate this provision.[68]

Assurances that the senate's instructions would be followed might not have been the reason to include a mention of approval in a charter or a public dedication. Liu has maintained that such statements amount to a group's assertion of its own "validation" in the eyes of the public. The extent to which these claims by individual groups reveal attempts at control from the authorities remains unclear, and the lack of similar statements from Egypt and the East is a complicating factor. The proliferation and presence of associations throughout the Mediterranean suggests that the impact of imperial decisions or senatorial legislation referred to by associations and even by the jurists themselves was less than sweeping.

A reference to senate regulations and imperial decrees pertaining to "approval" of groups may be less about legalities, although Liu is right to caution that this might have been a concern. Instead, including such language in texts, inscriptions, and monuments provided associations an opportunity for image crafting and social performance, akin to associations signaling ties to patrons and members of the local elite or aligning themselves with temples and religious cults in Roman Egypt. In defining themselves in this manner, associations seem to have co-opted Roman legal discourse in their own writings and public monuments. By making these statements, associations attempted to assert an "ancient" privilege, based on the approval they claim to have enjoyed and on their subsequent adherence to a senatorial action taken more than a century earlier, if they were referring to the *senatus consultum* or to the criteria Suetonius claims Augustus established for groups: that they must be *legitima et antiqua*. Ultimately, it seems that associations, not the authorities, were the ones taking an active interest in such definitions, which suggests that the people for whom these categories were meaningful were the craftsmen and merchants themselves. Adopting this public persona in its inscriptions enabled a group to distinguish itself from others and present its membership as reputable and trusted in another way besides trumpeting ties with influential members of the local community. In a sense, claims by these groups might have been less about

68. De Ligt 2000: 250; *CIL* VI 10234, VI 33885, X 444.

Roman oversight and any legal approval they gained and more about jockeying for position in competition with other groups at the local level.

Of course, certain associations might have actually sought and received some sort of approval or recognition from the authorities. Many groups in the west clearly felt that making a public statement to that effect mattered in terms of the image they projected. Influential groups may have procured letters from the emperor or officials and used these in a legal context or displayed them on public monuments. Two letters from emperors and addressed to associations of *navicularii*, for instance, were included in the Theodosian Code. Copies of the letters may have been preserved in imperial archives where the code's compilers found them. A letter issued under Constantine's name and addressed to the *navicularii* of the Orient rewarded those engaged in trade with immunity from service on councils and guardianship and extended privileges regarding inheritance.[69] Another letter addressed to an association of *navicularii* confirmed the privileges bestowed on them previously, including equestrian rank and immunity from service on local councils.

> We confirm the rank of the equestrian order that was conferred upon you by the sainted Constantine and Julian, eternal Emperors. Since this is so, if any person should dare to assail you with bodily injury, in violation of the interdicts of innumerable sanctions, he shall atone for the daring of this monstrous crime by a fitting expiation, and his office staff also shall be condemned to the supreme penalty, since it is the duty of the office staff, by their admonition and by their timely advice, to sustain the service of leading away from illicit actions judges who are perhaps aroused by vicious indignation.[70]

Letters like these were certainly valuable commodities. Individuals and groups copied such letters, kept them for reference, and used them when protection from state officials was necessary, as well as to ensure continued enjoyment of or to procure new privileges. The *navicularii* might have used the previously quoted letter to vindicate themselves against other groups that attempted to attach themselves to shipping associations by "misuse" of their name in order to obtain immunities, as the text describes.[71]

Influential individuals could boast of letters from the emperor with similar

69. *C.Th.* 13.5.7 (334 CE).
70. *C.Th.* 13.5.16 (380 CE), trans. Pharr (1952).
71. *C.Th.* 13.5.16.2 (380 CE).

effect.[72] A wealthy merchant from Ephesos named Lucius Erastus received a letter from Hadrian supporting Erastus' efforts to join the local council. Hadrian even offered to pay Erastus' entry fees.[73] The letter cites Erastus' "usefulness" (*chrēsimos*) to his country, using familiar terminology; but perhaps his greatest accomplishment and best career move was sailing with the emperor himself on two occasions.[74] Hadrian's attempts to gain a seat for Erastus on the Ephesian council may have met with local resistance, as both Pleket and van Nijf suggested.[75] Nevertheless, that the letter was inscribed on the marble facing of the council chamber signals that Erastus gained a council seat and was able to put his relationship with the emperor on display for others to see. As Carlos Noreña has maintained, such letters and, more importantly, the public reading or memorializing allowed recipients to lay claim to a type of social capital stemming from the trust and esteem with which the emperor viewed a particular individual or group.[76]

Not all associations could expect the same level of privileges or recognition as that enjoyed by the shipping associations or by influential individuals like Erastus. The spice merchants or glass makers of Oxyrhynchus and their leaders probably did not transact business or keep company with governors or prefects of the grain supply, as the leading members of shipping associations had done.[77] Associations that had gained some sort of imperial approval or attempted to assert that they had might be the exceptional cases and not necessarily the norm, although the state of the evidence on both sides of the debate makes it hard to be certain.

Associations and Provincial Governors

Pliny and the Firemen in Bithynia

It is difficult to measure to what extent the writings of the jurists, regulations in municipal charters, or concerns expressed by the likes of Cicero or Tacitus

72. On imperial letters, see Millar 1992: 469–72.
73. *I.Eph.* 1487 (128/9 CE). For a similar text of another merchant who was involved in shipping and had Hadrian's support in seeking a seat on the council, see *I.Eph.* 1488 (128/9 CE).
74. *I.Eph.* 1487, lines 9–11.
75. On this text, see Pleket 1984: 10; van Nijf 1997: 22.
76. Noreña 2007: 261.
77. For connections between a prefect of the *annona* (one who would later become prefect of Egypt in 203 CE) and associations, see *IG* XIV 917 (198–203 CE); *CIL* III 14165. On these texts, see Sirks 1991: 98, 103.

guided the actions of governors and local officials. Examples of governors getting involved in the affairs of associations offer an opportunity to assess how Roman officials dealt with the problems and legal questions described in both literary and documentary sources. Although general guidelines existed, each official could innovate and use a relatively free hand to deal with issues. Governors were essentially left to decide how to interpret and apply juristic discussions and legal statutes to situations that they confronted. This aspect of Roman rule allows for some variation in each situation and from governor to governor, which complicates attempts to find a single policy that was actually enforced.

The way in which Pliny handled associations during his term as proconsular governor of Bithynia-Pontus, as reported in his *Epistles,* details variations in approach.[78] On two occasions, Pliny referred questions about collegial organizations to the emperor. The request of a group in Amisus to organize themselves as an association ostensibly to support their colleagues, perceived to be among the poorer members of society, was granted, although with some caveats.[79] But Trajan denied Pliny's request to establish a *collegium* to serve as a fire brigade in Nicomedia.[80]

A fire that destroyed a number of public buildings prompted Pliny's query regarding the fire brigade. Not only were associations of craftsmen common, but some tended to provide these services.[81] Pliny seems surprised not to have found such an organization filling that need in Nicomedia. In his proposal for Trajan's consideration, Pliny implied that an association would be the way to move forward, but, anticipating apprehensions, he assured the emperor that the group would be small and therefore easily monitored. Given the ubiquitous nature of these groups and the public utility involved in their work, Trajan's concerns for sedition and unrest seem all the more interesting. The emperor's response, as Pliny reports it, admits that his decision not to approve Pliny's plan may actually go against expected norms.

> You may very well have had the idea that it should be possible to form a company of firemen [*collegium fabrorum*] at Nicomedia on the model of those existing elsewhere, but we must remember that it is societies like these which have been responsible for the political disturbances in your province, particularly in

78. On Pliny as governor and on his correspondence with Trajan, see Sherwin-White 1962; Woolf 2006; Noreña 2007; Gibson and Morello 2012: 251–59.
79. Pliny, *Ep.* 10.33–34.
80. Pliny, *Ep.* 10.92–93.
81. For *centonarii,* see Waltzing 1895–1900, vol. 2: 193–97; vol. 4: 78. See also Liu 2009: 126–60.

> its towns. If people assemble for a common purpose, whatever name we give them and for whatever reason, they soon turn into a political club. It is a better policy then to provide the equipment necessary for dealing with fires, and to instruct property owners to make use of it, calling on the help of the crowds which collect if they find it necessary.[82]

The correspondence suggests that Trajan's decision and the course of action that Pliny should take as governor had a great deal to do with the circumstances in the province and in that specific community. Pliny had been dispatched, we are told, to deal with a province perceived to be in some disorder: he complained of disarray in public accounts, dilapidated buildings, unfinished aqueducts, and fears of corruption. The province of Bithynia had perhaps also gained a reputation for unrest, as detailed in the writings of Dio Chrysostom. On a literary level, of course, all this provided Pliny with ample material to portray himself as the ideal provincial governor, one with especially close ties to the emperor.[83] As a result, although Pliny's implementation of Trajan's decision seems in line with some of the jurists' considerations, it probably should not be taken as an example of a universal policy.

Flaccus and Alexandria

Decades before Pliny and Trajan discussed associations, Aulus Avilius Flaccus took a stand against groups in Alexandria, as Egypt's prefect (32–38 CE).[84] Philo claims that upon assuming his post, Flaccus preemptively disbanded the *sunodoi* and *hetaireiai*—notorious hives of drunkenness, sedition, and villainy, as far as Philo was concerned.

> He judged important cases with the help of those in authority, humbled the arrogant and prevented any motley promiscuous horde of people from combining in opposition. The sodalities and clubs, which were constantly holding feasts under pretext of sacrifice in which drunkenness vented itself in political intrigue, he dissolved and dealt sternly and vigorously with the refractory.[85]

---

82. Pliny, *Ep.* 10.34, trans. Radice (Loeb).
83. This is pointed out in Sherwin-White 1966; see Dio Chrysostom, *Or.* 46.5–6, 11–13, for the story of a bread riot; for Dio on factions and the influence of groups, see *Or.* 45.7–10, 50.3.
84. On Flaccus and his time in Alexandria, see Alston 1997; Harker 2008.
85. Philo, *In Flaccum* 4, trans. Colson (Loeb).

Philo's use of the word *prophasis* (pretext) to characterize association religious activities emphasized his own incredulity about the actual nature of their activities, as well as his disdain for them. On this point concerning associations—and perhaps on this point alone, given the remainder of the account of Flaccus' time as prefect—Philo and Flaccus were in seeming agreement.

Philo's characterization of these groups may be quite familiar, and others doubtless shared his views; nevertheless, associations had been active for some time in and around Alexandria. Dedications reveal association-related honorific activity during the time of Augustus. A spice merchant serving as an official of a *sunodos*, for example, dedicated a statue to his association, according to the fragmentary inscription on the base.[86] An association dedicated to the emperor passed a decree awarding a member honors, titles, and extra portions at banquets.[87] It appears that the same association also provided a source of credit to its members, like groups found elsewhere.[88] There are even indications of women's associations.[89] Evidence shows that groups had been active in the Delta region prior to Roman rule, revealing that although Flaccus found associations suspect, they had already established themselves in Alexandria and surrounding communities.[90] It is therefore not surprising to see that Flaccus' decision seems to have had little impact. Papyri and inscriptions reveal that despite Flaccus' efforts to curb associations, their activities continued.[91] A dedication by a *sunodos* that is potentially from Alexandria and dates soon after Flaccus' time in Egypt suggests that any ban was fleeting.[92] All the evidence of associations from Tebtunis contained in Kronion's archive and throughout the Fayum tells a similar story. Associations had been and remained integral parts of the social, political, religious, and economic fabric of Egyptian communities.

That Flaccus was a governor famous for his failure should make us shrink from taking his actions to restrict associations as an illustration of normative practice, in a different way than the caution with which Pliny should be approached. Misunderstanding, mistranslation, and the importance of local

86. *I.Alex.Imp.* 96 (30 BCE–14 CE). See also *I.Alex.Imp.* 93 (14–15 CE), a dedication by a the former *prostatēs* of a *sunodos* to the members of the group; *I.Alex.Imp.* 97 (7 CE), a dedication of a statue from a *plēthos* of physicians; *IGR* I 1320 (24 CE), a dedication on a base that held a statue of a deity or perhaps a patron.

87. *SB* XXII 15460 (5 BCE).

88. *BGU* IV 1137 (6 BCE).

89. *I.Alex.Imp.* 70 (early I CE).

90. *I.Delta* I 446 (67 and 64 BCE).

91. Arnaoutoglou 2005 provides a catalog.

92. *IGR* I 1086 (40/41 CE).

knowledge shines through especially in the example of Flaccus. Moreover, Flaccus' handling of these organizations stands as an example of how not to govern. When he chose to disband associations, Flaccus did more than ignore what seems to have been prevailing custom in Alexandria and the rest of Egypt, as Philo makes clear.

Philo concludes his account of Flaccus' time in Egypt by pointing out two people in particular who helped mount the growing opposition against him. The first was a wealthy member of the community and a former gymnasiarch named Lampon; the other was a man named Isidorus, who Philo claims held sway with the associations—the very organizations that Flaccus had taken action against.[93] Flaccus' actions against associations damaged relationships with influential constituencies and the people that governors would have relied on to help govern—members of the local elite and, apparently, those with ties with associations, like Isidorus and Lampon. As one part of Flaccus' handling of different interest groups in Alexandria, his policies on associations betrays a failure to understand what others apparently had known: the place of associations and the important role they played in communities.

Stasis and the Bakers in Ephesos

The proconsul of Asia employed a different approach when called on to intervene in a riot that the Ephesian bakers caused in the second century. The proconsul's resolution of the disruption has been preserved as a lengthy, if somewhat fragmentary, inscription that receives frequent comment.

> And according to an agreement . . . thus it comes about at times that the people are plunged into disorder and tumults because of the meeting and insolence of the bakers in the market place, for which they ought to have been arrested and put on trial already. Since however it is necessary to consider the city's welfare more than the punishment of these men, I have resolved that it is necessary to bring them to their senses by an edict. I therefore order the bakers not to hold meetings as a faction nor to be leaders in recklessness, but strictly to obey the regulations made on behalf of the general welfare and to supply the city unfailingly with the labor essential for bread making. When from this time forward

93. Philo, *In Flaccum* 125–40.

> any one of them shall be caught in the act of attending a meeting contrary to orders, or of starting any tumult and *stasis,* he shall be arrested and shall be punished with the fitting penalty. And should anyone plot against the city dare to conceal himself, he shall in addition have *decuria* marked on his foot, and the receiver of such a man shall be liable to the same penalty.[94]

This example of a provincial official's interaction with local craft and merchant groups proves instructive for modeling the relations between imperial and local authorities and associations. The inscription does not indicate the particulars of the disturbance or the bakers' reasons. It seems safe to say that the potential work stoppage and the "disorder [*tarachos*] and tumult [*thorubous*]" that the bakers caused threatened economic activities in the marketplace. Unlike the Ephesian silversmiths' occupation of the theater, this disturbance (though described in similar terms) had been referred to the Romans. Prior to this moment, however, the authorities had not imposed any restrictions on this group of bakers.

Inscriptions from Ephesos attest to the integration of bakers into the local community. Some leading bakers had even attained positions on local councils or other bodies in Ephesos and elsewhere.[95] Various associations commemorated ties with influential members of the local and imperial elite. In the second century, the merchants and wool workers honored Vedius Antoninus, a former prytanis, gymnasiarch, and asiarch.[96] Bakers elsewhere in Asia Minor were also active in the marketplace and maintained connections with officeholders.[97] Additionally, many groups of craftsmen and merchants had been granted assigned places (*topoi*) in Ephesos, denoting a certain level of acknowledgment and acceptance of groups on the part of the authorities.[98]

What brought the Ephesian group to the attention of the local authorities and, eventually, the proconsul and Roman authorities was not that they had assembled as an association but that they had caused a disturbance. The way in which the disturbance was handled by the authorities is interesting. Though the

---

94. *I.Eph.* 215 (II CE), with *SEG* XXVIII 863, trans. Buckler (1923: 30–31, adapted). On this text, see Buckler 1923: 30–33.
95. *SEG* XXXVII 1309 = *MAMA* III 756; see van Nijf 1997: 21–22. See also Pleket 1984.
96. *I.Eph.* 727–28 (160–69 CE); see also 3075 (150 CE). For discussion of the Vedii Antonini and their relationship not only with associations but also with Ephesos as a whole, see Kalinowski 2002.
97. *TAM* V 966 (late II CE).
98. *I.Eph.* 444–45 (III CE), 547 (undated), 549 (undated); see also 2076–82 (III CE).

proconsul did not describe what had taken place as *stasis*, he assured them that future disruptions would be considered as such. The proconsul's choice to invoke *stasis*, a loaded term with a charged literary history, seems provocative. The silversmiths in Acts were cautioned not to be accused of *stasis*. Few other inscriptions attest to using *stasis* to describe some sort of civil disturbance, whether perpetrated by associations or anyone else.

Either the prefect of Egypt in 62 CE, Lucius Iulius Vestinus, or the scribe recording the relevant proceedings used similar terminology to describe the actions of the head of a weavers' association in Oxyrhynchus and two of his colleagues. Although the fragmentary nature of the text obscures some of the particulars, it appears that Sarapion, the *prostatēs* of the weavers' *plēthos*, and his associates have been accused of wrongdoing.

> Lucius Iulius Vestinus says: Sarapion son of Diogenes from the metropolis of the Oxyrhynchite (Nome), who is said to be the president of the guild of weavers and to have made exactions, having been summoned . . . with whom he is bringing [?] his associates contrary to [?] . . .–phris and Onnoprei[s] [?] . . . having been named as dissidents [*stasiodeis*] and the accomplices of Sarapion . . . I proclaim a fine and I allow it to stand [?], and if they fail to take notice in any respect I will employ the appropriate punishment against them.[99]

Although this text does not refer to a riot, the adjective describing the weavers, *stasiodeis*, implies that they had caused disorder in Oxyrhynchus that was brought to the prefect's attention. This is a reminder that *stasis* refers not only to violence but, perhaps more often, to factional strife in general, as Christina Kokkinia maintained.[100] Given the reference to "exactions," perhaps this case implies fiscal indiscretion. On a number of occasions, prefects issued edicts protecting people from the stereotypical rapacious tax collector, and it appears that the weavers may have gone too far in this case and invited the scorn of Vestinus, who fined them. In this context, *stasis* refers to unlawful activity, seditious in the sense that it goes against the wishes of the prefect and previously published edicts, though not necessarily a public disturbance.

Whatever the problem, Sarapion and his colleagues in the weavers' associa-

99. *P.Oxy.* LXXVI 5097 (62 CE), trans. Bowman.
100. Kokkinia 2004: 46–48.

tion from Oxyrhynchus appear to have been handled in a moderate manner, with fines and threats of future punishments. Although the actions of the Ephesian bakers presented a threat to the food supply, the proconsul also dealt with them moderately, at least in comparison to the hefty fines outlined in the *lex Irnitana* for occupying public places or to the penalty of five hundred drachmas suggested in the *Gnomon of the Idios Logos*. The proconsul and the local councilors apparently sought not to punish but to restore order. Like Vestinus, the proconsul threatened the bakers with arrest and trial for subsequent disruptions but did not dissolve their association, as may have been expected based on advice supplied by the jurists. The proconsul's claim that the bakers should have been put on trial allows him to display his magnanimity. He admonished the bakers to refrain from disruptive behavior in the future and not to hold any meetings that could be construed as seditious or to incite riots.

Belonging to an association of weavers in first-century Oxyrhynchus or an association of bakers in second-century Ephesos did not constitute illegal activity that caught authorities' attention. The authorities would notice an association of weavers or bakers that abused others while collecting taxes, committed acts of violence, or endangered the food supply, but taking disruptions and civil disobedience seriously on the part of local, provincial, or imperial officials does not imply a policy intended to restrict or ban associations indiscriminately. *Stasis* was not necessarily the natural state of associations, although groups (like the weavers in Oxyrhynchus) who participated in *stasis* and were described as *stasiodeis* could become disruptive.

Association activities were orientated outward toward the community too, whether they were completing construction projects and contracts or participating in honorific exchange. Craft and merchant associations were not unaware of this. It follows, then, that associations conscious of the element of social performance and reputation management in their actions would not have lightly made decisions to stage protests and cause unrest. Rather, a protest (big or small) might be better understood as a strategic social performance of its own, with its own rules and designated roles for people to play, and was not always a haphazard situation. In the cases of the bakers or the smiths, who seem to have played their roles quite well and to have leveraged a position of some strength and influence, the resolution of the protest confirmed and recognized their position in the community.

Conclusions

Evidence provided by papyri, inscriptions, and legal sources makes it hard to postulate that a uniform (and lasting) policy restricting association activities existed at the local, provincial, or imperial levels. The extent to which the existence of associations and *collegia* in Rome and throughout the empire required approval should continue to be debated. The role that the jurists of the second and third centuries have in that debate, as well as the correspondence between their discussions and communities' reality as observed in the documentary record, should also be questioned. Some jurists' concern with licit and illicit associations as distinct legal categories may be a legal and scholarly fiction. If nothing else, the distinction may have been invested with more meaning and importance by modern scholars than the average official or association member would have ascribed to it. Peachin suggests that even the jurists themselves probably envisioned the task on which they had embarked as being not only a legal exercise but a literary one; their intended audience included other jurists and members of the Roman elite for whom legal writing remained one of the proper literary pursuits.[101] As such, exclusive reliance on juristic commentaries may not help further our understanding of associations and their interactions with the authorities. Inscriptions, papyri, and even legal texts indicate that associations, craftsmen, and merchants concerned themselves with matters other than legal approval. Chief among those matters was establishing a reputation, forging meaningful connections with local and imperial elites, and accumulating social capital.

When determination of an association's status as licit or illicit and of the subversive nature of these groups becomes foundational for understanding their activities, it colors subsequent interpretation and creates a conflict that may not have been so pronounced between these groups and the authorities. Even an authority on elite attitudes such as Cicero, who condemned Clodius for his attachment to *collegia* at Rome, found much to recommend associations when they supported him.[102] Disruptions like that caused by the bakers in Ephesos or crackdowns like that initiated by Flaccus may not reflect normal practice. Examples of officials interacting with groups in different contexts point to the case-by-case approach they likely relied on with respect to associations.

101. Peachin 2011: 119–20.
102. Cicero, *De domo sua* 74.

To say that the imperial authorities were completely disinterested in the activities of associations is perhaps not quite accurate either. The discussion of government restrictions on associations that is outlined in the juristic writings cannot be entirely discounted or ignored, but it is only part of the story. The jurists reveal the complexities involved in relationships between associations and the authorities and also indicate the rights and privileges that groups had accumulated during the second and third centuries. The right of associations to possess common property (including slaves) and treasuries, inherit legacies, and have legal representation when needed are all specified in the writings of Gaius, Marcian, and others. It would seem, then, that the jurists discuss common practices among associations and, in effect, reflect the formalization of their organization and activities that is well illustrated by charters and other texts.

None of this means that the authorities had to listen to the cases made by the groups. Nor would the right to representation or an apparent lack of strict control over associations preclude local, senatorial, or imperial action with or without cause. Both going before the council and filing a petition entailed some risk. What determined the outcome in these situations was not strictly noted in any law or set of juristic writings. An association's influence and reputation and the social capital wielded by the group's representation or patrons probably determined who carried the day in disputes with the authorities, other associations, or unaffiliated individuals. In this sense, the reputation, esteem, and trust that associations enjoyed or lacked in a community and in the eyes of those charged with weighing in on a dispute impacted authorities' decisions and probably factored into associations' own strategic decisions as much as their understanding of formal legal constraints.

Above all, the jurists seem to accept associations as common features of communities, which might have prompted imperial officials to consider discussions of the phenomenon. Concern over associations and the actions taken by the authorities stemmed from the officials' overriding preoccupation with maintaining order, preserving public services, assuring tax collection, and meeting imperial needs. Good and effective Roman officials maintained order and established order when lacking. This certainly is the advice detailed in works such as Ulpian's *On the Duties of the Proconsul.* As sources of potential unrest and sedition, associations factored into the thinking of officials at Rome and in the provinces. Though this attention may imply a suspicion of these groups, it does not mean that officials followed Flaccus' example and imposed unilateral bans on associations as a matter of policy.

The negative view of associations, craftsmen, and merchants expressed in literature and reflected in juristic sources represented an informal constraint, but one that did not translate into limitations on their formation, their activities, or their proliferation throughout the Mediterranean. Likewise, formal restrictions on associations (the sort alluded to by the jurists or specified in municipal charters, reported in the literary sources, or occasionally referred to by associations themselves) may have had little sustained impact on association operations. The punishments, fines, and restrictions reported may very well have been only temporary measures; some, such as the restrictions Flaccus imposed, do not seem to have been applied or enforced evenly throughout Egypt itself. Associations had a strong presence in Asia Minor before the disruption caused by the bakers in Ephesos, and associations continued to be a prominent part of social and economic life afterward.

As Flaccus' actions and the situation in Alexandria revealed, completely hindering associations may not have made for good economic or legal policies. Instead of fear and anxiety, perhaps it is better to characterize the Roman policy toward associations as one of circumspect cooperation and collaboration—which may have been what groups expected. Anxieties remained, evidenced not only by the literary texts but by a juristic discussion that stretched over several centuries. Necessity and a lack of other alternatives ultimately promoted common interests between the imperial authorities, local officials, and associations.

CHAPTER 6

Associations in Late Roman Egypt

Halfway through the sixth century, Aphrodito, a rather large village in the Antaeopolite nome, became embroiled in a tax dispute. The village (or perhaps the leading members of one faction who acted on the village's behalf) contended that Aphrodito retained the right of *autopragia*—the privilege to collect its own taxes free from official interference, one that certain imperial officials in their nome had apparently been very good at disregarding. When other avenues failed to reach a satisfactory resolution, the village petitioned the emperor Justinian's wife, Theodora.[1] The petition was signed by fifty-one individuals—all presumably stakeholders in the community, with a keen interest in its tax status. In addition to the village's landowners and ecclesiastical officials, whose presence in the petition is not surprising, a wine merchant and the *kephalaiōtai* of six associations (wine merchants, shipbuilders, bronzesmiths, carpenters, weavers, and an unknown group) signed the petition. That association officials were included in the petition suggests that these men and their organizations enjoyed some level of trust and esteem in Aphrodito. Whether or not including association officials meant anything to Empress Theodora, it clearly mattered to some in the community and to the faction that authored the petition.

Their presence in the petition also suggests inclusion in a community, perhaps not unlike designated seats or allowances by local elites for associations to erect honorific statues and decrees in public places at an earlier time. Not only were associations a part of the community, but they were also part of a strategic attempt by the local landowners to present Aphrodito's case to the highest au-

1. *P.Cair.Masp.* III 67283 (547 CE).

thorities. As Klaas Worp pointed out in his analysis of occurrences of the terms *koinon* and *sunodos* during the late Roman period, there were many groups throughout Egypt for communities to lean on when possible and appropriate.[2]

A petition such as *P.Cair.Masp.* III 67283, combined with the other evidence of association activities during the fourth through seventh centuries, reflects a social, political, and economic reality at the local level that is sometimes not as readily recoverable from the legal codes on whose authority much of the social and economic history of late Roman associations has been written. The law codes paint a bleak picture of life led by craftsmen, merchants, and association members. The standard narrative for associations and their members during the late Roman period has been one of compulsion and control. In the wake of Diocletian's reforms, associations, craftsmen, and merchants supposedly suffered under increased intrusion into the social and economic lives of the taxpaying public, as manifested in the constraints documented by the late Roman legal codes. The codes seemingly describe a government focused on controlling the population's social and economic activities. Repeated entries in the codes reflect attempts to control mobility, social or otherwise, of people at all levels of society, which created what A. H. M. Jones once described as a "late Roman caste system," though one he believed was easily circumvented.[3]

It has been assumed that the authorities took steps to monitor the activities of craftsmen and merchants and to limit their geographic movement and social mobility, to ensure that certain trades had sufficient numbers to provide services and to facilitate collection of the trade tax (*chrysargyron* or *collatio lustralis*) instituted by Constantine and assessed every five years. The authority to impose this level of control ultimately appears to have derived from the various laws and edicts collected in the legal codes, although Alföldy would place it as early as the reign of Septimius Severus.[4] The laws and imperial decisions preserved in the Theodosian Code do refer to various restrictions imposed on association activities and individual craftsmen or merchants: all merchants and all men engaged in business were ordered to pay specific taxes (*C.Th.* 13.1.9); association members were ordered to be "dragged back" to cities to fulfill their obligations (14.7.1); and craftsmen in imperial workshops worked under specific restrictions (10.20.6). These entries, when read in light of the supposed universal application of the law codes and in the context of the low regard and

2. Worp 2012.
3. Jones 1974a; see also Sirks 1993: 159–60.
4. Alföldy 2011: 243–44.

mistrust for craftsmen and merchants, can imply that the government exercised control over economic activities and social movements in all sectors of the society and economy, on a different scale than during previous centuries.

Although this view is based largely (if not entirely) on the Theodosian Code, it is a selective reading of a set of material that it would be an understatement to call complicated. The Theodosian Code is a vast collection. The individual laws present themselves as authoritative pronouncements to be applied throughout the empire. Such application certainly was the aim of Theodosius and the compilers. But the laws also show themselves to be germane to a specific time and place and to particular questions of law and legal interpretation and to have been issued to resolve cases that could not be remedied through normal channels of dispute settlement or petition locally. As such, the law codes preserve the exceptional legal cases and questions brought to the attention of the authorities by people with enough economic or political standing and capital to have their cases heard.

Yet that is not all the codes say, nor is the restricted and limited image of craft and merchant activities borne out uniformly by the documentary record. Craftsmen, merchants, and association members continued to receive benefits from and maintained relationships with the local and imperial authorities. Special privileges enjoyed by segments of the craftsman and merchant population were confirmed by the central authorities and reiterated in the codes, which allude to a more complex relationship between associations and the local and imperial elites than is often assumed for the late Roman period. Reading papyri alongside legal texts in particular complicates what appear to be straightforward readings of the initial aims, enforcement, and application of the laws at local levels. Evidence suggests that associations remained influential in their communities in economic and political terms as well. In addition to Aphrodito's petition, tax registers and accounts document the substantial payments that some associations made, which at least provide another indication of the groups' relative economic standing in their communities. Other papyri point toward not increasing control but continued cooperation between associations and the local and imperial authorities. Beyond questioning the degree to which association membership was controlled by the imperial authorities, the papyri also reveal how associations operated and regulated themselves at the village and metropolitan levels. Law and the directives of the central authorities did not override but complemented, strengthened, and granted legitimacy to associations and their operations on the local level, including their own coercive actions.

Associations and the Legal Codes

The compilers of the Theodosian Code and the Corpus Iuris Civilis aimed at producing comprehensive, critical, and authoritative works that would address a host of issues facing the imperial administration during the fifth and sixth centuries. As Theodosius II laid out in the legislation describing the project and confirming the code, he aimed at collecting general imperial legislation (*constitutiones*) dating back to Constantine: the constitutions said to "rest upon the force of edicts or sacred imperial law of general force,"[5] described further as "all the edictal and general constitutions that have been ordered to be valid or to be posted in definite provinces or districts."[6] What Theodosius' editors included and excluded based on the criteria of *generalitas*, how the compilers interpreted *generalitas*, and the implications of their decisions for interpreting the law code has generated substantial debate. John N. Dillon, following John Matthews, claimed that the editors excluded private rescripts at the emperor's instruction but did aim at inclusion over exclusion, even of perceived obsolete and contradictory laws.[7] With respect to the *generalitas* ascribed to the individual laws collected, Matthews has cautioned us not to "fall victim to a simple logical fallacy" that equates generality with universality. Instead, Matthews asserted that the general nature of the laws included should be viewed as "enactments on specific subjects, large or small, *to be obeyed in all relevant circumstances.*"[8] Even with this interpretation of Theodosius' aims, Matthews would advise that we approach the code with circumspection.

The law code that resulted from the editorial process presents a number of issues, then, for those using the code to uncover the history of associations, their relationships with the imperial authorities, and what this information reveals about the activities of associations in their own communities. Among the legislation about ranks and privileges, taxation, liability for civic obligations, council membership, and economic concerns, which dominates the Theodosian Code, the editors included many laws that pertained to associations (*collegia* or *corpora*), their membership, and their activities. It is difficult, however, to ascertain a clearly articulated policy on associations from the varied and at

5. *C.Th.* 1.1.5 (429 CE), trans. Pharr (1952). On the editorial process, see Matthews 2000: 55–84; on *constitutiones,* Harries 1999: 19–26.
6. *C.Th.* 1.1.6 pr. (435 CE), trans. Pharr (1952).
7. Dillon 2012: 21–27.
8. Matthews 2000: 70 (italics in the original).

times contradictory responses relating to issues in far-flung parts of the empire. As described in fourth-century legislation, some groups of craftsmen and merchants known to have organized themselves as associations—including carpenters, goldsmiths and silversmiths, purple dyers, glass workers, and fullers–enjoyed privileges and exemptions from public obligations.[9] Detailed responses to questions about the obligations and privileges of the merchant shipowners (*navicularii*), many affiliated with associations based in their ports of call, indicate how legal regulations could encourage commercial enterprises, especially when their endeavors benefited the imperial treasury.[10]

Even some of these responses, however, refer to issues relevant at specific times and places and concern specific groups. A law dated to 324 CE, for instance, deals not necessarily with all groups of *navicularii* but with those arriving from Spain, although the compilers of the Theodosian Code may have assumed applicability in all similar scenarios.[11]

> If the ship of any shipmaster enter the port of the City of Rome from any shore of Spain whatsoever, provided this ship should carry a fiscal cargo, We command that the aforesaid ship shall depart without any claim by any person. It shall not be subject to any extraordinary burden, and thus it may more easily fulfill the services enjoined upon it.[12]

Associations of *navicularii* had been active in Spain (and throughout the Mediterranean), and the issues faced by this group likely would have been encountered elsewhere. The need to clarify privileges suggests that questions persisted and that tensions may have remained between local and imperial agents on the ground, even if the imperial authorities sought to facilitate their activities.

The codes do reference restrictions on associations and individual craftsmen and merchants, but they were imposed under certain circumstances. Restrictions on craftsmen working in imperial workshops (*C.Th.* 10.20.6) and directives to "drag back" (*retrahere*) association members to fulfill obligations in their communities (14.7.1) have been taken as general laws that indicate policies mandating membership in associations and placing craftsmen and merchants under long-term, hereditary obligations to remain in their trade. Besides main-

9. *C.Th.* 13.4.2 (337 CE).
10. *C.Th.* 13.5.5 (326 CE), 13.5.7 (334 CE), 13.5.9 (357 CE).
11. Matthews 2000: 65–70.
12. *C.Th.* 13.5.4 (324 CE), trans. Pharr (1952).

taining numbers to meet community and imperial needs, compulsory membership has been linked to tax collection, specifically of trade taxes incumbent on craftsmen, merchants, and "all men engaged in business" (*C.Th.* 13.1.9).

A. J. B. Sirks and, earlier, A. H. M. Jones suggested that legislation aimed at restricting mobility and controlling associations may not have had the far-reaching impact that inclusion in the legal compilations suggests.[13] But the authorities continued to show some interest in associations. Although Sirks claimed that membership was not obligatory or hereditary in a strict sense, he did suggest that groups associated with the food supply came under closer scrutiny, such as bakers in Rome and Constantinople.[14]

Other scholars have taken a different approach to the question of state intervention in craft and merchant economic activity and have argued that increased oversight was part and parcel of the increased compulsion and coercion of the period, what Alföldy maintains as a pervasive sense of "Unfreiheit."[15] J.-M. Carrié proposed that the regulations evidenced by the Theodosian Code did impact associations significantly. Carrié claimed that the authorities played a more direct role in structuring association activities and made membership in these organizations compulsory.[16] Carrié further suggested that all associations, not only groups involved with the food supply, were bound, in a sense, to provide services for the local and imperial authorities.

Reading the legislation in this way has created a sort of colonate for craftsmen and merchants, essentially tying people to their groups, their communities, and their trades. However, not all craftsmen, merchants, or associations mentioned in the law codes were on an equal footing in economic, social, political, or legal terms, in the eyes of the emperor or even in their communities. Closer scrutiny of the legislation contained in the Theodosian Code with reference to papyri and inscriptions reveals that the local and imperial authorities interacted differently with different groups, depending on the circumstances. As Sirks maintained, some associations were more closely tied to imperial interests. Close ties with imperial interests could result in privileges (and wealth) that had to be defended, clarified, and reiterated, which might have been a reason for the thirty-eight entries in the Theodosian Code concerning the *navicularii* (and an additional ten dealing with their property). In this case, a closer relationship with the authorities would not necessarily have been a negative.

13. Sirks 1993; Jones 1974a.
14. Sirks 1993. On the food supply, see Sirks 1991; Erdkamp 2005.
15. Alföldy 2011: 282.
16. Carrié 2002.

As comprehensive as the codes may appear, the legislation collected did not comment on every aspect of the associative phenomenon. Many of the groups operating in Egypt presumably did so without being mentioned in the legal codes.[17] The decision to exclude rescripts also suggests that *ad hoc* responses to individual groups were not considered general, although they remained a source of law and could provide precedents. As Jinyu Liu pointed out by way of example, the Theodosian Code included only three mentions of the associations of textile traders and weavers (*centonarii*) that she has studied exhaustively.[18] None of these three laws mandated membership or detailed tax policy; rather, each dealt with questions concerning relationships between associations, avoidance of obligations, and complications that may have arisen in Rome when nonmembers feigned membership in associations of *centonarii*.

Hereditary Obligations and Imperial Service

Among the people and groups specified in the Theodosian Code, many of the individual craftsmen and merchants and the groups to which they belonged were employed in imperial mines and quarries, weaving workshops and dye works, mints and bakeries.[19] Legislation that referred to hereditary obligations and required the return of delinquent individuals to service or that enumerated fines for harboring association members pertained to these groups. Orders addressed to the praetorian prefect in 372 CE by Valentinian, Valens, and Gratian, for instance, detailed problems with the operation of imperial weaving workshops.

> We have learned that workmen, who devote their labor to weaving linen garments to be used for Our issuance of supplies, have been solicited by very many persons. Therefore, We command that three pounds of gold shall be paid to the account of the treasury by each person who harbors such a weaver and by each weaver himself. Furthermore, the workmen shall be vindicated to the imperial weaving establishments for linen garments. But if any person should be detected as persisting in the aforesaid arrogance and should continue to detain a weaver, We command that he shall not undergo a fine as in previous times, but a proscription.[20]

17. Mention is made of the obligations incumbent on the members of associations (*corporati*) in Alexandria for work on the river at least until 436 CE, when a decision of the emperors relieved this obligation (*C.Th.* 14.27.2).
18. J. Liu 2009: 280; *C.Th.* 14.8.1 (329 CE), 14.8.2 (369 CE), 12.1.162 (399 CE).
19. *C.Th.* 10.20.16 (426 CE) = *CJ* 11.8.13.
20. *C.Th.* 10.20.6 (372 CE), trans. Pharr.

Concerns that the emperors expressed here echoed earlier legislation by Constantine and Constantius regarding weavers (*gynaecarii*) and slaves of imperial weaving workshops and mints issued to praetorian prefects.[21] Imperial weavers produced items of clothing for the military, the imperial service, and the court. In effect, they were members of the imperial service and were treated not unlike a member of the military. Operation and supplying of the *fabricae* fell under the jurisdiction of the praetorian prefect at this time, so it is fitting that the emperors would turn to the prefect to handle issues with linen production and supply.[22] Sometime in the fourth century, aspects of the oversight for *fabricae* and imperial arms workshops passed to the *magister officiorum* and to the count of the sacred largesses (*comes sacrarum largitionum*) but the prefect remained part of the administration of the *fabricae*.[23] The laws addressed to these officials attempted to keep imperial weavers working in *fabricae* and nowhere else, by imposing stiff fines to discourage proprietors of independent workshops from hiring them: one called for a fine of five pounds of gold for each weaver harbored from the imperial workshop at Scythopolis.[24]

The legal codes reveal that, like imperial weavers, imperial minters (*monetarii*) and their families or fishermen who collected the mollusks that provided the raw material for imperial purple dye (*murileguli* or *conchylioleguli*) also lived and worked under restrictions. For instance, fishermen who shirked their duties were recalled (*revocentur*) according to a law of 424 CE.[25] Imperial minters appear to have fared no better and were the subject of repeated attempts to prevent depletion of their numbers.[26] Restrictions were also placed on marriage among these groups, resulting in hereditary obligations in some cases. Children of a fisherman's daughter had to carry on the trade regardless of the father's status, for instance.[27] Marriage within the ranks of the minters was also encouraged by prohibiting marriages of daughters to individuals outside the group.[28]

There are examples of hereditary obligations beyond this circle of craftsmen and merchants. Legislation addressed by Constantine to the prefect of the city

21. *C.Th.* 10.20.1 (317 CE) = *CJ* 11.8.1; *C.Th.* 10.20.2 (358 CE).
22. Kelly 2004: 208.
23. Kelly 2004: 57–58. See also Kelly 1998: 165–66; Jones 1964: 341–47.
24. *C.Th.* 10.20.8 (374 CE); see also 10.20.6 (372 CE), 10.20.7 (372 CE) = *CJ* 11.8.5.
25. *C.Th.* 10.20.14 (424 CE) = *CJ* 11.8.11.
26. For imperial mints and minters, see Jones 1964: 435–37.
27. *C.Th.* 10.20.17 (426 CE) = *CJ* 11.8.15. See also *C.Th.* 10.20.15 (425 CE) = *CJ* 11.8.12; *C.Th.* 10.20.5 (371 CE).
28. *C.Th.* 10.20.1 (317 CE) = *CJ* 11.8.1; *C.Th.* 10.20.10 (380 CE) = *CJ* 11.8.7.

of Rome implied that service as a *navicularius* was hereditary.[29] As Sirks explored in detail, however, the hereditary rules in this case pertained not to individuals but to properties.[30] The imperial authorities took similar hereditary steps with associations of bakers and millers (*pistores*).[31] Nevertheless, the legal codes indicate that membership could also be somewhat fluid. Members of the *pistores* that became senators had to be certain that their previous obligations were met.[32] Bakers apparently could be expelled from their associations, although how that was achieved and in what circumstances is unclear.[33] The law only states that those expelled for any reason were not to be readmitted, and groups had historically reserved the right to expel, discipline, and punish their own membership, as described in charters. Legislation merely confirmed the course of action that associations sometimes pursued.

Overall, the legislation paints a bleak picture of life as a craftsman in the imperial service and indicates that bakers and millers operated under somewhat closer scrutiny, as might be expected. But, following Matthews' reading, the general nature of such legislation did not necessarily extend beyond the imperial service and speaks only to issues encountered by praetorian prefects, counts of the sacred largesses, and others administering *fabricae*. It is important not to confuse restrictions placed on individuals affiliated with imperial *collegia* or *corpora* working in *fabricae* with craftsmen or merchants who were active in Egypt or anywhere else and did not work in this environment—though certain other groups did supply goods to imperial workshops.[34] The hereditary requirements should thus be read with some circumspection as to their *generalitas*, regarding both the particular context that produced the imperial legislation and the extent to which the compilers intended that these requirements would be applied across the empire.

Compulsory Membership

Many of the laws dealing with *fabricae* declare that the workers should be "recalled" (*revocentur*) to their *collegia* or *corpora*. Instructions to "drag back" (*retrahere*) or "recall" (*revocare*) members to perform service in their communi-

29. *C.Th.* 13.5.1 (314 CE); see also 13.5.2 (315 CE), 13.5.3 (319 CE), 13.5.19 (390 CE).
30. Sirks 1993; see also *C.Th.* 13.6.1 (326 CE), 13.6.7 (375 CE), 13.6.8 (399 CE).
31. *C.Th.* 14.3.2 (355 CE); see also 14.3.14 (372 CE), 14.3.21 (403 CE).
32. *C.Th.* 14.3.4 (364 CE).
33. *C.Th.* 14.4.15 (377 CE).
34. *C.Th.* 11.1.24 (395 CE), trans. Pharr (1952); see also Jones 1964: 837.

ties have been taken as evidence for imperial control of membership in all associations. In the late fourth century CE, Arcadius and Honorius instructed the governor of Campania that,

> The competent judges shall assume the task of dragging back the guilds, that is, the guild members, and they shall order those who have departed to a distance to be dragged back, together with all their possessions, to their own municipalities, lest on account of the lack of such property it may not be possible to hold them to the place of their birth. With reference to their descendants, the general rule shall be observed that when the marriage is between persons of unequal status, the children shall follow the mother, but when it is legally recognized marriage, the children shall be freeborn and shall fall to the father.[35]

During the next century, emperors apparently made several attempts to limit the movement of association members. A law dating to 400 CE ordered that members of *collegia* should be not dragged back but recalled (*revocentur*).[36] A half century later, the emperors intervened on behalf of local communities served by councilors and association members. Theodosius and Valentinian took action against members of Rome's associations who tried to avoid obligations by joining the imperial service or the clergy.[37] Similar concerns had already been addressed by Arcadius and Honorius, who reminded the prefect of the city that spurious letters of privileges or exemptions from service would not excuse associations or council members from their obligations.[38] Leo and Majorian ordered the praetorian prefect to recall members of local councils and associations who had become tenants of imperial or private estates, although the emperors acknowledged that those who fled did so to avoid injustice at the hands of tax collectors and imperial officials.[39]

Being dragged back suggests violence and compulsion imposed by the imperial authorities and seems to indicate that association members occupied a weak and insecure social, legal, and economic position. But the fact that the language applied to associations was also commonly applied to council members points to the economic and social capital that associations and

35. *C.Th.* 14.7.1 (397 CE), trans. Pharr (1952).
36. *C.Th.* 12.19.1 (400 CE).
37. *N.Val.* 20 (445 CE); see also 7.1 (458 CE).
38. *C.Th.* 12.1.156 (397 CE).
39. *N.Maj.* 7.1.1–3 (458 CE).

their members possessed.[40] How these laws were directed and applied may not point to universal compulsory membership. Though the order issued at Milan in 397 CE (*C.Th.* 14.7.1) may have applied more widely, an earlier directive to drag back the association members, sent to the prefect of the city in 393 CE (14.17.12), related to the food supply in Constantinople and echoed familiar concerns.

A distinction should also be drawn between bakers' associations at Rome or Constantinople (and oversight of their activities) and bakers working elsewhere. Of the twenty-one laws related to bread making and the food supply that are preserved in book 14 of the Theodosian Code, more than half were addressed to the prefect of the city. Although the food supply remained a concern at all levels of the administration, bakers in Oxyrhynchus or Aphrodito operated under different levels of scrutiny. Even at Rome and Constantinople, not all bakers and millers worked in imperial bakeries. The *Notitia urbis Constantinopolitanae* listed twenty imperial bakeries and 120 private bakeries in Constantinople during the middle of the fifth century.[41] Individuals that belonged to associations and worked outside imperial establishments likely did so within a different institutional framework.

In addition, this legislation specified no further penalties apart from attempts to "drag" offending association members back. The same goes for the legislation aimed at delinquent council members. Returning individuals to their own municipalities reflects an interest in preserving a number of craftsmen and merchants to provide vital services. Beyond services, it also indicates common concerns, found throughout the legal codes, regarding tax collection and maintaining municipal and imperial treasuries. The authorities lacked a punishment aimed at preventing association or council members from taking the legal risk that came from shirking their responsibilities, and that may have provided them less coercion and control in reality.

The circumstances that led to the repeated responses from the emperors are not clear. But as Harries has reminded us, repetition does not imply imperial inefficacy or that laws were ignored.[42] Repetition may speak to the reliance on the law to bring a suit to a favorable conclusion in the mind of the litigants, even

40. For dragging back (*retrahere*) council members, see *C.Th.* 12.1.13 (326 CE), 12.1.49 (361 CE), 12.1.71 (370 CE), 12.1.74 (371 CE), 12.1.96 (383 CE), 12.1.114 (386 CE), 12.1.137 (393 CE), 12.1.188 (436 CE); for associations, see 14.7.1 (397 CE), 14.17.12 (393 CE).

41. Seeck 1876: 228–43.

42. Harries 1999: 82–88.

if only to confirm a previous decision. The issues surrounding the responses, as well as the possible motivations for bringing complaints to the attention of the authorities in the first place, suggest that the impetus to recall craftsmen, merchants, and council members might not have come from the imperial authorities. Relying on the legal framework, associations may have requested aid when members of their groups refused to fulfill obligations or follow through on contracts, such as the action the tow workers took against a delinquent member named Menas (described as their *homoergos*) in late fifth-century Oxyrhynchus, by filing a petition with a local official.[43]

Two fourth-century documents from Oxyrhynchus detailing disputes over membership in craft and merchant associations suggest different ways to approach the constraints supposedly imposed on groups by the imperial authorities. Both texts have been taken as bolstering claims of imperial efforts to enforce mandatory membership—and as reflecting a desire to "keep people in their place."[44] Yet the texts in question, *P.Ryl.* IV 654 (302–9 CE) and *P.Oxy.* XLIV 3192 (307 CE), may indicate that it was the craftsmen and merchants themselves, not the authorities, who sought to "drag back" association members.

The proceedings of a hearing before an imperial official (*iuridicus*) regarding a dispute between members of the builders' and weavers' associations in Oxyrhynchus, preserved as *P.Ryl.* IV 654 (already discussed in chapter 4, but quoted in full here), reveals something of the dynamics between associations and the authorities. According to the weavers, the builders had attempted to co-opt a weaver named Paul into their group. The weavers sought to check these abuses and defend their members' interests.

> Of the city of Oxyrhynchus, Apollinarius said: "He is a linen weaver by trade, and he is bound to be a *sundikos* in court for a man plying the same trade. For he has as fellow worker this Paul who, although an apprentice, has come to him for practice of the weaving trade. These men are in their own right of no small usefulness to the public services, and you, my lord, know—for they contribute abundantly to the *anabolicum*—how very much they have to produce. But the builders think it right, in a time of such pressing need, always to discuss only their own interests. For they are bent on making my client into a builder although he is a peaceful linen weaver, daring to perpetrate a very great wrong in

43. *P.Oxy.* XVI 1943 (late V CE).
44. Van Minnen 1986: 70 n. 141; see also Carrié 2002: 319.

the process. They are taking him away from the craft that he has learned, and they wish to teach him another, the builders' craft. Inasmuch, therefore, as he must be preserved for his own craft, it is fitting, in order that he suffer no violence from the builders, that the *strategos* and the *logistes* make provision for him. This is his request."

Maximianus, *vir perfectissimus*, *iuridicus Aegypti*, said: "The *strategos* and the *logistes* will make provision, in respect of his charges, that if he has learned the craft and is already in this trade, he is not to be transferred to another."[45]

The text does not preserve the builders' side of the story, nor does it clarify who Paul was or his trade. It seems that the weavers came to Paul's defense and that he welcomed their efforts, which suggests that he was affiliated with the weavers somehow. The involvement of the province's leading legal official indicates either that local and regional magistrates had referred the case to a higher authority or that the weavers and builders appealed earlier decisions. Maximianus' decision that Paul should remain a weaver if he was a weaver points toward the conservative tendencies of officials. The interests and actions of the administration err on preserving the *status quo*; any desire to "keep people in their place" appears passive at best.

Maximianus' decision was not necessarily inconsistent with the sentiment found in fourth-century legislation that ordered people to be dragged back to their councils or associations (with no further penalties). Yet the desire to exert control over membership and keep people in an association came from the craftsmen themselves, as was probably the case in many complaints. The authorities only learned of Paul's disputed membership on the basis of petitions alleging abuse by the builders who had tried to impress Paul into their service. The builders, not the imperial authorities, were the aggressors in this dispute. At least the weavers, who were no less interested in keeping Paul as a member of their group, attempted to cast the builders as the villains in this scenario.

Around the same time as the dispute between the weavers and the builders, a man named Aurelius Timotheus submitted a complaint to the *prytanis* of Oxyrhynchus about the donkey sellers, a trade group known to have organized themselves as an association.[46] Timotheus alleged that the donkey sellers of

45. *P.Ryl.* IV 654 (302–9 CE), *BL* X, 171 and XI, 191, trans. Youtie (1958: 401, adapted).
46. *P.Oxy.* LIV 3728 (306 CE).

Oxyrhynchus attempted to impose on him the burden of supplying donkeys to the official who supervised imperial estates (*magister rei privatae*). Even more troubling from Timotheus' perspective, he claimed that they did this even though he did not belong to the group.

> In the consulship of our lords Severus Augustus and Maximinus most illustrious Caesar. To Aurelius Dioscorus also called Helladius, [ex-?]gymnasiarch, councillor, prytanis-in-office of the glorious and most glorious city of the Oxyrhynchites, Aurelius Timotheus, son of Sarapiades, from the same city. Since the donkey-sellers of the same city have harassed me without justification concerning delegation of the delivery of two donkeys to the most perfect *magister rei privatae* on the ground that I am engaging in their trade, I accordingly declare, swearing by the fortune of our lords Imperatores Maximianus and Severus Augusti and Maximinus and Constantinus the most illustrious Caesares, that I have never yet practiced their trade nor do I do so. And if I am convicted in the future I will be subject to the divine oath and the risk to myself attaching thereto.[47]

The text does not provide the donkey sellers' side of the dispute; but, based on Timotheus' claims, they might have been trying to protect their own interests. Either they harassed Timotheus because he appeared to engage in their trade and ought to prevent this, or, as with Paul and the builders and weavers, the donkey sellers tried to press Timotheus into their association. The association presumably knew who belonged to their organization. Groups in Egypt do not appear to have been excessively large, and given regular meetings, participation in celebrations, and other group obligations, it would seem odd that the donkey sellers had the wrong man. If Timotheus was not a member, as he asserted he was not, perhaps he had fallen afoul of one of the donkey sellers, attempted to encroach on a contract, or committed some other slight. The builders in our other case might have been trying a similar tactic, only to see it backfire when challenged by the weavers, who were able to convince the *iuridicus* that the builders, not the weavers themselves, had perpetrated a "very great wrong."

Neither text reveals that the local or imperial officials sought to compel craftsmen or merchants to join the ranks of an association or to mandate membership. The agency remains with those party to the disputes, who seem more than able to

47. *P.Oxy.* XLIV 3192 (307 CE).

protect their interests and members. The imperial authorities do play a role, but only a minimal one. The officials seem to have supported the interests of groups like the weavers and associations' attempts to keep people within their ranks. Rather than examples of the authorities flexing administrative muscle, these texts illustrate different associations protecting their own interests, even at the expense of others, be it Paul the weaver/builder or Timotheus.

Membership and Taxation

Another argument made for compulsory association membership is the efficiency it supposedly brought to taxation, particularly for collecting the trade tax instituted by Constantine.[48] That tax was intended to be collected at five-year intervals, although emperors in the early fifth century acknowledged alternative payment arrangements.[49] The connection between assessing taxes and mandatory membership seems rooted in two assumptions: (1) that this method of tax collection only would have developed at the instigation of the authorities and (2) that it only could have been efficient if the government required every craftsman and merchant to belong to an association. Imperial legislation thus has been viewed as giving structure to association activities, perhaps to a greater extent than did the regulations associations imposed on themselves.

Carrié claims that besides assuring access to services and increasing efficiency, measures designed to enforce mandatory membership aimed at reducing the transaction costs involved in tax collection from the point of view of the imperial authorities. Carrié based these conclusions partly on a law issued by Valens, Valentinian, and Gratian and posted in Berytus in 372, which made a specific reference to associations of merchants.[50]

> All men now occupied in the pursuit of business, whether collectors of purple dye fish or merchants of any other guild, shall be compelled to the payment of the tax payable in gold which is levied upon tradesmen. For a special grant of imperial favor given to certain persons is a wrong committed upon the common people.[51]

48. For the *chrysargyron*, see Johnson and West 1949: 318–20; Bagnall 1992: 15–17.
49. *C.Th.* 13.1.20 (410 CE).
50. Carrié 2002: 318.
51. *C.Th.* 13.1.9 (372 CE), trans. Pharr (1952).

This law was one of a series confirming the liability of merchants (*negotiatores*) for the trade tax, although only two other laws mention associations of craftsmen or merchants.[52] As this legislation indicates, collecting the tax may not have been as difficult as figuring out who was liable to pay it. Even with imperial instructions, stipulations on what counted as merchant activity apparently caused confusion and left room for interpretation, negotiation, and circumvention. For instance, the imperial authorities did not hold estate tenants who marketed their own produce liable for the tax.[53] Potters and carpenters, both known to have organized themselves as associations in Egypt, were also exempt, as people considered to "seek and maintain their livelihood by manual labor."[54] Evidence from sixth-century Egyptian tax accounts and registers suggests that associations of carpenters possessed significant financial capital relative to other groups, owned land in the community, and were liable for other taxes.[55] Their inclusion in the petition to the empress points toward some standing in Aphrodito.[56] Their exclusion from the trade tax may reflect influence that they enjoyed elsewhere.

The law of 372 CE does explicitly mention the tax liability imposed on merchants and their associations for the trade tax. Nevertheless, it is difficult to know the exact circumstances that called for imperial intervention in this case. Perhaps the emperors were responding to complaints about exemptions and privileges enjoyed by some associations and not others. Their intervention may also have stemmed from questions about which tradesmen and associations were liable for what taxes or from appeals by influential associations regarding their tax burdens. The local and imperial authorities on the ground may have applied different policies to different situations, depending on the groups involved and the legal questions at hand. This could explain this law's reference to collectors of fish for purple dye, who worked in an industry monitored by the authorities. This law does not, however, contain any reference to compulsory membership in a group, and there is little evidence elsewhere—in the legal codes or otherwise—for such measures.

One law addressed to the governor of Numidia in 399 suggests that from at least the end of the fourth century, the collection of the *chrysargyron* fell to the

52. *C.Th.* 13.1.16 (399 CE), 13.1.17 (399 CE).
53. *C.Th.* 13.1.3 (361 CE), 13.1.13 (384 CE).
54. *C.Th.* 13.1.10 (374 CE). For potters, see *P.Oxy.* LIV 3766 (327 CE). For carpenters, see *P.Oxy.* I 53 (316 CE); *P.Aphrod.Reg.* (525/6 CE), col. 10, lines 361–81.
55. *P.Aphrod.Reg.* (525/6 CE), col. 10, lines, 361–81.
56. *P.Cair.Masp.* III 67283 (before 547 CE), line 16.

elected representatives of the associations, "as is done in almost all municipalities" (*sicut in omnibus fere civitatibus*).

> We are not ignorant of the fact that the lustral tax payment in gold is paid by tradesmen, and since the responsibility for tax assessment customarily reverts to those persons who are constrained by the necessity of the tax payment, decurions shall not be subject to this burden. Tradesmen shall know, therefore, that they must select supervisors from their own guilds [*corpora*], as is done in almost all municipalities, without any diminution of the resources of Our treasury; and the assessment of this alien tax shall be removed from the decurions.[57]

This stipulation implies that the practice of associations making payments or selecting a representative to do so on the group's behalf might have evolved out of arrangements that the associations made themselves. It would seem that this payment method proved beneficial in the estimation of both local and imperial authorities. Like *C.Th.* 13.1.9, issued in 372, this piece of legislation did not state explicitly that all craftsmen and merchants had to belong to an association. Besides the collection of the *chrysargyron*, the exemption of council members from the tax was no less the focus of this law. Perhaps associations in Numidia had not been operating according to what the authorities assumed to be standard operating procedure. Perhaps targets for tax collection had not been met, causing tension between the associations and the local council members. If that was the case, the imperial authorities became embroiled in the conflict as it played out in legal actions taken on each side, and not unlike in earlier disputes, the authorities were left to decide liabilities and privileges. Regardless, while the emperors indicated approval of managing taxes as a group, such approval does not amount to a mandate compelling association membership for merchants and craftsmen across the empire. The law seems to approve prevailing social or economic norms in most municipalities as a solution to whatever prompted the original complaint from Numidia.

Papyrological evidence indicates that from the fourth century onward, many associations made tax payments as a group and managed collection of the trade tax on their own. The responsibility for the collection of the *chrysargyron* and other taxes fell to association officers and seemingly comprised a

57. *C.Th.* 13.1.17 (399 CE), trans. Pharr (1952).

normal part of their duties as the group's representatives. During the late fourth century, for instance, the fullers in Oxyrhynchus apparently paid the trade tax in this manner for some time. A receipt that the fullers' *kephalaiōtai* issued to a colleague described as a *homotechnitēs* makes clear that associations collected the tax from and submitted payments on the behalf of members; the millers did something similar.[58] Over a century later, another group of fullers, this time from the Fayum, designated one of their officials (*epistatēs*) to collect the tax for their group.[59] According to two fifth-century texts, the goldsmiths' association from Oxyrhynchus designated a member to manage the trade tax.[60] A third text, possibly related to the same goldsmiths' association in Oxyrhynchus, preserves a group's stipulations for monthly tax collection, as well as provisions to help those who were in need or who were unable to pay what they owed.[61] Groups also helped manage liability for the taxes. A letter from a local official to the *mēniarchēs* of the carpet weavers in Oxyrhynchus, for instance, informed him that the name of a deceased association member had been removed from the roll for the trade tax, presumably after the association had made the request.[62] Although Libanius protested that the trade tax had reduced people to such poverty that they had to sell their children into slavery, at least the goldsmiths in Oxyrhynchus (and certainly others) had taken steps to assure payment and maintain good standing in the eyes of the public, provided, of course, that members followed through on their obligations. Nevertheless, the arrangements that groups made to manage the trade tax suggest that even in the late Roman period, members of associations would have been at a comparative advantage.

These texts indicate that associations and local officials collaborated (as alluded to in the legal sources) when it came to collecting the trade tax in villages and cities. Documents also indicate that associations collected and were liable for other assessments at this time. The fullers in Oxyrhynchus coordinated payments from their members for the *vestis militaris*,[63] and a fourth-century tax account lists the contributions that over twenty associations from an unknown community made for the same purpose.[64] This practice continued into the sixth

58. *SB* XVIII 13916 (386 CE); see also *PSI* VIII 884 (390 CE).
59. *SPP* VIII 852 (VI CE).
60. *SB* XVI 12260 (421 CE); *P.Rain.Cent.* 122 (429/30 CE). See Bagnall and Worp 1985: 67–70.
61. *PSI* XII 1265 (426 or 441 CE).
62. *P.Leid.Inst.* 62 (370, 385, or 400 CE).
63. *SB* XVI 12646 (326/7CE); on the *vestis militaris*, see Sheridan 1998.
64. *P.Gen.* I 24 (IV CE) = *SB* X 10258.

century, when a group of ironsmiths from an unknown community made a similar payment.[65] Associations also played a role in the collection of the head tax (*dēmosion*), according to a receipt signed by the *epistatēs* of an unspecified association.[66] Managing taxes as a group was not necessarily an innovation of the late Roman period. Associations handled collection and payment of taxes as a group in previous centuries; both the salt merchants and the *apolusimoi* from first-century Tebtunis managed taxes for their groups.[67]

Associations also seem to have assumed more official duties in communities and to have designated members to take up public service and obligations. When the monthly presidents of the tow workers' association in Oxyrhynchus nominated five members for a post in the mid-fourth century, they submitted a report to the *logistēs* pledging that these men were indeed "suitable" (*epitēdeios*) for service, using a term familiar from earlier nominations.[68] In the sixth century, we find that the authorities still sought nominations from within the ranks of associations. In response to a request by the *praeses,* the bleachers nominated one of their own as a *prōtodēmotēs*, a post involving uncertain responsibilities.[69] Three officials of Oxyrhynchus' association of sausage makers designated a member to take up an unspecified post early in the same century.[70] Not unlike the tow workers in the fourth century, the sausage makers asserted that their nominee was "wealthy and suitable." By this point, the lines between civic and association duties had become increasingly blurred, and perhaps the language employed reflects that. Nevertheless, associations continued to manage their affairs (even in cooperation with the authorities), relied on their networks, and trusted that their designated colleagues would perform their duties, at the risk of harming the entire association's relationship with the authorities.

Associations and Late Roman Egyptian Tax Registers

The order and uniformity hoped for and partly reflected in the law codes and association agreements to collect taxes is not always readily apparent in late

65. *SPP* VIII 850 (VI CE).
66. *P.Rain.Cent.* 138 (VI CE).
67. *P.Mich.* V 245 (47 CE), 244 (43 CE); for the salt merchants' tax payments, see also *P.Mich.* II 123r, col. XXII, line 27.
68. *P.Harr.* II 216 (343 CE).
69. *P.Oxy.* LIX 3987 (532 CE).
70. *SB* XX 14964 (517 CE); *BL* XI, 233. For earlier evidence, see *SB* XXII 15787 (IV CE).

Roman tax registers and accounts that document late Roman tax collection. Tax registers and account books compiled by local officials or estate employees that detail assessments on estate holdings and the tax liabilities of associations and ecclesiastical institutions and of entire communities are particularly varied: they record payments in money and grain by landowners, tenants, craftsmen, merchants, associations, churches, and monasteries. Despite the difficulty in working with these documents, tax registers offer a cross section of the economic, social, political, and religious life of the community. Perhaps more importantly for assessing association membership and its role in taxation, the registers provide additional insight into interactions between craftsmen, merchants, and the imperial administration in the form of tax collection.

Not only are the texts varied; they are also idiosyncratic. Gaps in information abound, as the scribes, tax collectors, and estate stewards responsible for producing the registers and account books were privy to more information than the record reflects about relationships described in a single line of text recording a tax payment. For example, we know that Apollos the carpenter submitted a payment on behalf of the heirs of Abraham, son of Heraklios, in a fiscal register from Aphrodito dating to 525/6 CE.[71] What led to these arrangements between the carpenter and Abraham's family is not known; it is unclear whether Apollos was an agent of Abraham's family, associated with or related to them in some other way, or a subtenant, as well as whether the relationship was long lasting or for the single tax year covered by the register. Even with information gaps, these documents illustrate different strategies, beyond submitting individual payments, that people used to meet their obligations: they turned to family, to agents or employees, and to associations. The registers and accounts also reveal how these different relationships and individual and group obligations were rendered intelligible to local officials and, by extension, the layers of imperial bureaucracy—for which there was seemingly no set way either.

With respect to associations and taxes, the evidence is diverse. Registers confirm that associations did pay taxes and other imposts collectively. Perhaps somewhat perplexing, given the assumed connection between tax payments and compulsory association membership, the registers also show that craftsmen and merchants paid taxes on their own behalf, on behalf of others, and on behalf of families, in addition to payments already made by their trade group. This complicates the efficiency argument for compulsory membership. Belong-

71. *P.Aphrod.Reg.*, line 327.

ing to a group did not necessarily reduce members' individual agency or limit their options for interacting with the authorities in one of the most visible manifestations of Roman power: taxation. Membership continued to be just one element (although an important one) of their social, economic, legal, and taxpaying lives.

Taxing Associations at the Village Level: Aphrodito

Not surprisingly, documents from Aphrodito indicate persistence of association organization and participation in the community in many ways.[72] Associations partnered with landowners, as indicated by an agreement with an association of shepherds to protect their fields.[73] Associations also owned property and paid taxes accordingly. There is ample sixth-century evidence of what appear to be Aphrodito's associations paying taxes as collectives, including the fiscal register of village property published and analyzed by Constantin Zuckerman (*P.Aphrod.Reg.*, 525/6 CE). More than oppressed taxpayers, Aphrodito's associations appear as stakeholders in the community. Associations also possessed some standing and influence with certain members of the landowning elite and leading ecclesiastical officials, according to the petition to Empress Theodora with which this chapter began. Giovanni Ruffini has pointed out that only a select number of the village's association officials (and probably a subset of the landowners) were among the fifty-one individuals to have signed the petition, which suggests that it may not depict a "unified" Aphrodito.[74] Instead, the petition reflects the interests of one influential faction, a group centered around Dioscorus; those absent from the document might have represented or been aligned with another.[75]

How associations, craftsmen, and merchants were assessed and handled tax liabilities looms large in the documentary evidence from Aphrodito. A fragmentary account of military expenses, for instance, records the payments made by eleven associations as a group; the payments ranged from the single solidus that the fullers paid to the twenty solidi paid by the shipbuilders.[76] A second

72. For additional citations, see Worp 2012.
73. *P.Cair.Masp.* I 67001 (514 CE).
74. Ruffini 2008b: 177–79.
75. Ruffini 2008a: 163–68.
76. *P.Cair.Masp.* II 67147 (532 CE): individual trades mentioned include fullers (*gnapheis*), shipbuilders (*paktōnopoioi*), cobblers (*skuteis*), stonemasons or inscription carvers (*glupheutai*), smiths (*chalkeis*), embroiderers or tailors (*raptai*), weavers (*linouphoi*), carpenters (*tektones*), bakers (*katharourgoi*), oil

account records tax payments submitted by associations (described as the *suntēchnitai*) alongside Aphrodito's landowners.[77] The account records association payments for three tax assessments that together total roughly 10 percent of the amount collected. Over forty-five solidi were collected from eleven associations for the *kanonika*, taxes due to the imperial treasury but not otherwise designated for military needs.[78] A smaller amount totaling, thirty-two solidi, was collected from the same associations for the *dēmosia*.[79] Additionally, for what is described as *sunētheia*, which usually refers to salaries received by officials, six associations made lower payments totaling just over two solidi.[80]

Assuming that there is a connection between economic standing and the amounts paid by associations and individual craftsmen and merchants as recorded in tax registers and accounts like *P.Cair.Masp.* II 67147 or *P.Hamb.* I 56, those living and operating in this milieu and the associations they formed remained somewhat influential in their communities. Since the groups making the three highest payments recorded in *P.Cair.Masp.* II 67147 were the shipbuilders (twenty solidi), carpenters (nine solidi), and weavers (five solidi), it is perhaps not unexpected to find their representatives included among the signers of the petition to Theodora. These associations had or were perceived to have possessed significant economic capital and therefore an elevated standing even among other groups. The account recorded in *P.Hamb.* I 56 tells a similar story. For instance, the carpenters' payments that totaled eighteen solidi represented over 20 percent of the amount assessed on associations, second only to the twenty solidi paid by the shepherds, who, although they did not sign the petition, maintained connections with landowners in Aphrodito (even if this sometimes caused conflict).[81]

Another detailed sixth-century tax register, *P.Cair.Masp.* III 67288, lists 151 individuals as taxpayers, partners with others, or agents of taxpayers for an unspecified collection. Numerous ecclesiastical institutions, associations, and

---

workers (*elaiourgoi*), and barbers (*koureis*).

77. *P.Hamb.* I 56 (VI/VII CE).

78. *P.Hamb.* I 56, col. 5, lines 1–20: individual trades mentioned include carpenters (*tektones*), bakers (*artokollutoi*), cloak makers (*kaunakoplokoi*), fullers (*gnapheis*), embroiderers or tailors (*raptai*), the *exōpulitai*, shipbuilders (*paktōnopoioi*), bronzesmiths (*chalkotupoi*), cobblers (*skuteis*), *gnōsteroi*, and shepherds (*poimenes*). On this tax, see Zuckerman 2004: 179–80.

79. *P.Hamb.* I 56, col. 6, lines 1–13.

80. *P.Hamb.* I 56, col. 6, lines 17–22: individual trades mentioned include shipbuilders (*paktōnopoioi*), bronzesmiths (*chalkotupoi*), bakers (*artokollutoi*), funerary workers (*nekrotaphoi*), embroiderers or tailors (*raptai*), and cobblers (*skuteis*).

81. *P.Cair.Masp.* I 67001 (514 CE).

groups of heirs also appear in the document as taxpayers. Although much of the first column has been lost, the text originally contained six columns of individual entries (five on the recto and a sixth on the verso). Like *P.Cair.Masp.* II 67147, the document belonged to the archive of Dioscorus and recorded all the payments in money. Of the people listed, forty-seven separate individuals practicing eighteen different trades are identified.[82] It is difficult to know how many of these trades had organized themselves as associations, but many likely belonged to groups active at this time in Aphrodito. The account also lists collective payments made by what would appear to be six associations: tailors, shipbuilders, bronzesmiths, cobblers, cloak makers, and fullers.

Although evidence suggests that taxes were assessed on associations as collectives in Aphrodito, the forty-seven craftsmen and merchants listed as taxpayers in *P.Cair.Masp.* III 67288 made individual payments. On several occasions, people paid on their own behalf and on behalf of a family member. Palos the butcher, for example, contributed one solidus for himself and his brother.[83] Another butcher, Lakon, paid one solidus on behalf of himself and his son.[84] Some appear to have partnered with others who did not have the same trade (or were not identified as having one), like Phib the vegetable seller and his partner Pachumios.[85] In total, the account lists fifteen different partnerships of this kind, including those that existed between family members.

Everyone identified as a craftsman or merchant in *P.Cair.Masp.* III 67288 paid between one-third of a solidus to a single solidus, no more or less than payments made by those not associated with a particular trade. Without knowing the nature of the collection, it is difficult to say if this speaks to a smaller economic gap between craftsmen, merchants, and the other landowners (or tenants) represented in the account. Since the text dates to a time after the reign of Anastasius and the abolition of the *chrysargyron*, the trade tax seems unlikely. The document may instead record tax liabilities on land owned or rented by the individuals and associations listed.

The nine individuals identified as specialty bakers (*katharourgoi*) repre-

82. *P.Cair.Masp.* III 67288 (VI CE): individual trades mentioned included butchers (*mageiroi*), dyers (*bapheis*), weavers (*linophoi*), bakers (*katharourgoi*), beekeepers (*melissourgoi*), millers (*molunarchoi*), shipbuilders (*paktōnopoioi*), fullers (gnapheis), vegetable merchants (*obriopōlai*), bronzesmiths (chalkotupoi), potters (*keramoplastai*), cobblers (*skuteis*), goldsmiths (*chrusochooi*), carpenters (*tektones*), barbers (*koureis*), smiths (*chalkeis*), embroiderers or tailors (*raptai*), and cloak makers (*kaunakopoioi*).

83. *P.Cair.Masp.* III 67288 (VI CE), col. 2, line 1.

84. *P.Cair.Masp.* III 67288, col. 2, line 5.

85. *P.Cair.Masp.* III 67288, col. 3, line 13.

sented the single largest professional group assessed, seven bakers at one-third of a solidus and two more at one-half of a solidus. Unlike these bakers, who, if they belonged to an association, still paid their tax individually, several associations submitted payments as a group, some in amounts similar to those of a single baker. The local cobblers, for instance, made one payment of one-half of a solidus, as did the fullers.[86] The tailors, with their assessment of one and one-third solidi, more than doubled the payments of the fullers and cobblers.[87] The bronzesmiths (col. 3, line 17) and the cloak makers (col. 4, line 5) each made the comparatively large payment of two solidi, four times the amount of the cobblers and fullers.[88] The shipbuilders' payment is unfortunately not preserved. These payments serve as a reminder that even between associations, there was a range of economic and social capital.

There are examples recorded in *P.Cair.Masp.* III 67288 of tradesmen who made individual payments but plied trades for which an association had also made a collective payment. Despite the fact that the fullers had paid one-half of a solidus as a group, seven fullers made their own payments.[89] Two tailors paid one-third of a solidus, as did two bronzesmiths. Only the cloak makers and the cobblers appear solely as a group, with no individuals paying taxes.

The account does not reflect a preference on the part of the official, landowner, or steward compiling the list—in this case, possibly Dioscorus—for a particular method of reporting taxes collected from associations or individual craftsmen and merchants. If anyone would have been well versed in law and policies regarding taxes, it should have been Dioscorus, a member of the local elite, an imperial official, and presumably the author of the petition to Theodora. Apparently, some payments remained outstanding, such as the one-third of a solidus owed by Phanes the specialty baker.[90] Whether the presence of an outstanding payment has a negative connotation is unclear. Outstanding payments may relate to different payment schedules or to neglect on the taxpayer's part, but they also might reveal the existence of a credit relationship between, for example, Phanes and Dioscorus. A one-size-fits-all strategy does not work

86. *P.Cair.Masp.* III 67288, col. 3, line 30; col. 4, line 20.
87. *P.Cair.Masp.* III 67288, col. 2, line 22.
88. *P.Cair.Masp.* III 67288, col. 3, line 17. The editor expanded the abbreviation to the singular *chalkotupos*, but there does not seem to be space for a name of someone identified as a *chalkotupos*; instead, reading *chalkotupoi* would seem consistent with the plural *gnapheis* (fullers) at col. 4, line 20, and the plural reading of *skuteis* (cobblers) at col. 3, line 30. Other texts from Aphrodito suggest that there was in fact an association of chalkotupoi operating at this time; see *P.Cair.Masp.* III 67283, line 15.
89. *P.Cair.Masp.* III 67288, col. 5, lines 20 (Abraam), 21 (Viktor).
90. *P.Cair.Masp.* III 67288, col. 2, line 20.

in these cases. It seems clear that craftsmen and merchants neither relied only on their associations to manage tax payments or to interact with local officials and tax collectors nor were expected to do so exclusively. Landowners, their managers, and local officials like Dioscorus did not require payment as a group in all situations or even assume that would be the case.

A register of taxes collected on village property (categorized as *kometika*) from Aphrodito, compiled in 525/6 CE, provides more evidence of not only collective payments but also payments by individual craftsmen and merchants operating outside (or in addition to) their membership in an association.[91] The register was produced by three different individuals, including the *boethos,* who collaborated with the local landowners to oversee assessment and collection, and the *hypodektēs*, who conveyed the taxes to the provincial treasury.[92] The register contained three separate accounts spread across eighteen columns of text, largely devoted to taxes assessed on land and paid in cash to the treasury of the village over the course of the year. The entries reveal similarities with other accounts: taxpayers included ecclesiastical institutions (who apparently owned 6.3 percent of the village land recorded in the register), individuals, and partnerships. Families show up in the register as groups of heirs, whose payments, according to Zuckerman's analysis, account for 40 percent of the entries, a higher proportion than what is found in *P.Cair.Masp.* III 67288.[93] Additionally, payments were routinely made on behalf of others or through agents.

Included among the over two hundred individual taxpayers listed, craftsmen, merchants, and their heirs were specified as taxpayers (or as agents of taxpayers) in sixteen entries. These entries reveal something of the financial capacity of the individuals listed and of the personal networks of craftsmen and merchants. Viktor the oil worker, for example, made two payments potentially as an agent or subtenant of another Viktor described as *lamprotatos*, which indicates connections with elite levels of society.[94] Paulos the goldsmith had a financial relationship with a man named Triadelphos, possibly a landowner, for whom he made two payments.[95] Others appear to have been landowners in the community who were operating on their own or who at least paid taxes on their

91. The register consists of *P.Flor.* III 297 combined with three leaves from Strasbourg; see Zuckerman 2004; all citations of this register (*P.Aphrod.Reg.*) refer to Zuckerman's edition.
92. On the *boethos*, see Zuckerman 2004: 128–33.
93. Zuckerman 2004: 234.
94. *P.Aphrod.Reg.*, lines 80, 134.
95. *P.Aphrod.Reg.*, lines 83, 164.

own, such as the carpenter Ibeis, son of Sarapion.[96] Some may have had their own agents or subtenants, such as the bronzesmith John (son of Besios), who made payments not only on his own (line 402) but also through an agent (line 525). Increased imperial efforts to control craftsmen and merchants, accompanied by the increasing sense of "Unfreiheit" that supposedly characterized their existences, may not have altered social and economic relations dramatically for everyone.

Although many craftsmen and merchants made individual payments, the register confirms the importance of associations and their place as taxpayers in the community. In particular, the tenth column alone details the taxes assessed presumably on property that associations owned. Associations of carpenters (*tektones*), fullers (*gnapheis*), funeral workers (*nekrotaphoi*), bakers (*artokollutai*), cloak makers (*kaunakopoioi*), and the enigmatic *lōtkoi* (perhaps a gloss or mistake for shipbuilders, according to Zuckerman) all appear as collective and potentially landowning taxpayers.[97] The register also indicates through whom each group made their payments, with the exception of the fullers.[98] All the groups paid once except the carpenters, who made multiple payments through several individuals: Mousaios, son of Viktor the carpenter[99]; Paulos the *dekanos*[100]; another Paulos, son of Hermaos[101]; Mousaios, son of Pibentios[102]; and Viktor the *dekanos*, who made six payments on the carpenters' behalf.[103] What this means besides using different methods to coordinate the group's payments is not clear. The individuals who submitted payments on a group's behalf were association officials or members designated for the task, which is how Zuckerman interprets the title *dekanos*. Only the fullers are listed without any indication of who made the actual tax payment. The variation indicates that methods of making and recording payments varied even for the same tax assessment. Taking into account this information regarding Aphrodito, it seems that what counted as efficient for taxpayers and collectors may have differed from community to community and within a given location.

Based on evidence contained in other documents, the tenth column of the

96. *P.Aphrod.Reg.*, line 101.
97. Zuckerman 2004: 225.
98. *P.Aphrod.Reg.*, line 368.
99. *P.Aphrod.Reg.*, line 364.
100. *P.Aphrod.Reg.*, line 367.
101. *P.Aphrod.Reg.*, line 373.
102. *P.Aphrod.Reg.*, line 375.
103. *P.Aphrod.Reg.*, lines 369, 372, 374, 376, 377, 380.

Aphrodito register does not appear to preserve a comprehensive list of all associations operating in Aphrodito around this time. Zuckerman estimates that 3.2 percent of overall revenue from these collections came from imposts on the groups listed, a small but perhaps not insignificant amount, considering it constituted the payments from only six associations. The amount paid by the associations compared fairly well with the amounts that the account listed for ecclesiastical institutions, for instance; the total was only half of the taxpaying footprint left by churches and monasteries. The amount paid by the six associations does, however, nearly match up with the amount owed by Aphrodito's nine churches, which totaled 3.7 percent of the revenue according to Roger Bagnall.[104] Given the repeated emphasis on the economic power and influence of the church at this time, it seems significant that associations appear to have paid a similar amount of tax. Factionalism aside, the village's accounts help explain the place of associations alongside landowners and ecclesiastical officials in the petition to Empress Theodora.

Associations and Taxation at the Village Level: Temseu Skordon

A tax register that covers the village of Temseu Skordon (as well as a hamlet identified as Topos Demeou) in the Hermopolite nome, published by Roger Bagnall, James Keenan, and Leslie MacCoull, offers a comparison to what can be gleaned from Aphrodito's registers and accounts.[105] Like the fiscal register that Zuckerman edited, the Temseu Skordon codex is an account of village property. The text's date, 546/7, places it within the same time frame as those from Aphrodito.[106] The codex, composed of twenty-seven folios and an additional fragment, records payments in money by what the editors describe as a "principal scribe" and at least one other, who wrote mainly in Greek but also used Coptic.[107] The taxes, presumably on land, were paid at different intervals throughout the year, as the assessor and his assistant (*boethos*) visited villages to collect the payments (primarily in bronze coins, along with the occasional gold solidus, from landowners and institutions, as the editors describe).[108]

Of the 284 individuals, institutions, or families listed as taxpayers in Tem-

104. Bagnall 2008: 184.
105. Originally *P.Lond.Copt.* 1075, now published as a new edition by Bagnall, Keenan, and MacCoull (2011).
106. Bagnall, Keenan, and MacCoull 2011: 33.
107. Bagnall, Keenan, and MacCoull 2011: 13–21, on paleography and language.
108. Bagnall, Keenan, and MacCoull 2011: 34.

seu Skordon, at least 31 individuals—roughly 11 percent of the total—were identified by occupations often linked to associations of craftsmen or merchants. In addition, the codex lists three vinedressers (*ampelourgoi*), a doctor, a grain measurer, a scribe, and two soldiers, which, if added to the first group, brings the percentage of taxpayers identified by an occupation to 13.7 percent. The largest subset consisted of those workers involved in construction (twelve taxpayers), followed closely by those involved in food production (ten taxpayers, including the three vinedressers). Of the craftsmen, many appear to have been small-scale holders in the community. Nevertheless, while none compare to Enoch the *oikonomos,* whose payment of roughly 9.8 solidi (244,900 talents at a rate of 25,000 talents to the solidus) is the largest sum contributed and accounts for 2.7 percent of the 354 solidi to be collected, several craftsmen and merchants had relatively large holdings based on total payments: the bronzesmith Tatianos, son of Banos, contributed 2.6 solidi; Menas the butcher, 1.9 solidi; and a butcher named Georgios, roughly 2.2 solidi. Although payments varied widely from a few carats to almost 3 solidi, the 31 individuals involved in craft and merchant activities contributed 15.3 solidi, about 4.3 percent of the total collected. Including the vinedressers and the "service providers" (as identified by the editors) would bring the total to 22.9 solidi, or 6.5 percent of the total, even though this number is somewhat skewed by Sarapion the *sitometres,* who paid just over 4 solidi.

As in other cases, it is difficult to determine whether or not any of the individuals identified by occupation belonged to an association. Two groups, however, the tow workers and the cobblers, made their tax payments collectively. The cobblers made five payments totaling 0.6 of a solidus (14,900 talents).[109] The contribution of the tow workers and their identification as an association in the register are more ambiguous. The tow workers appear in the heading of an account contained within the text labeled "the account of the tow workers," dated to Tybi 9 and collected through a man identified as Viktor the *gnoster.*[110] There is no specific payment made by the tow workers, but they may have been responsible for collecting the thirteen payments listed under the heading, which totaled just over one solidus. Whether those listed under the heading were themselves tow workers is unclear; two men are identified by different trades: Viktor the baker and Makarios the builder. A third man, Esaias, is iden-

109. 8v, line 13; 13v, line 25; 15v, line 24; 24r, lines 15, 32.
110. 10v, line 1.

tified as a priest. One group of heirs, the heirs of Kah, also paid into the account of the tow workers. If this account represents the share of the village tax incumbent on the tow workers based on land they had leased out to the individuals named in the account, it may point to another way in which associations were embedded within the community, but it is difficult to be certain about what is going on here.

The editors of the codex rightly caution that the use of the plurals *skuteis* and *sippourgoi* may simply mean that there were a minimum of two individuals involved in the transaction. Parallels would suggest, however, that they refer to associations of cobblers and tow workers, since both are attested elsewhere, as are associations for any number of the occupations attested in the codex. If the two entries reflect payments submitted by an association of cobblers and tow workers, these associations may also have owned land, as was likely the case for groups listed in the tenth column of the Aphrodito fiscal register: the *tektones*, *nekrotaphoi*, *gnapheis*, *artokollutai*, *kaunakopoioi*, and *lōktoi*.[111] Given that the Aphrodito account only concerns land classified as *kometika*, it is possible that other trade groups might have owned land categorized differently and therefore would not be attested in this document. Be that as it may, the likelihood that the two groups mentioned in the Temseu Skordon register owned property indicates that associations enjoyed some economic standing that may have translated into social, political, and legal capital in the community, like the groups that lent their capital to Aphrodito's petition to the empress. Assuming that 6.4 percent of the tax liability amounts to the ratio of landownership in the community, the craft and merchant segment's collective capital would rival that of the ecclesiastical institutions listed in Aphrodito's village account.

The wealth of the craft and merchant sector in Temseu Skordon and the corresponding social and political capital attached to it, though significant, did not quite rise to the same level as the power and influence of the ecclesiastical institutions.[112] Based on its payment of fifty-one solidi (roughly 14 percent of the total collected), the Holy Church of Hermopolis (the bishop's seat), which the account describes as the "Holy Church," was the largest landowner in the village. Only one other ecclesiastical institution shows up as a taxpayer in the Temseu Skordon codex, the Holy Martyrion, which made a total payment of 4.8 solidi. This is a reminder that the standing of influential constituencies in com-

111. Zuckerman 2004: 225.
112. On ecclesiastical institutions in the codex, see Bagnall, Keenan, and MacCoull 2011: 53–55.

munities varied from place to place, sometimes quite considerably. Nevertheless, craftsmen and merchants, whether they belonged to associations or not, might have had a place at the table, so to speak, in Temseu Skordon as well.

Tax Collection in the Metropoleis at the End of Roman Rule

Tax collection in the metropoleis appears to have been conducted in a variety of ways, as evidenced by the Hermopolite Fiscal Codex (*P.Sorb.* II 69, 618/9 or 633/4 CE), a substantial codex consisting of sixty-seven leaves. The codex preserves payments by individuals and organizations throughout the nome, mostly in grain, unlike what the accounts from Aphrodito and Temseu Skordon show. Nevertheless, the Hermopolite codex provides a sense of craftsmen and merchants in the final years of Roman rule in Egypt and shows some continuity with what has been observed elsewhere in terms of tax collection and relationships between authorities and taxpayers. Among the craftsmen and merchants listed, Jean Gascou, the text's editor, counted twenty-one different professions, which reflects a similar variety found in texts from Aphrodito and Temseu Skordon. The carpenters were the largest group, with eight individual taxpayers scattered across various locations. The largest single payment of a craftsman or merchant, however, was made by the goldsmith Hadrianus, who paid four artabae of wheat.[113]

Other trades were represented by a single taxpayer. Whether this means that Viktor was the only beekeeper, for example, is not clear; that may be unlikely, based on parallels.[114] Three beekeepers from the village of Aphrodito alone are listed in *P.Cair.Masp.* III 67288.[115] That the Hermopolite Codex contained a listing for a single beekeeper may imply that the beekeeper Viktor of *P.Sorb.* II 69 was a leading member of the trade who happened to own land and was perhaps liable for taxes above and beyond other beekeepers.

Some craftsmen and merchants made multiple payments. Viktor the carpenter made three payments; a man named Monios, identified as a tow worker and a priest, made two payments.[116] There is no explicit indication that either Viktor or Monios belonged to an association, although associations of carpenters and tow workers existed during the late Roman period,

113. *P.Sorb.* II 69, at 40 C3.

114. *P.Sorb.* II 69, at 45 C7. Victor made a payment of one-third of an artaba.

115. *P.Cair.Masp.* III 67288, col. 2, lines 23–25.

116. For the payments by Viktor the carpenter, see *P.Sorb.* II 69, at 85 A14, 88 B7, 120 A16; for the payments of Monios, see *P.Sorb.* II 69, at 54 D5, 84 E9; a third payment by Monios' heirs is made at 108 B8.

including an association of tow workers elsewhere in the Hermopolite nome, in Temseu Skordon.[117]

As the sixth-century tax registers from Aphrodito make clear, it does not seem that payments had to be made by associations as collectives. The two payments of one-half and five-eighths of an artaba made by Sarapion the son of Thunis, the only fuller mentioned in the Hermopolite text, at least as it survives, do not seem so dissimilar from other payments to suggest that he made them not on his own behalf but on that of an association.[118] As in other accounts, the details behind a single entry can be obscured. Recorded payments were often made on behalf of or through the agency of another person or group. But such arrangements likely would have been noted in a tax register or account. The scribes responsible for the registers from Aphrodito made these arrangements clear by using the terms *dia* or *huper* in entries for payments made through or on behalf of another person or persons. Had someone like Sarapion made a payment on behalf of another individual or an association, it would have been indicated.

Other texts indicate that associations contributed collectively for various local financial burdens and to support local civic institutions. For instance, a fragmentary tax list from the Arsinoite nome details the payments made by many trade groups that likely were organized as associations: porters, bakers, specialty bakers, flower merchants, salt merchants, dyers, fullers, and two other groups, the *kuthrobrochoi* and the *erektai*.[119] An early seventh-century document (*P.Lond.* III 1028) records contributions for upkeep of the circus building and personnel in Hermopolis and provides a counterpoint to the Hermopolite Fiscal Codex.[120] The first column contains payments totaling over sixty-eight solidi made by thirteen associations (two of which are unidentifiable due to the state of the papyrus), ranging from just over one solidus made by the wreath makers to ten solidi made by the oil makers.[121] The second column of the text details payments from estates, ecclesiastical institutions, and the merchants working in the market near the old temple of Serapis, who made a substantial

117. For example, for tow workers, see *P.Harr.* II 216 (343 CE); *P.Oxy.* XVI 1943 (V CE); *P.Stras.* IV 287 (VI CE). For carpenters, see *P.Oxy.* I 53 (316 CE); *P.Cair.Masp.* II 67147 (VI CE); *P.Aphrod.Reg.*, line 368.
118. For Sarapion the fuller, see *P.Sorb.* II 69, at 110 A15, A 21.
119. *P.Prag.* I 25 (VI/VII CE).
120. *P.Lond.* III 1028 (VII CE).
121. *P.Lond.* III 1028, lines 4, 9.

payment of six hundred solidi.[122] Collection of taxes as a group or on behalf of an institution or a fiscal unit was not necessarily reserved only for associations: two payments on behalf of streets or districts are also recorded.[123]

Reading this seventh-century record, *P.Lond.* III 1028, alongside the Hermopolite codex helps place the individual craftsmen and merchants listed there in context, especially since the codex records no single payment from an association, though associations clearly made some payments collectively at other times. The individual craftsmen and merchants listed in the codex may have belonged to the groups that made contributions for the maintenance of circus buildings and staff, but we cannot be certain. This text offers a different yet, in many respects, complementary picture of associations and their involvement in their communities found in Aphrodito and elsewhere throughout late Roman Egypt. It also suggests that these associations had some social and economic standing (and shouldered a portion of the financial and tax burdens) in the community, along with estates and ecclesiastical institutions.

Managing Tax Collection as a Group

It has been debated whether the variety present in these tax accounts and registers provides evidence for the activities of craftsmen and merchants who were not affiliated with associations. Fikhman claimed that *P.Cair.Masp.* III 67288 in particular provided evidence for individuals who did not belong to associations and remained free to practice their professions without interference either from a local association or the authorities.[124] This may be the case. There remains the possibility that these individuals might have belonged to an association but that the tax assessment was managed differently among the groups. Some may have chosen to pay as individuals, whereas others paid collectively.

Different interpretations are possible. The text may record payments of taxes incumbent on craftsmen and merchants besides trade taxes, most likely taxes on land that individuals or the association owned or rented, something that was not uncommon. The account preserved as *P.Cair.Masp.* III 67288 cannot be securely dated and thus may date from a time after Anastasius had done away with the trade tax. If this is the case, perhaps we would not expect that associations continued to submit tax payments as collectives once the iron

122. *P.Lond.* III 1028, line 17.
123. *P.Lond.* III 1028, lines 19, 24.
124. Fikhman 1994.

hand of the state removed that constraint. It may be that no uniform policy existed and that officials on the ground who were charged with tax collection did the best they could depending on circumstances. There also may not be a link between compulsory membership and taxation. Instead, association membership was one among many ways to meet tax liabilities and to engage in other social, economic, legal, and religious activities, as these groups had done during earlier centuries.

If a uniform policy for tax collection pertaining to craftsmen and merchants did exist, it may have been subject to interpretations at any number of levels by those to whom the task of tax collection fell. The tax registers from Aphrodito and Temseu Skordon provide a look into the workings of tax assessment in sixth-century villages. It is tempting to assume that similar documents would have been produced elsewhere to organize tax collection. But what worked for one tax collector may not have worked for others. The differences in these documents may simply suggest variations in whatever passed for protocol locally in Aphrodito, Temseu Skordon, Hermopolis, and other locations. Differences may also indicate alternate views of what was deemed efficient not by the imperial authorities, who cared only that they received their payments, but by local officials and taxpayers themselves.[125]

According to these documents, local officials, organizations, and individual craftsmen and merchants used different strategies to fulfill obligations at different times and places. The local authorities did rely on associations to collect taxes, but this does not necessarily amount to coercion of associations or the craftsmen and merchants that belonged to these groups—certainly not any more coercion than other taxpayers experienced. Besides payment as a collective, the same avenues for payment were available for craftsmen and merchants who would have belonged to associations as for anyone else: reliance on partnerships, family networks, and agents, all of which point to complicated social and economic relationships that may have overlapped with association membership and the obligations to a particular group. As long as the tax payments continued to line imperial and local coffers, how associations made payments did not matter. In fact, a protected right to manage their own collection may have been a real privilege that saved association members from coercion, besides the pressure, of course, that associations applied to their own membership.

---

125. J.-M. Carrié has suggested that *P.Cair.Masp.* III 67288 does not necessarily imply that the men listed were not members of an association; see Carrié 2002: 312–13.

Collective tax payment may not have had a negative connotation. Association members may have benefited from this method of tax collection. By coordinating tax payments through craft and merchant associations, as the law codes and various papyri indicate, members may have been spared from encounters with the stereotypical rapacious tax collector, about whom no shortage of imperial legislation exists. One complaint from late fourth-century Oxyrhynchus alleges abuse by a *boethos* in his attempts to collect the *chrysargyron.*[126] In this sense, group payments may have reflected not a dependent and powerless position on the part of associations, craftsmen, and merchants but, rather, their influence. Perhaps as a corrective to possible abuse or a nod to their standing in the community, associations had acquired the right to serve as their own tax collectors. Like designated seating in theaters or arenas, not everyone enjoyed this privilege and the protections it provided. Coordinating payments in this manner may have appeared beneficial to elites and to the individuals contracted to collect the tax prescribed by the imperial authorities. Efficiency for the imperial authorities may not have been the only concern.

Self-Regulation and Social Capital

The tax registers and accounts seem to suggest that late Roman legal constraints imposed from above did not necessarily serve as the dominant force that structured the lives of craftsmen, merchants, and association members. Though the Egyptian accounts reflect that membership was not required for paying taxes, the need to make tax payments certainly factored into how groups handled their liabilities and organized their activities. The continued designation of officials by groups implies not only a sense of continuity with earlier organizations but also that associations sought to regulate themselves. But even during the late Roman period, self-regulation was facilitated among the membership by more than the coercive power of officials. Evidence suggests that for associations in villages and cities, reliance on practices familiar from first-century association charters and attention to social capital remained critical for the success of the group and its members.

A variety of documents indicate that associations and their leadership concerned themselves with more than paying taxes and demonstrate the attention

126. *P.Oxy.* XLIX 3480 (360–90 CE).

that craftsmen and merchants continued to pay to trust, reputation, and esteem. For example, the ironsmiths of Hermonthis, an association of about a dozen or so smiths living in the Theban area and active at least between 283/4 and 333/4 CE, seemed to operate as any other group had in the past, according to a dossier of six inscriptions documenting their ritual activities.[127] The group met annually, on the new year, at the temple of Hatshepsut in Deir el-Bahari; like other groups, the ironsmiths probably met regularly elsewhere. During their gathering at Deir el-Bahari, certainly a special occasion for members who traveled some twenty kilometers from Hermonthis to attend, they conducted sacrifices (specifically a donkey sacrifice) and shared a banquet.

The ironsmiths documented the attendees, their positions, and even the individuals who supplied beer and tended to the donkey. The inscriptions show that three officials presided at the celebrations and that a scribe recorded the proceedings; although the scribe Hatres, son of Horion, held the post for a decade, the officials seem to have rotated. The inscriptions recording the sacrifices and banquets on the wall where the group would return each year speak to the meaning attached to attendance at the sacrifice and perhaps also to commemorating the officials who presided and those who were present. Though there is no association charter or evidence of honorific activities among the dossier, the inscribed records imply the importance of social capital accumulated within the group through participation—and of sharing information about members and their past actions. In some sense, then, the inscriptions not only served as *proskunēmata* documenting the group's devotion but may have also highlighted a member's devotion to the group over time, like the honorific statues displayed or decrees recited (often repeatedly) at association banquets. In the case of the ironsmiths, group members who came each year not only saw the continuity of the association and its particular brand of piety but were also reminded of each other's position in the group and of who had (and perhaps, by omission, who had not) attended and followed through on what was probably an obligation to attend. As among the first-century groups in Tebtunis and associations elsewhere, attendance offered a chance to renew or develop bonds of trust, to measure each other's actions and piety, and to gain information about colleagues' relative trustworthiness.

The association of goldsmiths in fifth-century Oxyrhynchus was more deliberate about social capital and its place in the group's approach to their ac-

127. On the ironsmiths, see A. Łajtar 2006: 94–104, 244–65.

tivities. The document that preserves the election of a man named Aurelius Chairemon as *kephalaiōtēs* by at least ten members to manage and collect their taxes, is imbued with the language of trust and esteem: the group described Chairemon as a man "worthy of trust."[128] The text is not just a record of an election and reveals that the goldsmiths concerned themselves with more than tax collection and choosing officials. A good portion of the text elucidates the group's expectations for members: to obey the *kephalaiōtēs* or face penalties (lines 7–8), to attend meetings (lines 8–9), and to help others or risk incurring the "customary penalties" for failing to do so (lines 10–12). Though the group empowered Chairemon to "prosecute" and "compel" delinquent members, the goldsmiths, not unlike other associations, set up a system that allowed them to evaluate their colleagues' actions against an agreed-on standard of accepted practices and norms (which did not change very much in several centuries).

When an association that referred to themselves as "hunters" (*agreutai*) and had some connection to an estate in sixth-century Aphrodito agreed on the appointment of a *kephalaiōtēs*, they similarly included a series of obligations for members, providing insights into the concerns that structured their activities.[129] Like the goldsmiths, the hunters specified obedience to association officers "in all good works pleasing to men and to God" (lines 12–13). The officer may have been the one charged with collecting the taxes (*dēmosia*) referred to in a fragmentary portion of the document (line 32). Provisions called for contributions of wine on the occasion of marriages and births, which indicate that the group held banquets together to commemorate significant events in members' lives (lines 18–19). Such celebrations also presumably provided all members an opportunity to amass goodwill and build up social capital—and to assure everyone that they would make their tax payments. Additional regulations regarding sale and pricing of boats (*paktones*) betray that the group's interests extended beyond hunting. More than likely, the group also owned (and leased out) or built boats used for river transport. Specifically, members were enjoined not to steal customers from colleagues, for which they would face fines (lines 21–26). Members were also prohibited from stealing or misappropriating wood, which might suggest an attempt by the group to manage the supply of raw materials used for making the boats

128. *PSI* XII 1265 (426 or 441 CE), line 4.

129. *SB* III 6704 (538 CE). On this text, see Johnson and West 1949: 154; van Minnen 1987: 66–67; Fikhman 1994: 38–40.

(lines 26–29). Abiding by the norms regarding social and economic concerns spelled out here and in *PSI* XII 1265 helped members establish a trustworthy reputation, repair a damaged one, and accomplish group and individual goals while minimizing risk and uncertainty in their pursuits.

The goldsmiths acknowledged the importance of cultivating esteem and perpetuating a trustworthy reputation in the community as well. The supposed support outlined in *PSI* XII 1265 for those who had fallen on hard times may be aimed at assuring their participation in public processions and celebrations in honor of imperial victories, as associations did elsewhere.[130] According to the description of Justinian's triumphal return to Constantinople in 559 (the first of several accounts of imperial triumphs contained in the *Book of Ceremonies* compiled by the emperor Constantine VII Porphyrogenitus for his son), all the associations, along with the silversmiths and merchants, welcomed the emperor into the city.[131] Associations apparently maintained a public presence in communities and showed concern for maintaining their place and their public persona, as the example of the goldsmiths of Oxyrhynchus suggests. Perhaps Justinian's wife, Theodora, might not have found the presence of six associations in a petition from Aphrodito so out of the ordinary after all.

Conclusions

Reassessing the discussions in the legal codes and juristic writings in light of documentary sources shows that the imperial authorities did not necessarily impose mandatory membership or constrain association activities in novel ways. Groups tied to the food supply or working in imperial workshops are discussed at greater length in the legal sources, which reveals, not surprisingly, an increased level of supervision from the imperial authorities. It is difficult, however, to read legislation concerned with workers in *fabricae* as general laws that pertain to all craftsmen, merchants, and associations. Members of Egyptian associations lived and worked outside imperial establishments and, in some sense, beyond direct imperial control, although requirements to declare prices, collect taxes, and take on local obligations show that they could not operate without any regard for the authorities.

130. *PSI* XII 1265, lines 12–13; see also McCormick 1986: 204–7.
131. Constantine Porphyrogenitus, *De imp. exped.* C 715–16 (ed. J. F. Haldon).

Late Roman tax accounts and registers indicated that groups maintained a high level of economic vitality (relative to the rest of the population). The documents considered here also suggest that these groups continued to rely on trust, reputation, and esteem to lower transaction costs, bridge information gaps, confront risk and uncertainty, and possibly exert control over their own members. Social mobility and actual relocation from one place to another may have caused anxiety for imperial officials, local councilors, and other association members; they would have been left to meet tax burdens or service obligations when their colleagues departed. In light of this, repeated legislation to keep members of associations and local councils in their communities may not have originated from a fear that a system of rank and privilege was breaking down. Rather, the legislation can be viewed as a response to something more concrete that faced local and imperial officials: concerns expressed by important constituencies—such as local councils, large landowners, or associations—over tax liability not being met or over obligations and their accompanying expenses being passed to others. Furthermore, the urge to keep people in their place seems to have originated with the associations themselves, as indicated by the petitions from Oxyrhynchus regarding disputes with the builders, weavers, and donkey sellers.

Rather than limit or diminish the role played by association members, the imperial constitutions seem to have supported their activities and their prerogatives in certain circumstances. Obtaining privileges and exemptions speaks to the important position that associations occupied at local levels, something the emperors and their legal advisors acknowledged. Specific decisions were crafted to encourage continued activity by craftsmen and merchants, which would benefit these individuals, their organizations, and the empire as a whole. Many of the imperial constitutions that specified privileges likely had a positive impact on the activities of craftsmen and merchants that was not limited to economic benefits derived from immunity from obligations alone. The benefits may have extended to protections from abuse at the hands of officials. According to the legal texts, associations even assumed new responsibilities (and burdens) that blurred the line between public and private.

That associations continued to thrive amid structural and administrative change is not necessarily surprising. The administrative and tax regimes may have undergone reorganizations by Diocletian, and craftsmen, merchants, and associations had to navigate the assessment and collection of a new trade tax. With the spread of Christianity, ecclesiastical institutions began to wield an increasing amount of power and influence as landowners in communities. All these factors may have somewhat altered the playing field, if not necessarily the rules of the game. The compilation and codification of the legal corpora under Theodosius II and Justinian reveal the restrictions under which some groups operated, but the law codes also indicate the privileges enjoyed by others and how few constraints impacting day-to-day operations were placed on individual associations and their members. Daily operations remained in the hands of the groups themselves, organized still with an eye to the importance of social capital and their own norms for assuring compliance and even the tax collection with which the legal sources were so concerned. In this sense, too, members remained in a position of relative strength.

Conclusion

The persistence and vitality of association organization into the seventh century CE suggests that membership remained a viable strategy to mitigate risk and uncertainty, manage transaction costs, and confront challenges in personal and professional life. In this sense, for individuals who could afford to belong (craftsmen, merchants, or otherwise), association membership helped to deal with a multitude of the issues that faced people living and working in an economic environment where information was scarce and transaction costs were high. As Geertz observed, in such environments, like the bazaars he studied, the need for information is pressing, and knowledge is "intensely valued."

> The level of ignorance about everything from product quality and going prices to market possibilities and production costs is very high, and much of the way in which the bazaar functions can be interpreted as an attempt to reduce such ignorance for someone, increase it for someone, or defend someone against it.[1]

Association membership provided one means of confronting these challenges and facilitated the efforts of individual members to reduce their ignorance, defend their interests, and, presumably, increase the ignorance of others. For instance, when the salt merchants in Tebtunis used their charter to enjoin members of their association "not to sell more than a stater's worth of salt to a merchant," they were probably not looking to help others who were engaged in the trade but did not belong to the group.

1. Geertz 1978: 29.

Members of Egyptian groups (and, doubtless, other associations) reduced their own ignorance and therefore more than likely increased their profit margin, at least in part, through reliance on their networks and the advantages that accumulating social capital provided them. Theoretically, the advantages provided, including information about prices, materials, and demand, as well as access to information about the reputation and habits of others plying the same trade and those within their networks, made an association member who plied the weaving trade, for instance, a more successful weaver who operated on a more solid social and economic footing. So, too, did benefits like financial support (not limited to trade-specific activities but including loans and legal aid) and assistance with burial, which it can be said that members invested in by maintaining their membership within an association. Assurances not to interfere with, slander, or prosecute colleagues also would have improved an individual's position by alleviating some of the dangers that could potentially accompany the contracts and agreements that craftsmen and merchants made in their economic lives.

Associations and group members made reliance on their networks clear in a variety of documents encountered here. Individual contracts, receipts, and accounts show that members pooled their resources and collaborated with each other in professional and personal economic endeavors, to complete large orders, provide loans, and coordinate the exchange of information about goods, colleagues, clients, and competitors. Petitions also reveal that groups tried to represent their own interests, acted on behalf of individual members, and helped manage relations with local and imperial officials.

The archaeological evidence of honorific exchanges and dedications from Egypt suggests that groups there invested in social capital beyond the confines of their own association. These texts indicate that groups sought to cultivate and communicate a specific reputation and to develop esteem in the public sphere, suggesting that the Egyptian evidence should be read in conversation with what is found elsewhere. Making dedications to shrines or financial donations to temples or erecting honorific stelai sent messages that the people and groups mentioned showed attention to *eunoia*, *aretē*, and *philotimia*. All of this had an economic impact.

The charters that governed association activities perhaps best explain how members themselves conceived of their collaborations, what they expected from each other, and the importance they placed on trust, reputation, and esteem. Egyptian association charters reveal a common set of activities (and concerns) that compared well to what is found elsewhere in the ancient world. Even amid changes in administrative structure, organization, and taxation that occurred during Roman rule, groups continued to abide by an agreed-on set of behavioral norms and to delineate obligations to support and not hinder colleagues, organized professional activities, shared rituals and celebrations, and managed their own affairs.

Based on what the evidence suggests, associations accomplished all of this not necessarily as separate from the community in which they lived and worked, to compensate for some deficiency, but as active participants in their community (though participation may have meant different things for different groups and their members). The documents also articulate the importance that members placed on cultivating trust between colleagues through adhering to charters and the norms spelled out therein. Membership may have reduced transaction costs and increased profits, but charters make it clear that members were supposed to pursue and achieve these goals with a sense of honor, at least displayed principally to those within the group or their immediate network. The reliance on public honorific exchange would suggest that they wanted the community to assume the group's honor as well, whether it was a reality or not.

For the most part, the state did not involve itself in the day-to-day operations of associations or of individual craftsmen or merchants, nor did it seek to impose its own form of organization on associations. Even in the face of supposed increased state interference in associations and the lives of potential members—and in the economy in general—during the late Roman period, what continued to set the parameters of association activities and organization remained members' own concerns regarding trust, reputation, and esteem. This does not mean that the state was a nonfactor or had no bearing on association activities and organization. The state and its potential coercive force, as well as its role in granting benefits, privileges, and exemptions, would seem to have been very much a part of the reality for associations and the strategies they adopted. Whether fulfilling a contract, filing a petition, or mounting a formal protest, associations interacted with the authorities and sought their protection according to established norms and modes of communication. It is to the state that associations turned (whether in the face of challenges or otherwise) to solidify their own position, to increase their standing, and, at the most basic level, for legitimation.

This study has traced a path through a period of economic expansion and growth in the first several centuries CE, followed by decline starting in the third century (though exactly when and how precipitous of a decline remains a point of contention). The nature and extent of the growth has been debated, though that the economy experienced some growth (either measured in the aggregate and fueled by population increase or measured per capita and powered by an increase in production, the two options Bowman and Wilson describe) seems to be emerging as somewhat of a consensus opinion.[2] Even more conservative stances on the subject allow for moderate aggregate growth beginning in the imperial period, the "gentle growth curve" suggested by Saller.[3] Egypt certainly experienced some of this growth.[4] Elio Lo Cascio points out, in his search for growth through the lens of urbanization, that Egypt and Italy provide some of the best quantitative evidence for such trends.[5] How this study's observations about the place of associations in large or small Egyptian communities during this period relate to patterns of economic growth is worth considering.

In some sense, common administrative strategies adopted by the Romans and put in place in Egypt apparently contributed to observed growth and propelled momentum toward urbanization and municipalization.[6] At the risk of drastic oversimplification, it can be said that more extensive private landownership ushered in under Roman rule created a new elite (as Bagnall and others have described), who sponsored this urbanization in nome capitals where they were based.[7] This may have also impacted the development of many associations engaged in the economy and society from the start of Roman rule and may have partly supported growth in a craft and merchant economy. The extent to which the seeming explosion in popularity of groups relates to economic trends and political developments that accompanied Roman rule in the first centuries CE is difficult to judge for sure. Although the associative phenomenon in Egypt and elsewhere predates Roman rule, the presence and variety of associations seems to increase following the battle of Actium and the annexation of Egypt, which suggests that a correlation cannot be ruled out. At the very least, population increase and economic growth (however slight or robust it may have been), coupled with a favorable institutional environment that did

2. Bowman and Wilson 2009a: 3–5, 28–69. See also, for example, Patterson 1998; Hitchner 2005; Scheidel, Morris, and Saller 2007: 1–12; Bang 2008: 26–36, 122–27; Lo Cascio 2009.
3. Saller 2005: 237; see also Kehoe 2007.
4. Rathbone 2007.
5. LoCascio 2009, with Bagnall 2009; see also Bagnall 2005a.
6. See Monson 2012 for a detailed analysis.
7. Bagnall 2005a: 198–99; see also Bowman and Rathbone 1992; on urbanization, see Rathbone 2007: 705–9.

not hinder forming associations for economic (among other) reasons, may have produced fertile ground in which groups flourished, particularly those organized around craft or commercial pursuits. Population increase, urbanization, and increased building activity sponsored by the local elite certainly called for additional craftsmen, and documents indicate that associations responded to the need through contracts with the local authorities.

To what extent the associations themselves provided evidence of intensifying investment in order to increase productivity and thus contribute to the perceived overall economic growth is difficult to measure and unclear. If growth was occurring as it is supposed to have been, individual members certainly played a part and may have invested their surplus accordingly, leading to aggregate growth. Association common funds were used for many things, including purchase of property. The sheep and cattle herders in Tebtunis used donations to the common fund to mark individual investment in livestock or purchase of property by members. The same group also adopted policies to protect the investments and households of members, but this action is different than the group itself making such an investment to increase productivity in some way that led to growth. Investing in more workshop space and therefore more production capacity, for instance, may have been left to individual practitioners, like Isidorus, the would-be foreman weaver who had many weavers working for him.

It is clear that associations invested heavily in social capital, a key factor to success for groups and individual members. That groups helped members respond to a host of fundamental economic issues may explain the persistence of association organization at village and city levels even after growth began to taper off in the third century and into the fourth. In times of growth and decline, the benefits of investing in social capital to secure advantages remained. In times of decline, the advantages relative to the rest of the community and other members of the nonelite may have become even more pronounced.

Bibliography

Adams, C. E. 2007. *Land Transport in Roman Egypt: A Study of Economics and Administration in a Roman Province*. Oxford: Oxford University Press.

Akerlof, G. A. 1970. "The Market for 'Lemons': Quality Uncertainty and the Market Mechanism." *Quarterly Journal of Economics* 84: 488–500.

Alföldy, G. 2011. *Römische Sozialgeschichte*. Wiesbaden: Franz Steiner.

Allen, R. C. 2009. "How Prosperous Were the Romans? Evidence from Diocletian's Price Edict (301 AD)." In A. K. Bowman and A. Wilson, eds., *Quantifying the Roman Economy: Methods and Problems*, 327–45. Oxford: Oxford University Press.

Alston, R. 1997. "Philo's In Flaccum: Ethnicity and Social Space in Roman Alexandria." *Greece and Rome* 44: 165–75.

Alston, R. 1998. "Trade and the City in Roman Egypt." In H. Parkins and C. Smith, eds., *Trade, Traders, and the Ancient City*, 168–202. London: Routledge.

Alston, R. 2002. *The City in Roman and Byzantine Egypt*. London: Routledge.

Ando, C. 2000. *Imperial Ideology and Provincial Loyalty in the Roman Empire*. Berkeley: University of California Press.

Andreau, J. 1999. *Banking and Business in the Roman World*. Translated by Janet Lloyd. Cambridge: Cambridge University Press.

Andreau, J. 2002. "Twenty Years after Moses I. Finley's *The Ancient Economy*." In W. Scheidel and S. Von Reden, eds., *The Ancient Economy*, 33–49. Edinburgh: Edinburgh University Press.

Archibald, Z. H., J. K. Davies, and V. Gabrielsen, eds. 2005. *Making, Moving, and Managing: The New World of Ancient Economies, 323–31 BC*. Oxford: Oxbow Books.

Archibald, Z. H., J. K. Davies, V. Gabrielsen, and G. J. Oliver, eds. 2001. *Hellenistic Economies*. London: Routledge.

Arnaoutoglou, I. N. 2002. "Roman Law and *Collegia* in Asia Minor." *Revue Internationale des droits de l'Antiquité* 49: 27–44.

Arnaoutoglou, I. N. 2003. Thusias heneka kai sunousias*: Private Religious Associations in Hellenistic Athens*. Athens: Academy of Athens.

Arnaoutoglou, I. N. 2005. "*Collegia* in the Province of Egypt in the First Century CE." *Ancient Society* 35: 197–216.

Arnaoutoglou, I. N. 2011. "Craftsmen Associations in Roman Lydia—A Tale of Two Cities?" *Ancient Society* 41: 257–90.

Ascough, R. A., P. A. Harland, and J. S. Kloppenborg, eds. 2012. *Associations in the Greco-Roman World: A Sourcebook*. Waco: Baylor University Press.

Ascough, R. A., P. A. Harland, and J. S. Kloppenborg, eds. *Associations in the Greco-Roman World: A Companion to the Sourcebook*. Accessed November 23, 2015. http://www.philipharland.com/greco-roman-associations/.

Axelrod, R. 2006. *The Evolution of Cooperation*. Revised edition. Cambridge, MA: Basic Books.

Bagnall, R. S. 1992. "The Periodicity and Collection of the Chrysargyron." *Tyche* 7: 15–17.

Bagnall, R. S. 1993. *Egypt in Late Antiquity*. Princeton: Princeton University Press.

Bagnall, R. S. 1995. *Reading Papyri, Writing Ancient History*. London: Routledge.

Bagnall, R. S. 2000. "Governmental Roles in the Economy of Late Antiquity." In E. Lo Cascio and D. W. Rathbone, eds., *Production and Public Powers in Classical Antiquity*, 86–91. Cambridge Philological Society Supplementary Volume 26. Cambridge: Cambridge University Press.

Bagnall, R. S. 2004. "The Last Donkey Sacrifice at Deir el-Bahari." *JJP* 34: 15–21.

Bagnall, R. S. 2005a. "Evidence and Models for the Economy of Roman Egypt." In J. G. Manning and I. Morris, eds., *The Ancient Economy: Evidence and Models*, 186–204. Stanford: Stanford University Press.

Bagnall, R. S. 2005b. "Village and City: Geographies of Power in Byzantine Egypt." In J. Lefort, C. Morrisson, and J.-P. Sodini, eds., *Les Villages dans l'Empire byzantin (IVe–XVe siècle)*, 553–65. Réalités Byzantines 11. Paris: Lethielleux.

Bagnall, R. S., ed. 2007. *Egypt in the Byzantine World, 300–700*. Cambridge: Cambridge University Press.

Bagnall, R. S. 2008. "Village Landholding at Aphrodito in Comparative Perspective." In J.- L. Fournet, ed., *Les archives de Dioscore d'Aphrodité cent ans après leur découverte: Histoire et culture dans l'Egypte byzantine; Actes du Colloque de Strasbourg, 8–10 décembre 2005*, 181–90. Paris: De Boccard.

Bagnall, R. S. 2009. "Response to Elio Lo Cascio." In A. K. Bowman and A. Wilson, eds., *Quantifying the Roman Economy: Methods and Problems*, 107–12. Oxford: Oxford University Press.

Bagnall, R. S., and B. W. Frier. 1994. *The Demography of Roman Egypt*. Cambridge: Cambridge University Press.

Bagnall, R. S., J. G. Keenan, and L. S. B. MacCoull. 2011. *A Sixth-century Tax Register from the Hermopolite Nome. American Studies in Papyrology* 51. Durham: Americna Society of Papyrologists.

Bagnall, R. S., and D. W. Rathbone. 2004. *Egypt from Alexander to the Early Christians: An Archaeological and Historical Guide*. London: British Museum Press.

Bagnall, R. S., and K. A. Worp. 1985. "Two Nominations of Goldsmiths to Collect Taxes." *ZPE* 59: 67–70.

Bailey, D. M. 1991. *Excavations at El- Ashmunein*. Vol. 4, *Hermopolis Magna: Buildings of the Roman Period*. London: British Museum Press.

Balch, D. L., and C. Osiek, eds. 2003. *Early Christian Families in Context: An Interdisciplinary Dialogue*. Grand Rapids: W. B. Eerdmans.

Banaji, J. 2007. *Agrarian Change in Late Antiquity: Gold, Labour, and Aristocratic Dominance*. Revised edition. Oxford: Oxford University Press.

Bang, P. F. 2006. "Imperial Bazaar: Towards a Comparative Understanding of Markets in the Roman Empire." In P. F. Bang, M. Ikeguchi, and H. G. Ziche, eds., *Ancient Economies, Modern Methodologies*, 51–88. Bari: Edipuglia.

Bang, P. F. 2007. "Trade and Empire: In Search of the Organizing Concepts of the Roman Economy." *Past and Present* 195: 3–54.

Bang, P. F. 2008. *The Roman Bazaar: A Comparative Study of Trade and Markets in a Tributary Empire*. Cambridge: Cambridge University Press.

Bang, P. F., M. Ikeguchi, and H. G. Ziche, eds. 2006. *Ancient Economies, Modern Methodologies*. Bari: Edipuglia.

Bernand, E. 1993. "Τόπος dans les inscriptions grecques d'Egypte." *ZPE* 98: 103–10.

Bierbrier, M. L., ed. 1997. *Portraits and Masks: Burial Customs in Roman Egypt*. London: British Museum Press.

Boak, A. E. R. 1937. "The Organization of Guilds in Greco-Roman Egypt." *TAPA* 68: 212–20.

Bollmann, B. 1998. *Römische Vereinshäuser: Untersuchungen zu den Scholea der römischen Berufs-, Kult- und Augustalen-Kollegien in Italien*. Mainz: Von Zabern.

Bowman, A. K. 1971. *The Town Councils of Roman Egypt*. American Studies in Papyrology 11. Toronto: Hakkert.

Bowman, A. K. 1986. *Egypt after the Pharaohs*. Berkeley: University of California Press.

Bowman, A. K., R. A. Coles, N. Gonis, D. Obbink, and P. J. Parsons, eds. 2007. *Oxyrhynchus: A City and Its Texts*. London: Egypt Exploration Society.

Bowman, A. K., and D. Rathbone. 1992. "Cities and Administration in Roman Egypt." *JRS* 82: 107–27.

Bowman, A. K., and E. Rogan, eds. 1999. *Agriculture in Egypt from Pharonic to Modern Times*. Proceedings of the British Academy 96. Oxford: Oxford University Press.

Bowman, A. K., and A. Wilson. 2009a. "Quantifying the Roman Economy: Integration, Growth, Decline?" In A. K. Bowman and A. Wilson, eds., *Quantifying the Roman Economy: Methods and Problems*, 3–86. Oxford: Oxford University Press.

Bowman, A. K., and A. Wilson, eds. 2009b. *Quantifying the Roman Economy: Methods and Problems*. Oxford: Oxford University Press.

Bradley, K. 1991. *Discovering the Roman Family: Studies in Roman Social History*. Oxford: Oxford University Press.

Brennan, G., and P. Pettit. 2004. *The Economy of Esteem*. Oxford: Oxford University Press.

Broekaert, W. 2011. "Partners in Business: Roman Merchants and the Potential Advantages of Being a *Collegiatus*." *Ancient Society* 41: 221–56.

Brookhiser, R., ed. 1997. *Rules of Civility*. New York: Free Press.

Bryen, A. 2008. "Visibility and Violence in Petitions from Roman Egypt." *GRBS* 48: 181–200.

Bryen, A. Z. 2013. *Violence in Roman Egypt: An Interpretation*. Philadelphia: University of Pennsylvania Press.

Buckler, W. H. 1923. "Labour Disputes in the Province of Asia." In W. H. Buckler and W. M. Calder, eds., *Anatolian Studies Presented to Sir W. M. Ramsay*, 27–50. Manchester: Manchester University Press.

Burford, A. 1972. *Craftsmen in Greek and Roman Society*. Ithaca: Cornell University Press.

Burt, R. S. 2005. *Brokerage and Closure: An Introduction to Social Capital*. Chicago: University of Chicago Press.

Burton, G. P. 1975. "Proconsuls, Assizes, and the Administration of Justice under the Empire." *JRS* 65: 92–106.

Burton, G. P. 2001a. "The Imperial State and Its Impact on the Role and Status of Local Magistrates and Councillors in the Provinces of the Empire." In L. De Blois, ed., *Administration, Prosopography, and Appointment Policies in the Roman Empire*, 202-14. Amsterdam: Gieben.

Burton, G. P. 2001b. "The Roman Imperial State (A.D. 14—235): Evidence and Reality." *Chiron* 31: 249–80.

Burton, G. P. 2004. "The Roman Imperial State, Provincial Governors, and the Public Finances of Provincial Cities, 27 B.C.–A.D. 235." *Historia* 53: 312–42.

Capasso, M., and P. Davoli, eds. 2007. *New Archaeological and Papyrological Researches on the Fayyum: Proceedings of the International Meeting of Egyptology and Papyrology*. Lecce: Congeddo.

Capponi, L. 2005. *Augustan Egypt: The Creation of a Roman Province*. London: Routledge.

Carrié, J.-M. 2002. "Les associations professionnelles à l'époque tardive: Entre *munus* et convivialité." In J.-M. Carrié and Rita Lizzi Testa, eds., *Humana Sapit: Mélanges en l'honneur de Lellia Cracco Ruggini*, 309–22. Turnhout: Brepols.

Carroll, M. 2006. *Spirits of the Dead: Roman Funerary Commemoration in Western Europe*. Oxford: Oxford University Press.

Casson, L. 1989. *The "Periplus Maris Erythraei": Text with Introduction, Translation, and Commentary*. Princeton: Princeton University Press.

Clarysse, W., and D. J. Thompson. 2004. *Counting the People in Hellenistic Egypt*. Cambridge: Cambridge University Press.

Coase, R. H. 1937. "The Nature of the Firm." *Economica* 4: 386–405.

Coase, R. H. 1960. "The Problem of Social Cost." *Journal of Law and Economics* 3: 1–44.

Coase, R. H. 1990. *The Firm, the Market, and the Law*. Chicago: University of Chicago Press.

Cockle, H. 1981. "Pottery Manufacture in Roman Egypt: A New Papyrus." *JRS* 71: 87–97.

Coleman, J. S. 1988. "Social Capital in the Creation of Human Capital." *American Journal of Sociology* 94: S95–S120.

Coles, R. A. 1980a. "*P.Harr.* 73 and 160 Revised." *ZPE* 37: 229–39.

Coles, R. A. 1980b. "*P.Oxy.* I 85 Revised." *ZPE* 39: 115–23.

Cotter, W. 1996. "The Collegia and Roman Law: State Restrictions on Voluntary Associations, 64 BCE–200CE." In J. S. Kloppenborg and S. G. Wilson, eds., *Voluntary Associations in the Graeco-Roman World*, 74–89. London: Routledge.

Craver, S. E. 2010. "Urban Real Estate in Late Republican Rome." *Memoirs of the American Academy in Rome* 55: 135-158.

Crawford, M. 1996. *Roman Statutes.* Bulletin of the Institute of Classical Studies Supplement 64. London: Institute of Classical Studies, School of Advanced Study, University of London.

Crook, J. A. 1967. *Law and Life of Rome, 90 B.C.–212 A.D.* Ithaca: Cornell University Press.

D'Arms, J. 1981. *Commerce and Social Standing in Ancient Rome.* Cambridge, MA: Harvard University Press.

Davoli, P. 2007. "The Temple Area of Soknopaiou Nesos." In M. Capasso and P. Davoli, eds., *New Archaeological and Papyrological Researches on the Fayyum: Proceedings of the International Meeting of Egyptology and Papyrology*, 97–124. Lecce: Congeddo.

de Cenival, F. 1972. *Les associations religieuses en Égypte, d'après les documents démotiques.* Bibliotheque d'Étude 46. Cairo: IFAO.

de Cenival, F. 1977. "Deux papyri inédits de Lille, avec une révision du P. dem. Lille 31." *Enchoria* 7: 1–49.

de Cenival, F. 1986. "Comptes d'une association religieuse Thébaine datant das années 29 à 33 du roi Amasis (*P.Démot.* Louvre E 7840 Bis)." *Revue d'Égyptologie* 37: 13–29.

de Ligt, L. 1993. *Fairs and Markets in the Roman Empire.* Amsterdam: Gieben.

de Ligt, L. 2000. "Governmental Attitudes towards Markets and *Collegia*." In E. Lo Cascio, ed., *Mercati permanenti e mercati periodici nel mondo romano: Atti degli Incontri capresi di storia dell'economia antica (Capri 13–15 ottobre 1997)*, 237–52. Pragmateiai 2. Bari: Edipuglia.

de Ligt, L. 2001. "*D.* 47, 22, 1, pr.-1 and the Formation of Semi-Public *Collegia*." *Latomus* 60: 345–58.

de Ligt, L., E. A. Hemelrijk, and H. W. Singor, eds. 2004. *Roman Rule and Civic Life: Local and Regional Perspectives.* Amsterdam: Gieben.

Derda, T. 1991. "Necropolis Workers in Graeco-Roman Egypt in the Light of the Greek Papyri." *JJP* 21: 13–36.

De Robertis, F. M. 1971. *Storia delle corporazioni e del regime associativo nel mondo romano.* Bari: Adriatica.

Dillon, J. N. 2012. *The Justice of Constantine: Law, Communication, and Control.* Ann Arbor: University of Michigan Press.

Dunand, F. 1979. "L'artisanat du textile dans l'Égypte lagide." *Ktema* 4: 47–69.

Duncan-Jones, R. P. 1982. *The Economy of the Roman Empire: Quantitative Studies*. Second edition. Cambridge: Cambridge University Press.

Duncan-Jones, R. P. 1990. *Structure and Scale in the Roman Economy*. Cambridge: Cambridge University Press.

Dyck, A. R. 1996. *A Commentary on Cicero, "De officiis."* Ann Arbor: University of Michigan Press.

Erdkamp, P. 2005. *The Grain Market in the Roman Empire: A Social, Political, and Economic Study*. Cambridge: Cambridge University Press.

Evans, J. A. S. 1961. "The Social and Economic History of an Egyptian Temple in the Greco-Roman Period." *YCS* 17: 143–283.

Farr, J. R. 1988. *Hands of Honor: Artisans and Their World in Dijon, 1550–1650*. Ithaca: Cornell University Press.

Farr, J. R. 2000. *Artisans in Europe, 1300–1914*. Cambridge: Cambridge University Press.

Fikhman, I. F. 1969. "Grundfragen der handwerklichen Produktion in Ägypten vom 4. bis zur Mitte des 7. Jahrhunderts." *JWG* 4: 149–71.

Fikhman, I. F. 1971. "Die Bevölkerungszahl von Oxyrhynchos in byzantinischer Zeit." *APF* 21: 111–20.

Fikhman, I. F. 1991–92. "State and Prices in Byzantine Egypt." *Scripta Classica Israelica* 11: 139–48.

Fikhman, I. F. 1994. "Sur quelques aspects socio-économiques de l'activité des corporations professionnelles de l'Égypte Byzantine." *ZPE* 111: 19–40.

Fikhman, I. F. 1996. "On Onomastics of Greek and Roman Egypt." In R. Katzoff, ed., *Classical Studies in Honor of David Sohlberg*, 403–14. Ramat Gan: Bar-Ilan University Press.

Finley, M. I. 1983. *Politics in the Ancient World*. Cambridge: Cambridge University Press.

Finley, M. I. 1999. *The Ancient Economy*. Revised edition. Berkeley: University of California Press.

Finnestad, R. B. 1997. "Temples of the Ptolemaic and Roman Periods: Ancient Traditions in New Contexts." In B. E. Shafer, ed., *Temples of Ancient Egypt*, 185–237. Ithaca: Cornell University Press.

Flohr, M. 2013. *The World of the* Fullo: *Work, Economy, and Society in Roman Italy*. Oxford: Oxford University Press.

Forbis, E. 1996. *Municipal Virtues in the Roman Empire*. Beiträge zur Altertumskunde 79. Stuttgart: Teubner.

Foucart, P. 1873. *Des Associations religieuses chez les Grecs*. Paris: Klincksieck.

Fournet, J.-L. 1999. *Hellénisme dans l'Égypte du sixième siècle: La bibliothèque et l'oeuvre de Dioscore d'Aphrodito*. 2 vols. Cairo: IFAO.

Fournet, J.-L., ed. 2008. *Les archives de Dioscore d'Aphrodité cent ans après leur découverte: Histoire et culture dans l'Egypte byzantine; Actes du Colloque de Strasbourg, 8–10 décembre 2005*. Paris: De Boccard.

Frankfurter, D. 1998. *Religion in Roman Egypt: Assimilation and Resistance*. Princeton: Princeton University Press.

Frier, B. W. 1980. *Landlords and Tenants in Imperial Rome*. Princeton: Princeton University Press.

Frier, B. W., and D. P. Kehoe. 2007. "Law and Economic Institutions." In W. Scheidel, I. Morris, and R. P. Saller, eds., *The Cambridge Economic History of the Greco-Roman World*, 113–43. Cambridge: Cambridge University Press.

Gabrielsen, V. 2001. "The Rhodian Associations and Economic Activity." In Z. H. Archibald, J. K. Davies, V. Gabrielsen, and G. J. Oliver, eds., *Hellenistic Economies*, 215–44. London: Routledge.

Gabrielsen, V. 2007. "Brotherhoods of Faith and Provident Planning: The Non-public Associations of the Greek World." *Mediterranean Historical Review* 22: 183–210.

Gabrielsen, V., and C. A. Thomsen, eds., *Private Associations and the Public Sphere: Proceedings of a Symposium held at the Royal Danish Academy of Sciences and Letters, 9-11 September 2010*. Scientia Danica. Series H, Humanistic, 8 vol. 9. Copenhagen: The Royal Danish Academy of Sciences and Letters.

Gagos, T., and P. van Minnen. 1994. *Settling a Dispute: Toward a Legal Anthropology of Late Antique Egypt*. Ann Arbor: University of Michigan Press.

Galsterer, H. 1988. "Municipium Flavium Irnitanum: A Latin Town in Spain." *JRS* 78: 78–90.

Garnsey, P. 1970. *Social Status and Legal Privilege*. Oxford: Oxford University Press.

Garnsey, P., K. Hopkins, and C. R. Whittaker, eds. 1983. *Trade in the Ancient Economy*. Berkeley: University of California Press.

Garnsey, P., and R. Saller. 1987. *The Roman Empire: Economy, Society, and Culture*. Berkeley: University of California Press.

Gascou, J. 1994. *Un codex fiscal Hermopolite* (*P.Sorb.* II 69). American Studies in Papyrology 32. Atlanta: Scholars Press.

Gascou, J., and L. S. B. MacCoull. 1987. "Le cadastre d'Aphrodito." *Travaux et Mémoires* 10: 103–58.

Gascou, J., and K. A. Worp. 1990. "Un dossier d'ostraca du VIe siècle: Les archives des huiliers d'Aphrodito." In M. Capasso, G. M. Savorelli, and R. Pintaudi, eds., *Miscellanea Papyrologica in occasione del bicentenario dell' edizione della charta borgiana*, 217–44. Papyrologica Florentina 19. Florence: Gonnelli.

Geertz, C. 1963. *Peddlers and Princes: Social Change and Economic Modernization in Two Indonesian Towns*. Chicago: University of Chicago Press.

Geertz, C. 1978. "The Bazaar Economy: Information and Search in Peasant Marketing." *American Economic Review* 68, no. 2: 28–32.

Gibbs, M. 2008. "Professional and Trade Associations in Ptolemaic and Roman Egypt." PhD diss., Oxford University.

Gibbs, M. 2011. "Trade Associations in Roman Egypt: Their Raison d'Être." *Ancient Society* 41: 291–315.

Gibson, R. K, and R. Morello. 2012. *Reading the* Letters *of Pliny the Younger: An Introduction*. Cambridge: Cambridge University Press.

Goffart, W. 1974. *Caput and Colonate: Towards a History of Late Roman Taxation*. Toronto: University of Toronto Press.

Goffman, E. 1959. *Presentation of the Self in Everyday Life*. Garden City, NY: Doubleday.

Gonis, N. 2004. "Notes on Oxyrhynchus Papyri III." *ZPE* 150: 197–202.

Gonzalez, J., and M. Crawford. 1986. "The *Lex Irnitana*: A New Copy of the Flavian Municipal Law." *JRS* 76: 147–243.

Granovetter, M. 1985. "Economic Action and Social Structure: The Problem of Embeddedness." *American Journal of Sociology* 91, no. 3: 481–510.

Granovetter, M., and R. Swerdberg, eds. 2001. *The Sociology of Economic Life*. Second edition. Westview.

Greif, A. 1989. "Reputation and Coalitions in Medieval Trade: Evidence on the Maghribi Traders." *Journal of Economic History* 49, no. 4: 857–82.

Greif, A. 1993. "Contract Enforceability and Economic Institutions in Early Trade: The Maghribi Traders' Coalition." *American Economic Review* 83, no. 3: 525–48.

Greif, A. 2006. *Institutions and the Path to the Modern Economy: Lessons from Medieval Trade*. Cambridge: Cambridge University Press.

Greif, A., P. Milgrom, and B. R. Weingast. 1994. "Coordination, Commitment, and Enforcement: The Case of the Merchant Guild." *Journal of Political Economy* 102, no. 4: 745–76.

Grey, C. 2007. "Contextualizing *Colonatus*: The *Origo* of the Late Roman Empire." *JRS* 97: 155–75.

Grey, C. 2011. *Constructing Communities in the Late Roman Countryside*. Cambridge: Cambridge University Press.

Hagedorn, D. 2007. "The Emergence of Civic Offices in the Nome Capitals of Egypt." In A. K. Bowman, R. A. Coles, N. Gonis, D. Obbink, P. J. Parsons, eds., *Oxyrhynchus: A City and Its Texts*, 194–204. London: Egypt Exploration Society.

Hall, J. M. 2004. *Hellenicity*. Chicago: University of Chicago Press.

Hardin, G. 1968. "The Tragedy of the Commons." *Science* 162: 1243–47.

Harker, A. 2008. *Loyalty and Dissidence in Roman Egypt: The Case of the Acta Alexandrinorum*. Cambridge: Cambridge University Press.

Harland, P. 2003. *Associations, Synagogues, and Congregations: Claiming a Place in Ancient Mediterranean Society*. Minneapolis: Fortress.

Harries, J. 1999. *Law and Empire in Late Antiquity*. Cambridge: Cambridge University Press.

Harries, J., and I. Wood, eds. 1993. *The Theodosian Code*. Ithaca: Cornell University Press.

Hawkins, C. 2006. "Work in the City: Roman Artisans and the Urban Economy." PhD diss., University of Chicago.

Hermansen, G. 1982. *Ostia: Aspects of Roman City Life*. Calgary: University of Alberta Press.

Hickey, T. M. 2007. "Aristocratic Landholding and the Economy of Byzantine Egypt." In R. S. Bagnall, ed., *Egypt in the Byzantine World*, 288–308. Cambridge: Cambridge University Press.

Hickey, T. M. 2008. "Papyrology." In R. Cormack, J. F. Haldon, and E. Jeffreys, eds., *The Oxford Handbook of Byzantine Studies*, 115–28. Oxford: Oxford University Press.

Hickey, T. M. 2009. "Writing Histories from the Papyri." In R. S. Bagnall, ed., *The Oxford Handbook of Papyrology*, 495–520. Oxford: Oxford University Press.

Hickey, T. M. 2012. *Wine, Wealth, and the State in Late Antique Egypt: The House of Apion at Oxyrhynchus*. Ann Arbor: University of Michigan Press.

Hitchner, B. W. 2005. "'The Advantages of Wealth and Luxury': The Case for Economic Growth in the Roman Empire." In J. G. Manning and I. Morris, eds., *The Ancient Economy: Evidence and Models*, 207–22. Stanford: Stanford University Press.

Hobson, D. W. 1983. "Women as Property Owners." *TAPA* 113: 311–21.

Hobson, D. W. 1985. "The Village of Heraklia in the Arsinoite Nome." *BASP* 22: 101–15.

Hobson, D. W. 1986. "The Inhabitants of Heraklia." *BASP* 23: 99–123.

Hobson, D. W. 1989. "Naming Practices in Roman Egypt." *BASP* 25: 157–74.

Holleran, C. 2012. *Shopping in Ancient Rome: The Retail Trade in the Late Republic and the Principate*. Oxford: Oxford University Press.

Honoré, T. 2010. *Justinian's Digest: Character and Compilation*. Oxford: Oxford University Press.

Hopkins, K. 1983a. *Death and Renewal*. Cambridge: Cambridge University Press.

Hopkins, K. 1983b. Introduction to P. Garnsey, K. Hopkins, and C. R. Whittaker, eds., *Trade in the Ancient Economy*, ix–xxv. Berkeley: University of California Press,.

Husselman, E. 1970. "Procedures of the Record Office of Tebtunis in the First Century AD." In D. H. Samuel, ed., *Proceedings of the Twelfth International Congress of Papyrology, Ann Arbor, 13—17 August 1968*. American Studies in Papyrology 7. Toronto: Hakkert.

Johnson, A. C. 1936. *An Economic Survey of Ancient Rome*. Vol. 2, *Roman Egypt to the Reign of Diocletian*. Edited by Tenney Frank. Baltimore: Johns Hopkins Press.

Johnson, A. C., and L. C. West. 1936. *Currency in Roman and Byzantine Egypt*. Princeton: Princeton University Press.

Johnson, A. C., and L. C. West. 1949. *Byzantine Egypt: Economic Studies*. Princeton: Princeton University Press.

Johnstone, S. 2011. *A History of Trust in Ancient Greece*. Chicago: University of Chicago Press.

Jolowicz, H. F., and N. Barry. 1972. *Historical Introduction to the Study of Roman Law*. Third edition. Cambridge: Cambridge University Press.

Jones, A. H. M. 1964. *The Later Roman Empire: 284–602*. 2 vols. Norman: University of Oklahoma Press.

Jones, A. H. M. 1974a. "The Caste System in the Later Roman Empire." In P. A. Brunt, ed., *The Roman Economy: Studies in Ancient Economic and Administrative History*, 396–417. Oxford: Blackwell. Originally published in *Eirene* 8 (1970): 79–96.

Jones, A. H. M. 1974b. "The Cloth Industry under the Roman Empire." In P. A. Brunt, ed., *The Roman Economy: Studies in Ancient Economic and Administrative History*, 350–64. Oxford: Blackwell. Originally published in *Economic History Review* 13 (1960): 183–92.

Jones, N. 1999. *The Associations of Classical Athens: The Response to Democracy*. Oxford: Oxford University Press.

Jongman, W., and M. Kleijwegt, eds. 2002. *After the Past: Essays in Ancient History in Honour of H. W. Pleket*. Leiden: Brill.

Joshel, S. R. 1992. *Work, Identity, and Legal Status at Rome: A Study of the Occupational Inscriptions*. Norman: University of Oklahoma Press.

Kalinowski, A. 2002. "The Vedii Antonini: Aspects of Patronage and Benefaction in Second-Century Ephesos." *Phoenix* 56: 109–49.

Keenan, J. G. 1975. "On Law and Society in Late Roman Egypt." *ZPE* 17: 237–50.

Keenan, J. G. 1980. "Aurelius Phoibammon, son of Triadelphus: A Byzantine Egyptian Entrepreneur." *BASP* 17: 145–54.

Keenan, J. G. 1984. "The Aphrodite Papyri and Village Life in Byzantine Egypt." *Bulletin de la Société d'Archéologie Copte* 26: 51–63.

Keenan, J. G. 1993. "Papyrology and Byzantine Historiography." *BASP* 30: 137–44.

Keenan, J. G. 1995. "The Aphrodito Murder Mystery: A Return to the Scene of the Crimes." *BASP* 32: 57–63.

Keenan, J. G. 2009. "Egypt's 'Special Place.'" In E. P. Cueva, S. N. Byrne, and F. Benda, eds., *Jesuit Education and the Classics*, 177–92. Newcastle upon Tyne, UK: Cambridge Scholars Publishing.

Kehoe, D. P. 2007. "The Early Roman Empire: Production." In W. Scheidel, I. Morris, and R. P. Saller, eds., *The Cambridge Economic History of the Greco-Roman World*, 543–69. Cambridge: Cambridge University Press.

Kelly, B. 2007. "Riot Control and Imperial Ideology in the Roman Empire." *Phoenix* 61: 150–76.

Kelly, B. 2011. *Petitions, Litigation, and Social Control in Roman Egypt*. Oxford: Oxford University Press.

Kelly, C. 1998. "Emperors, Government, and Bureaucracy." In A. Cameron and P. Garnsey, eds., *Cambridge Ancient History*, vol. 13, *The Late Empire, A.D. 337–425*, 138–83. Cambridge: Cambridge University Press.

Kelly, C. 2004. *Ruling the Later Roman Empire*. Cambridge, MA: Harvard University Press.

Klein, D. B., ed. 1997. *Reputation: Studies in the Voluntary Elicitation of Good Conduct*. Ann Arbor: University of Michigan Press.

Kloppenborg, J. S. 1996. "*Collegia* and *Thiasoi*: Issues in Function, Taxonomy, and Membership." In J. S. Kloppenborg and S. G. Wilson, eds., *Voluntary Associations in the Graeco-Roman World*, 16–30. London: Routledge.

Kloppenborg, J. S., and R. S. Ascough, eds. 2011. *Greco-Roman Associations: Texts, Translations, and Commentary*. Vol. 1, *Attica, Central Greece, Macedonia, and Thrace*. New York: De Gruyter.

Kloppenborg, J. S., and S. G. Wilson, eds. 1996. *Voluntary Associations in the Graeco-Roman World*. London: Routledge.

Knight, F. H. (1921) 2006. *Risk, Uncertainty, and Profit*. Mineola, NY: Dover.

Kokkinia, C. 2004. "Ruling, Inducing, Arguing: How to Govern (and Survive) a Greek Province." In L. De Ligt, E. A. Hemelrijk, H. W. Singor, eds., *Roman Rule and Civic Life: Local and Regional Perspectives*, 39–58. Amsterdam: Gieben.

Łajtar, A. 1991. "Proskynema Inscriptions of a Corporation of Iron-Workers from Hermonthis in the Temple of Queen Hatshepsut in Deir el-Bahari: New Evidence for Pagan Cults in Egypt in the 4th century AD." *JJP* 21: 53–70.

Łajtar, A. 2006. *Deir el-Bahari in the Hellenistic and Roman Periods: A Study Based on Greek Sources*. Journal of Juristic Papyrology Supplement 4. Warsaw: Institute of Archaeology, Warsaw University.

Lefort, J., C. Morrisson, and J.-P. Sodini, eds. 2005. *Les Villages dans l'Empire byzantin (IVe–XVe siècle)*. Réalités Byzantines 11. Paris: Lethielleux.

Lendon, J. E. 1997. *Empire of Honour: The Art of Government in the Roman World*. Oxford: Oxford University Press.

Lewis, N. 1983. *Life in Egypt under Roman Rule*. Oxford: Oxford University Press.

Lewis, N. 1993a. "Εὐσχήμονες in Roman Egypt." *BASP* 30: 105–13.

Lewis, N. 1993b. "Notationes Legentis." *BASP* 30: 27–33.

Lewis, N. 1997. *The Compulsory Public Services of Roman Egypt*. Second edition. Papyrologica Florentina 28. Florence: Gonnelli.

Liebeschuetz, J. H. W. G. 1972. *Antioch: City and Imperial Administration in the Later Roman Empire*. Oxford: Oxford University Press.

Liebeschuetz, J. H. W. G. 2001. *Decline and Fall of the Roman City*. Oxford: Oxford University Press.

Lippert, S., and M. Schentuleit, eds. 2008. *Graeco-Roman Fayum: Texts and Archaeology; Proceedings of the Third International Fayum Symposion, Freudenstadt, May 29–June 1, 2007*. Wiesbaden: Harrassowitz.

Liu, J. 2005. "Local Governments and Collegia: A New Appraisal of the Evidence." In J.- J. Aubert and Z. Varhelyi, eds., *A Tall Order: Writing the Social History of the Ancient World*, 285–316. Munich: Saur.

Liu, J. 2008. "The Economy of Endowments: The Case of Roman *Collegia*." In K. Verboven, K. Vandorpe, and V. Chankowski-Sable, eds., Pistoi dia tèn technèn*: Bankers, Loans, and Archives in the Ancient World; Studies in Honour of Raymond Bogaert*, 231–56. Studia Hellenistica 44. Louvain: Peeters.

Liu, J. 2009. Collegia Centoniariorum*: The Guilds of Textile Dealers in the Roman West*. Columbia Studies in the Classical Tradition 34. Leiden: Brill.

Lo Cascio, E. 2009. "Urbanization as a Proxy of Demographic and Economic Growth." In A. K. Bowman and A. Wilson, eds., *Quantifying the Roman Economy: Methods and Problems*, 87–106. Oxford: Oxford University Press.

Luijendijk, A. M. 2010. "A New Testament Papyrus and Its Documentary Context: An

Early Christian Writing Exercise from the Archive of Aurelius Leonides." *JBL* 129: 575–96.

Lupton, D. 1999. *Risk*. New York: Routledge.

Ma, J. 2007. "Hellenistic Honorific Statues and Their Inscriptions." In Z. Newby and R. Leader-Newby, eds., *Art and Inscriptions in the Ancient World*, 203–20. Cambridge: Cambridge University Press.

MacCoull, L. S. B. 1984. "Notes on the Social Structure of Late Antique Aphrodito." *Bulletin de la Société d'Archéologie Copte* 26: 65–77.

MacCoull, L. S. B. 1987. "Money and People in the Late Antique Hermopolite: BM 1075 and Related Texts." *Tyche* 2: 99–105.

MacCoull, L. S. B. 1988. *Dioscorus of Aphrodito: His Work and His World*. Berkeley: University of California Press.

MacCoull, L. S. B. 1990. "The Aphrodito Murder Mystery." *JJP* 20: 103–7.

MacMullen, R. 1963. "A Note on Roman Strikes." *Classical Journal* 58: 269–71.

MacMullen, R. 1964. "Social Mobility and the Theodosian Code." *JRS* 54: 49–53.

MacMullen, R. 1974. *Roman Social Relations*. New Haven: Yale University Press.

MacMullen, R. 1992. *Enemies of the Roman Order*. New York: Routledge.

Manning, J. G. 2010. *The Last Pharaohs: Egypt under the Ptolemies, 305–30 BC*. Princeton: Princeton University Press.

Manning, J. G., and Ian Morris, eds. 2005. *The Ancient Economy: Evidence and Models*. Stanford: Stanford University Press.

Manning, P. 1991. "Drama as Life: The Significance of Goffman's Changing Use of the Theatrical Metaphor." *Sociological Theory* 9: 70–86.

Martinez, D. 1997. "*P.Erasm.* I 10: An Order for Payment from a Cult Association." *ZPE* 118: 263–66.

Martinez, D., and M. Williams. 1997. "Records of Loan Receipts from a Guild Association." *ZPE* 118: 259–63.

Matthews, J. F. 1984. "The Tax Law of Palmyra: Evidence for Economic History in a City of the Roman East." *JRS* 74: 157–80.

Matthews, J. F. 2000. *Laying Down the Law: A Study of the Theodosian Code*. New Haven: Yale University Press.

Mattingly, D. J., and J. Salmon, eds. 2001. *Economies beyond Agriculture in the Classical World*. New York: Routledge.

Mayer, E. 2012. *The Ancient Middle Classes: Urban Life and Aesthetics in the Roman Empire, 100 BCE–250 CE*. Cambridge, MA: Harvard University Press.

Mayerson, P. 1997. "The Role of Flax in Roman and Fatamid Egypt." *JNES* 56: 201–7.

Mazza, R. 2001. *L'archivio degli Apioni: Terra, lavoro e proprieta' senatoria nell'Egitto tardoantico*. Bari: Edipuglia.

McCormick, M. 1986. *Eternal Victory: Triumphal Rulership in Late Antiquity, Byzantium, and the Early Medieval West*. Cambridge: Cambridge University Press.

McMillan, J. 2002. *Reinventing the Bazaar*. New York: Norton.

Meeks, W. A. 1983. *The First Urban Christians: The Social World of the Apostle Paul*. New Haven: Yale University Press.

Meiggs, R. 1973. *Roman Ostia*. Oxford: Oxford University Press.

Millar, F. 1977. *The Emperor in the Roman World, 31 BC–AD 337*. Ithaca: Cornell University Press.

Millar, F. 1983. "Empire and City, Augustus to Julian: Obligations, Excuses, and Status." *JRS* 73: 76–96.

Mitthof, F., and A. Papathomas. 1994. "Das Archiv des ἐλαιουργός Sambas. Unterhaltszahlungen in Ol an die Bediensteten eines Gutes." *ZPE* 103: 53–84.

Mommsen, T. 1943. *De collegiis et sodaliciis Romanorum*. Kiel: Libraria Schwersiana.

Monson, A. 2006. "The Ethics and Economics of Ptolemaic Religious Associations." *Ancient Society* 36: 221–38.

Monson, A. 2007a. "Private Associations in the Ptolemaic Fayyum: The Evidence of Demotic Accounts." In M. Capasso and P. Davoli, eds., *New Archaeological and Papyrological Researches on the Fayyum: Proceedings of the International Meeting of Egyptology and Papyrology*, 179–96. Lecce: Congeddo.

Monson, A. 2007b. "Religious Associations and Temples in Ptolemaic Tebtunis." In J. Frösén, T. Purola, and E. Salmenkivi, eds., *Proceedings of the 24th International Congress of Papyrology, Helsinki, 1st–7th of August 2004*, 769–79. Commentationes Humanarum Litterarum 122. Helsinki: Societas Scientiarum Fennica.

Monson, A. 2012. *From the Ptolemies to the Romans: Political and Economic Change in Egypt*. Cambridge: Cambridge University Press.

Montserrat, D. 1997. "Death and Funerals in the Roman Fayum." In M. L. Bierbrier, ed., *Portraits and Masks: Burial Customs in Roman Egypt*, 33–44. London: British Museum Press.

Mooren, L., ed. 2000. *Politics, Administration, and Society in the Hellenistic and Roman World*. Louvain: Peeters.

Morrisson, C., ed. 2012. *Trade and Markets in Byzantium*. Dumbarton Oaks Byzantine Symposia and Colloquia. Washington, DC: Dumbarton Oaks.

Mouritsen, H. 2011. *The Freedman in the Roman World*. Cambridge: Cambridge University Press.

Muhs, B. 2001. "Membership in Private Associations in Ptolemaic Tebtunis." *JESHO* 44: 1–21.

Muszynski, M. 1977. "Les 'associations religieuses' en Égypte." *Orientalia Lovaniensia Periodica* 8: 145–74.

Nelson, C. A. 1979. *Status Declarations in Roman Egypt*. American Studies in Papyrology 19. Amsterdam: Hakkert.

Nelson, C. A. 1995. "Protest against Nomination to a Liturgy (P.Berol.Inv. 25609)." *JJP* 25: 147–52.

Newby, Z., and R. Leader-Newby, eds. 2007. *Art and Inscriptions in the Ancient World.* Cambridge: Cambridge University Press.

Nicholas, B. 1962. *An Introduction to Roman Law.* Oxford: Oxford University Press.

Nock, A. D., C. Roberts, and T. C. Skeat. 1936. "The Guild of Zeus Hypsistos." *HTR* 29: 39–88.

Noreña, C. F. 2007. "The Social Economy of Pliny's Correspondence with Trajan." *AJP* 128: 239–77.

North, D. C. 1981. *Structure and Change in Economic History.* New York: Norton.

North, D. C. 1990. *Institutions, Institutional Change, and Economic Performance.* Cambridge: Cambridge University Press.

Ogilvie, S. 2007. "'Whatever Is, Is Right'? Economic Institutions in Pre-industrial Europe." *Economic History Review* 60, no. 4: 649–84.

Ogilvie, S. 2011. *Institutions and European Trade: Merchant Guilds, 1000–1800.* Cambridge: Cambridge University Press.

Palme, B. 2007. "The Imperial Presence: Government and Army." In R. Bagnall, ed., *Egypt in the Byzantine World, 300–700*, 244–70. Cambridge: Cambridge University Press.

Parássoglou, G. M. 1973. "Five Private Letters from Roman Egypt." *Hellenika* 26: 277–79.

Parkins, H. M., ed. 1997. *Roman Urbanism: Beyond the Consumer City.* London: Routledge, 1997.

Parkins, H. M., and C. J. Smith, eds. 1998. *Trade, Traders, and the Ancient City.* London: Routledge.

Parsons, P. J. 2007. *The City of the Sharp-Nosed Fish: Greek Lives in Roman Egypt.* London: Weidenfeld and Nicolson.

Patterson, J. R. 1998. "Trade and Traders in the Roman World: Scale, Structure, and Organization." In H. Parkins and C. J. Smith, eds., *Trade, Traders, and the Ancient City*, 145–63. London: Routledge.

Patterson, J. R. 1992. "Patronage, *Collegia*, and Burial in Imperial Rome." In S. Bassett, ed., *Death in Towns: Urban Responses to Death and Dying, 100–1600*, 15–27. Leicester: Leicester University Press.

Peachin, M. "The Jurists and the Law in the Early Roman Empire." In L. de Blois, ed., *Administration, Prosopography, and Appointment Policies in the Roman Empire: Proceedings of the First Workshop of the International Network Impact of Empire (Roman Empire, 27 BC—AD 406), Leiden, June 28–July 1, 2000*, 109–20. Amsterdam: Gieben.

Perpillou-Thomas, F. 1993. *Fêtes d'Egypte ptolémaïque et romaine d'après la documentation papyrologique grecque.* Louvain: Centre national de la recherche scientifique.

Perry, J. S. 2006. *The Roman* Collegia*: The Modern Evolution of an Ancient Concept.* Leiden: Brill.

Pestman, P. W. 1993. *The Archive of the Theban Choachytes (Second Century B.C.): A Survey of the Demotic and Greek Papyri Contained in the Archive.* Louvain: Peeters.

Pharr, C. 1952. *The Theodosian Code and Novels.* Princeton: Princeton University Press.

Pleket, H. W. 1984. "Urban Elites and the Economy of the Greek Cities of the Roman Empire." *MBAH* 3: 3–35.

Poland, F. 1909. *Geschichte des griechischen Vereinswesens*. Leipzig.

Putnam, R. D. 2000. *Bowling Alone: The Collapse and Revival of American Community*. New York: Simon and Schuster.

Rathbone, D. W. 1990. "Villages, Land, and Population in Graeco-Roman Egypt." *PCPS* 36: 103–42.

Rathbone, D. W. 1991. *Economic Rationalism and Rural Society in Third-Century A.D. Egypt: The Heroninos Archive and the Appianus Estate*. Cambridge: Cambridge University Press.

Rathbone, D. W. 2007. "Roman Egypt." In W. Scheidel, I. Morris, and R. P. Saller, eds., *The Cambridge Economic History of the Greco-Roman World*, 698–719. Cambridge: Cambridge University Press.

Rathbone, D. W. 2009. "Earnings and Costs: Living Standards and the Roman Economy (First to Third Centuries AD)." In A. K. Bowman and A. Wilson, eds., *Quantifying the Roman Economy: Methods and Problems*, 299–326. Oxford: Oxford University Press.

Rauh, N. K. 1993. *The Sacred Bonds of Commerce: Religion, Economy, and Trade Society at Hellenistic Roman Delos, 166–87 B.C.* Amsterdam: Gieben.

Rea, J. R. 1982. "P.Lond.Inv. 1562 Verso: Market Taxes in Oxyrhynchus." *ZPE* 46: 191–209.

Rees, B. R. 1953–54. "The *Curator Civitatis* in Egypt." *JJP* 7–8: 83–105.

Reymond, E. A. E., and J. W. B. Barns, eds. 1973. *Four Coptic Martyrdoms from the Pierpont Morgan Coptic Codices*. Oxford: Oxford University Press.

Rich, J., and A. Wallace-Hadrill, eds. 1991. *City and Country in the Ancient World*. London: Routledge.

Riggs, C. 2005. *The Beautiful Burial in Roman Egypt: Art, Identity, and Funerary Religion*. Oxford: Oxford University Press.

Rosenstein, N. 2008. "Aristocrats and Agriculture in the Middle and Late Republic." *JRS* 98: 1-26.

Rostovtzeff, M. 1941. *Social and Economic History of the Hellenistic World*. Oxford: Oxford University Press.

Rostovtzeff, M. 1957. *Social and Economic History of the Roman Empire*. Second edition. Oxford: Oxford University Press.

Roueché, C. 1993. *Performers and Partisans at Aphrodisias in the Roman and Late Roman Periods*. Journal of Roman Studies Monographs 6. London: Society for the Promotion of Roman Studies.

Roueché, C. 1995. "Aurarii in the Auditoria." *ZPE* 105: 37–50.

Rowlandson, J. 1996. *Landowners and Tenants in Roman Egypt: The Social Relations of Agriculture in the Oxyrhynchite Nome*. Oxford: Oxford University Press.

Royden, H. L. 1988. *The Magistrates of the Roman Professional Collegia in Italy from the First to the Third Century A.D.* Pisa: Giardini editori e stampatori.

Ruffini, G. R. 2006. "Genealogy and the Gymnasium." *BASP* 43: 71–99.

Ruffini, G. R. 2008a. "Factions and Social Distance in Sixth-Century Aphrodito." In J.-L. Fournet, ed., *Les archives de Dioscore d'Aphrodité cent ans après leur découverte: Histoire et culture dans l'Egypte byzantine; Actes du Colloque de Strasbourg, 8–10 décembre 2005*, 163–68. Paris: De Boccard.

Ruffini, G. R. 2008b. *Social Networks in Byzantine Egypt*. Cambridge: Cambridge University Press.

Ruffini, G. R. 2011. *A Prosopography of Aphrodito*. Durham, NC: American Society of Papyrologists.

Saller, R. P. 2003. "Women, Slaves, and the Economy of the Roman Household." In D. L. Balch and C. Osiek, eds., *Early Christian Families in Context: An Interdisciplinary Dialogue*, 185–204. Grand Rapids: W. B. Eerdmans.

Saller, R. P. 2005. "Framing the Debate over Growth in the Ancient Economy." In J. G. Manning and I. Morris, eds., *The Ancient Economy: Evidence and Models*, 223–38. Stanford: Stanford University Press.

Saller, R. P. 2007. "Household and Gender." In W. Scheidel, I. Morris, and R. P. Saller, eds., *The Cambridge Economic History of the Greco-Roman World*, 87–112. Cambridge: Cambridge University Press.

San Nicolò, M. 1913. *Ägyptisches Vereinswesen zur zeit der Ptolemäer und Römer*. Munich: Beck.

Sarris, P. 2006. *Economy and Society in the Age of Justinian*. Cambridge: Cambridge University Press.

Scheidel, W. 2010. "Real Wages in Early Economies: Evidence for Living Standards from 1800 BCE to 1300 CE." *JESHO* 53: 425–62.

Scheidel, W., and S. J. Friesen. 2009. "The Size of the Economy and the Distribution of Income in the Roman Empire." *JRS* 99: 61–91.

Scheidel, W., I. Morris, and R. P. Saller, eds. 2007. *The Cambridge Economic History of the Greco-Roman World*. Cambridge: Cambridge University Press.

Scheidel, W., and S. Von Reden, eds. 2002. *The Ancient Economy*. New York: Routledge.

Seeck, O. ed. 1876. *Notitia Urbis Constantinopolitanae*. Berlin.

Seland, T. 1996. "Philo and the Associations of Alexandria." In J. S. Kloppenborg and S. G. Wilson, eds., *Voluntary Associations in the Graeco-Roman World*, 110–27. London: Routledge.

Sennett, R. 2008. *The Craftsman*. New Haven: Yale University Press.

Sennett, R. 2012. *Together: The Rituals, Pleasures and Politics of Cooperation*. New Haven: Yale University Press.

Shafer, B., ed. 1997. *Temples of Ancient Egypt*. Ithaca: Cornell University Press.

Sharp, M. 1999. "The Village of Theadelphia in the Fayyum: Land and Population in the Second Century." In A. K. Bowman and E. Rogan, eds., *Agriculture in Egypt from Pharonic to Modern Times*, 159–92. Proceedings of the British Academy 96. Oxford: Oxford University Press.

Sharp, M. 2007. "The Food Supply." In A. K. Bowman, R. A. Coles, N. Gonis, D. Obbink, and P. J. Parsons, eds., *Oxyrhynchus: A City and Its Texts*, 218–30. London: Egypt Exploration Society.

Sheridan, J. A. 1998. *Columbia Papyri IX: The* Vestis Militaris *Codex*. American Studies in Papyrology 39. Atlanta: Scholars Press.

Sherk, A. K. 1988. *The Roman Empire: Augustus to Hadrian*. Cambridge: Cambridge University Press.

Sherwin-White, A. N. 1962. "Trajan's Replies to Pliny: Authorship and Necessity." *JRS* 52: 114–25.

Sherwin-White, A. N. 1966. *The Letters of Pliny: A Historical and Social Commentary*. Oxford: Oxford University Press.

Sijpesteijn, P. J. 1969. "A New Document concerning Hadrian's Visit to Egypt." *Historia* 18: 109–18.

Sijpesteijn, P. J. 1980. "List of Nominations to Liturgies." In *Miscellanea Papyrologica*, 341–47. Florence: Gonnelli, 1980.

Sirks, A. J. B. 1991. *Food for Rome: The Legal Structure of the Transfer and Processing of Supplies for the Imperial Distributions in Rome and Constantinople*. Amsterdam: Gieben.

Sirks, A. J. B. 1993. "Did the Late Roman Government Try to Tie People to Their Profession or Status?" *Tyche* 8: 159–75.

Smith, A. 1977. *An Inquiry into the Nature and Causes of the Wealth of Nations*. Edited by E. Cannan. Chicago: University of Chicago Press.

Smith, A. 2009. *Theory of Moral Sentiments*. Edited by R. P. Hanley. New York: Penguin Classics.

Smith, R. R. R. 1998. "Cultural Choice and Political Identity in Honorific Portrait Statues in the Greek East in the Second Century A.D." *JRS* 88: 56–93.

Smith, R. R. R. 1999. "Late Antique Portraits in a Public Context: Honorific Statuary at Aphrodisias in Caria, A.D. 300–600." *JRS* 89: 155–89.

Sodini, J.-P. 1979. "L'artisanat urbain a l'époque paléochrétienne." Ktema 4: 71–119.

Solomon, R. C. 2008. "Free Enterprise, Sympathy, and Virtue." In P. J. Zak, ed., *Moral Markets: The Critical Role of Values in the Economy*, 16–41. Princeton: Princeton University Press.

Swarney, P. R. 1970. *The Ptolemaic and Roman Idios Logos*. American Studies in Papyrology 5. Toronto: Hakkert.

Tacoma, L. 2006. *Fragile Hierarchies*. Leiden: Brill.

Tacoma, L. 2011. "The Councillor's Dilemma: Political Culture in Third-Century Roman Egypt." In O. van Nijf and R. Alston, eds., *Political Culture in the Greek City after the Classical Age*, 243–61. Louvain: Peeters.

Taubenschlag, R. 1955. *The Law of Greco-Roman Egypt in the Light of the Papyri, 332 B.C.–640 A.D.* Second edition. New York: Herald Square Press.

Temin, P. 2012. *The Roman Market Economy*. Princeton: Princeton University Press.

Tilly, C. 2005. *Trust and Rule*. Cambridge: Cambridge University Press.

Toynbee, J. M. C. 1971. *Death and Burial in the Roman World*. Ithaca: Cornell University Press.

Treggiari, S. 1979. "Lower Class Women in the Roman Economy." *Florilegium* 1: 65–85.

Trigger, B. G., B. J. Kemp, D. O'Connor, and A. B. Lloyd. 1983. *Ancient Egypt: A Social History*. Cambridge: Cambridge University Press.

Trümper, M. 2006. "Negotiating Religious and Ethnic Identity: The Case of Clubhouses in Late Hellenistic Delos." *Hephaistos* 24: 113–50.

Trümper, M. 2011. "Where the Non-Delians Met in Delos: The Meeting-Places of Foreign Associations and Ethnic Communities in Late Hellenistic Delos." In O. van Nijf and R. Alston, eds., *Political Culture in the Greek City after the Classical Age*, 49–100. Louvain: Peeters.

Tsantsanoglou, K. 1975. "P. Yale Inv. 554 Verso." *ZPE* 16: 137–38.

van Minnen, P. 1987. "Urban Craftsmen in Roman Egypt." *MBAH* 6: 31–88.

van Minnen, P. 1994. "The Roots of Egyptian Christianity." *APF* 40: 71–85.

van Minnen, P. 2000. "Euergetism in Graeco-Roman Egypt." In L. Mooren, ed., *Politics, Administration, and Society in the Hellenistic and Roman World*, 437–69. Louvain: Peeters.

van Minnen, P. 2002. "Aἱ ἀπὸ γυμνασίου: 'Greek' Women and the 'Greek' Elite in the Metropoleis of Roman Egypt." In H. Melaerts and L. Mooren, eds., *Le role et le statut de la femme en Egypte hellenistique, romaine et Byzantine*, 337–53. Louvain: Peeters.

van Nijf, O. 1997. *The Civic World of Professional Associations in the Roman East*. Amsterdam: Gieben.

van Nijf, O. 2000. "Athletics, Festivals, and Greek Identity in the Roman East." *PCPS* 45: 176–200.

van Nijf, O. 2002. "*Collegia* and Civic Guards: Two Chapters in the History of Sociability." In W. Jongman and M. Kleijwegt, eds., *After the Past: Essays in Ancient History in Honour of H. W. Pleket*, 305–39. Leiden: Brill.

van Nijf, O. 2011. "Public Space and the Political Culture of Roman Termessos." In O. van Nijf and R. Alston, eds., *Political Culture in the Greek City after the Classical Age*, 215–42. Louvain: Peeters.

van Nijf, O., and R. Alston, eds. 2011. *Political Culture in the Greek City after the Classical Age*. Louvain: Peeters.

Venticinque, P. F. 2009. "Common Causes: Guilds, Craftsmen, and Merchants in the Economy and Society of Roman and Late Roman Egypt." PhD diss., University of Chicago.

Venticinque, P. F. 2010. "Family Affairs: Guild Regulations and Family Relationships in Roman Egypt." *GRBS* 50: 273–94.

Venticinque, P. F. 2013. "Matters of Trust: Associations and Social Capital in Roman Egypt." *Center for Hellenic Studies Research Bulletin*, Volume 1, Issue 2.

Venticinque, P. F. 2015. "Courting the Associations: Cooperation, Conflict, and Interaction in Roman Egypt," in V. Gabrielsen, C. A. Thomsen, eds., *Private Associations and the Public Sphere: Proceedings of a Symposium held at the Royal Danish Academy of Sciences and Letters, 9-11 September 2010*. Scientia Danica. Series H, Humanistic, 8 vol. 9, 314–40. Copenhagen: The Royal Danish Academy of Sciences and Letters.

Venticinque, P. F. 2016. "P.Mich.Inv. 424: Packing List of a *Katholikos*." *BASP* 53.

Venticinque, P. F. Forthcoming. "Dying to Belong: Associations and the Economics of Funerals in Egypt and the Roman World." In A. Cazemier and S. Skaltsa, eds., *Associations in Context: Rethinking Associations and Religion in the Post-Classical Polis.*

Verboven, K. 2007. "The Associative Order: Status and Ethos among Roman Businessmen in the Late Republic and Early Empire." *Athenaeum* 95: 861–93.

Verboven, K. 2011. "Professional Collegia: Guilds or Social Clubs?" *Ancient Society* 41: 187–95.

Vleeming, S. P. 2001. *Some Coins of Artaxerxes and Other Short Texts in the Demotic Script Found on Various Objects and Gathered from Many Publications.* Sterling, VA: Peeters.

Wace, A. J. B., A. H. S. Megaw, and T. C. Skeat. 1959. *Hermopolis Magna, Ashmunein: The Ptolemaic Sanctuary and the Basilica.* Alexandria: Alexandria University Press.

Walker-Ramisch, S. 1996. "Graeco-Roman Voluntary Associations and the Damascus Document: A Sociological Analysis." In J. S. Kloppenborg and S. G. Wilson, eds., *Voluntary Associations in the Graeco-Roman World*, 128–45. London: Routledge.

Wallace, S. L. 1938. *Taxation in Egypt*. Princeton: Princeton University Press.

Wallace-Hadrill, A. 1991. "Elites and Trade in the Roman Town." In J. Rich and A. Wallace-Hadrill, eds., *City and Country in the Ancient World*, 241–72. London: Routledge.

Waltzing, J.-P. 1895–1900. *Étude historique sur les corporations professionnelles chez les Romains depuis les origines jusqu'à la chute de l'Empire d'Occident.* 4 vols. Louvain: Peeters.

Waterfield, R., trans. 1998. *Herodotus.* The Histories. With introduction and notes by C. Dewald. Oxford World's Classics. Oxford: Oxford University Press.

Watson, A., ed. 1985. *The Digest of Justinian.* With Latin text edited by Theodor Mommsen with the aid of Paul Krueger. Philadelphia: University of Pennsylvania Press.

Westermann, W. L. 1924. "The Castanet Dancers of Arsinoe." *JEA* 10: 133–44.

Westermann, W. L. 1932. "Entertainment in the Villages of Graeco-Roman Egypt." *JEA* 18: 16–27.

Whittow, M. 1990. "Ruling the Late Roman and Early Byzantine City: A Continuous History." *Past and Present* 129: 3–29.

Wickham, C. 1998. "Gossip and Resistance among the Medieval Peasantry." *Past and Present* 160: 3–24.

Williamson, C. 1987. "Monuments of Bronze: Roman Legal Documents Written on Bronze Tablets." *CA* 6: 160–83.

Wipszycka, E. 1965. *L'industrie textile dans l'Égypte Romaine.* Wrocław: Zakład Narodowy im. Ossolińskich.

Woolf, G. 2006. "Pliny's Province." In T. Bekker-Nielsen, ed., *Rome and the Black Sea Region: Domination, Romanisation, Resistance*, 93–108. Aarhus: Aarhus University Press.

Worp, K. A. 2012. "Corporations of Craftsmen and Other Professionals in Graeco-Roman Egypt." *MBAH* 30: 1–8.

Youtie, H. C. 1958. "Notes on Papyri and Ostraca." *TAPA* 89: 374–407.

Youtie, H. C. 1964. "Notes on Papyri." *TAPA* 95: 303–32.

Zak, P. J., ed. 2008. *Moral Markets: The Critical Role of Values in the Economy*. Princeton: Princeton University Press.

Zimmermann, C. 2002. *Handwerkervereine im Griechischen Osten des Imperium Romanum*. Mainz: Verlag des Romisch-Germanischen Zentralmuseums.

Zuckerman, C. 2004. *Du village à l'Empire: Autour du Registre fiscal d'Aphroditô (525/526)*. Centre de Recherche d'Histoire et Civilisation de Byzance Monographies 16. Paris: Association des amis du centre d'histoire et civilisation de Byzance.

Zuiderhoek, A. 2007. "The Ambiguity of Munificence." *Historia* 56: 196–213.

Zuiderhoek, A. 2008. "On the Political Sociology of the Imperial Greek City." *GRBS* 48: 417–45.

Zuiderhoek, A. 2009. *The Politics of Munificence in the Roman Empire: Citizens, Elites, and Benefactors in Asia Minor*. Cambridge: Cambridge University Press.

Zuiderhoek, A. 2011. "The Oligarchs and Benefactors: Elite Demography and Euergetism in the Greek East of the Roman Empire." In O. van Nijf and R. Alston, eds., *Political Culture in the Greek City after the Classical Age*, 185–96. Louvain: Peeters.

Index

Literary Sources

Papyri and Ostraca

Inscriptions

Legal Sources